Praise Him
with Your Very Life

A Collection of Plays

by

Mother Mary Francis, P.C.C.

Catholic Heritage Curricula

1-800-490-7713   www.chcweb.com

This collection of plays may be read for their sheer literary delight or presented on stage as entertainment in full dramatic flair. Whether acted out or read aloud, these plays are inspirational masterpieces which deepen our awareness of God's love. They provide an excellent dramatic tool for hands-on reinforcement of the truths of our Faith. We thank Mother Mary Francis for sharing her sterling collection of plays with Catholic families.

The Publisher

ISBN: 978-1-946207-22-7

© 2001, 2005 The Community of Poor Clares of New Mexico, Inc.

This collection is under copyright, as is each individual play. No part of this collection may be reproduced for use in any commercial production in any form by any means—electronic, mechanical, or graphic—without prior written permission from the Community of Poor Clares of New Mexico, Inc.
Poor Clare Monastery of Our Lady of Guadalupe
809 East 19th Street
Roswell, New Mexico 88201

The Community of Poor Clares of New Mexico, Inc. encourages the dramatic performance of these plays. Permission is extended to families and groups to make copies for use in staging small performances where there is no admission fee charged. If a printed program is used, please give the following credit:
Playwright credit: Mother Mary Francis, P.C.C.

Cover image: "St. Francis Supported by an Angel" by Orazio Gentileschi, Copyright © Museo del Prado, Madrid, Spain.

Printed by Bookmasters
Ashland, Ohio
March 2019
Print code: 28242

Contents

About the Author

The late Mother Mary Francis, P.C.C. was the Abbess of the Poor Clare Monastery of Our Lady of Guadalupe in Roswell, New Mexico. Her literary work of more than 50 years includes several collections of poetry, thirteen books, and many articles. *A Right to be Merry,* her best-selling book, has been published in six languages. Her plays have been produced on and off the stage for years, including a production off-Broadway by the Blackfriars' Guild. Through her tireless dedication, the Immaculate Heart Federation of Poor Clare Nuns has expanded to eleven monasteries throughout the United States and one in Holland.

For vocation information on the Poor Clare life, write to:

Poor Clare Monastery of Our Lady of Guadalupe
809 East 19th Street
Roswell, New Mexico 88201

Website: www.poorclares-roswell.org

Praise Him with your very life.
—St. Clare

The Wolf of Gubbio

A Drama in One Act

© 1980, 2005 The Community of Poor Clares of New Mexico, Inc.

Author's Note

The story of St. Francis and the Wolf of Gubbio has profound significance for the twenty-first century. Through the laughter it engenders runs the gravity of sobering truth. Like all genuine comedy, it alerts us to the profound meaning of life in its sobriety. Here is its significance for our era.

Cast of Characters

BROTHER FRANCIS . . . . the Saint of Assisi

BROTHER JOHN THE SIMPLE . . . . loyal follower of Francis

LUCHESIUS . . . . a wealthy Italian lawyer who has been converted to a new way of life by Francis

BELLADONNA . . . . his beautiful wife

and

THE WOLF OF GUBBIO

The Wolf of Gubbio

SCENE. *A meadow outside Gubbio in Italy, about 1216. Enter* LUCHESIUS, *very well-dressed and carrying a bulging portfolio. He sits down immediately on a rustic bench, but carefully dusts the other half of it before spreading out on it the papers from the portfolio. He weights each stack down with a small rock from the ground, first polishing the rock on his silk breeches. He rises and comes Downstage to address the audience.*

LUCHESIUS. (*points back at the bench*) There is the symbol of my life. You'll agree it is neat enough. Respectable. A monument, in its way, to prudence. Not one business deal left unrecorded. As for the sale of farm lands where I nipped the lads a little, the legal language is, I modestly admit, real literature. It shows me, (*draws himself up*) Master Luchesius, as a model of right dealing, a man who earned his gold honestly and under a smiling Heaven. (*walks to side*) Furthermore, my wife was not called Belladonna for nothing. Even without the assistance of twenty velvet mantles with veils of silk in matching colors and sizable diamonds for her ears, Belladonna is enough to stop Italian traffic any day.

(*sighs*) All I can say is, it was a good life while it lasted. (*forward, confidential*) If you see an undersized little fellow in a brown robe tied with a rope, avoid him like the very plague. That is, unless you want your life turned upside down. (*looks cautiously around*) His name is Francis di Bernardone. He calls himself Brother Francis. (*pause*) He called *me* "Brother Luchesius" one day. (*pause*) Don't ask me what happened after that. But I'll tell you this much. (*moves back to bench*)

I've lost my art. You know,—cutting a few corners here and there. Good business is what it is called.

That's what I called it, before I met Brother Francis. (*He picks up some of the papers.*) He called it cheating. (*begins to tear them up and to strew them on the ground*) He doesn't speak our language,—doesn't know the art of the soft word. (*sweeps the rocks onto the ground and throws one high in the air, catching it expertly behind his back*) Just keep out of Brother Francis' way, that's all I have to tell you, unless you want to end up like me,—the happiest fool in the world! (*begins to whistle and move Offstage*) (*turns back and stops short*) But, oh, my wife! Oh, dear Belladonna! There's another story! (*exit Right*)

(*enter* BROTHER FRANCIS *and* BROTHER JOHN THE SIMPLE, *Left, singing*)

FRANCIS. I wish someone might be inspired to give us a fiddle.

JOHN. Who would play it?

FRANCIS. Brother John, if we had a fiddle, I would pray the good God to send me a fiddler. If we had a fiddling brother, the people back in Gubbio (*gestures Offstage, Left*) might feel better.

JOHN. But they're terrified of the wolf, Brother Francis.

FRANCIS. Very true, poor people. They have lost their joy. They need a fiddler.

JOHN. You mean that the wolf could devour them to music instead of a cappella?

FRANCIS. No, Brother John. Fear had devoured their souls before the wolf came. It is only the body he devours.

JOHN. He does not seem to ask more.

FRANCIS. I wish we would meet him.

JOHN. (*sprints to far side of stage*) The wolf?

FRANCIS. Our brother, the wolf.

JOHN. He's no kin of mine.

FRANCIS. (*walks over to* JOHN, *earnestly*) That's just it, Brother John. No one cares about him. Everyone hates him. What can you expect of the wolf? He is only living down to everyone's expectations.

JOHN. But the wolf is not a human being.

FRANCIS. The trouble with the wolf is that his reactions are surprisingly human. He is hated, and so he hates in return. No one remembers his dignity, so he despises the dignity of everyone else. If he were treated more like a wolf and less like a murdering man, we might expect great things from the wolf.

JOHN. You expect great things from all creatures, Brother Francis.

FRANCIS. It is my right. They were made by a great God.

JOHN. Suppose we prove you are wrong? What will you say if you discover your brother the wolf is only a murderous monster (*turns away*), and Brother John is only a simple-minded fool?

FRANCIS. (*laughs*) I shall still be right in the end. For I shall tell the murderous monster of the loving God, and he will repent of his ways. And I shall urge Brother John to be a very faithful fool, since the world is sore pressed for the lack of the right kind of fools. (*He stoops and picks up two sticks which he holds in position like a fiddle and bow.*) See, my brother! I have found a fiddle!

JOHN. (*spontaneously snatches the sticks from* FRANCIS) And God has now burdened you with a fiddling brother! (*puts one stick under his chin and begins to bow with the other*) What will you hear?

FRANCIS. (*jumps on the bench, enthusiastically*) I will hear the praises of God! I will hear the praises of the fools who love Him! I will sing of the wise fools who serve Him! (JOHN *follows him, fiddling vigorously, and* FRANCIS *directs him from the bench like a conductor.*)

FRANCIS. Some are fools for money's sake
And some are fools for power's sake.
Many are the fools of fear,
But few the fools for God's sake!

(*Enter* LUCHESIUS, *Right, unnoticed, with portfolio.*)

Come, learn, my brothers, in my school
A very few and simple rules:
Money and power are spent in an hour,
But God and eternity last a long time.
Yes, Heaven will last for quite a long time,
And nobody gains it but God's fools!

(*He sees* Luchesius *and jumps down from the bench to embrace him.*)

My Brother Luchesius!

JOHN. My Brother Luchesius!

LUCHESIUS. (*little bow*) Brother Francis! (*toward* JOHN) And this is?

JOHN. (*deep bow*) Brother John the Simple.

LUCHESIUS. Are you simple-minded, Brother?

JOHN. It is not so much an attainment as a goal.

LUCHESIUS. (*still smiling*) Is it beyond my strength?

JOHN. (*very serious*) Not if you are willing to pay the price.

LUCHESIUS. Which is—?

JOHN. The price is,—to remember you have a soul.

LUCHESIUS. (*no longer smiling, he fingers the portfolio*) It is costing me a great deal already to remember that. I must say I always liked the idea of having a soul,—just knowing it was there, I mean. But *remembering* it can be very trying, especially for a business man.

(*Enter* BELLADONNA *Right, unnoticed. She is very richly attired and has a short train which she kicks out of her way from time to time. She carries a small gilt box.*)

FRANCIS. Do things go badly?

LUCHESIUS. They do. People are beginning to trust me. (*turns away*) I can hardly bear the shame of it.

FRANCIS. Yes, my Brother Luchesius, the trust of good men is a fearsome responsibility. And heavier yet is the burden of their love.

LUCHESIUS. It is too heavy, brother, for a man to bear. When he deserves to be hated and is loved instead...

FRANCIS. But there is a way to make the burden light.

LUCHESIUS. Teach it to me!

FRANCIS. It is to love still more in return.

JOHN. (*nodding*) It is to love still more in return.

BELLADONNA. (*high, excited voice*) It is to love still more in return! Master Luchesius, do you know or do you not know there is a wolf in Gubbio?

LUCHESIUS. (*goes to her*) My darling, my lady, my most esteemed wife!— I do.

BELLADONNA. Then why are you not back in the town helping to prepare defenses instead of frittering away your time with these—(*kicks train*)—people.

FRANCIS. How do you do.

JOHN. How do you do.

BELLADONNA. (*icily*) I did very well before my husband began acting the fool instead of attending to his business affairs.

JOHN. Brother Francis just composed two beautiful verses for fools. Would you like to hear them? (*He holds his two sticks in fiddle position.*)

BELLADONNA. No, thank you. (*loud aside to* LUCHESIUS) What is he doing with those sticks?

LUCHESIUS. He uses them for a fiddle and a bow.

FRANCIS. When I sing, Brother John accompanies me on this fiddle the Lord has provided.

BELLADONNA. Oh, kind heaven!

FRANCIS. Oh, madame, you are so right!

BELLADONNA. What's that?

FRANCIS. Heaven is the habitat of kindness, for kindness is the little sister of love.

BELLADONNA. My dear Brother Francis, there are better times for sermons on love than when a wolf is killing off the citizens of Gubbio as fast as his digestion will permit! (*kicks at her train*)

FRANCIS. On the contrary, madame, I think there could not be a better time.

JOHN. On the contrary indeed, there could not be a better time.

BELLADONNA. (*to* LUCHESIUS) Who *is* that person? (*points at* JOHN)

LUCHESIUS. Pardon my manners, my sweet, my darling wife. (*deep bow*) Mistress Belladonna, most truly named, this is Brother John the Simple.

BELLADONNA. I believe it.

JOHN. Oh, thank you! But really I only strive.

BELLADONNA. (*Bewildered, she begins to cry.*) Luchesius, how can you stand around listening to simpletons rub sticks together when our lives are in danger! Look, I was so frightened by the wolf that I ran out of the house without packing anything except two changes of earrings! (*thrusts gilt box at him*)

LUCHESIUS. My poor darling! I had to attend to some business. I am just returning. I will protect you.

BELLADONNA. (*brightens*) Business?

LUCHESIUS. (*pats the portfolio*) I had to close a few deals.

BELLADONNA. (*reaches out eagerly for the portfolio*) Let me see! (*opens it and stares into it unbelievingly*) It's empty! (*turns it upside down and shakes it*) Empty!

JOHN. I guess he closed the deals rather thoroughly.

BELLADONNA. (*shrilly*) Where are the contracts?

LUCHESIUS. (*low voice, looking down*) I tore them up.

BELLADONNA. (*a real shriek*) What!

LUCHESIUS. (*miserably*) They weren't honest.

BELLADONNA. (*begins to cry again*) Oh, what is to become of us? (*shakes the empty portfolio and throws it angrily on the ground*) What am I to do with a mad husband and an empty portfolio?

JOHN. I could carry my fiddle in the portfolio. (*picks it up and fits the two sticks into it*) And maybe Luchesius could join our brotherhood.

BELLADONNA. (*in a perfect fury*) I am going back home! I would rather be with the wolf! (*kicks her train out of her way and exits, Left*)

LUCHESIUS. What can I do, Brother Francis? It's not so easy for a married man to change his ways when he cannot change his wife. How can I make Belladonna see?

FRANCIS. You can't.

LUCHESIUS. (*surprised and crestfallen*) I thought you would help me.

FRANCIS. I *am* helping you.

JOHN. He *is* helping you.

LUCHESIUS. I don't know how.

FRANCIS. I have told you that you can't *make* her see things differently. But you can teach her to *want* to see them differently.

LUCHESIUS. How? Oh, how, Brother Francis?

FRANCIS. By endurance. Love outlasts hate. Patience is stronger than fury.

LUCHESIUS. Shall I go after her, then?

FRANCIS. Yes, do, brother, in the name of God Who loves all of us poor wretches so much.

JOHN. Indeed He has loved us. One wonders sometimes at His taste.

FRANCIS. (*hand on* LUCHESIUS' *shoulder*) God is patient as eternity, my brother. All will be well in the end.

JOHN. I have observed that to be always patient is more than to put one's head on the block. Brother ax is swift and sure. Our sister patience is a devotee of the art of waiting. For myself, I would take the ax.

(*Exit* LUCHESIUS, *Left*)

FRANCIS. Our sister Belladonna has a mighty voice.

JOHN. She has a mighty glance.

FRANCIS. Really? I did not notice. I never look at women.

JOHN. (*sighs*) I never thought of that, but I intend to try it.

(*scream Offstage. . . both* BROTHERS *start and run to the Left*)

JOHN. It's Belladonna!

(BELLADONNA *streaks onto the stage, her long skirts caught up in one arm and the gilt box still grasped in the other hand.*)

BELLADONNA. The wolf! The wolf! (*She runs off, Right.*)

JOHN. Let's go!

(LUCHESIUS *chases on after* BELLADONNA.)

LUCHESIUS. The wolf! The wolf of Gubbio! Run for your lives! (*races off Right*)

JOHN. (*pulls* FRANCIS *by the arm*) Let's go! (*starts pulling him along, but* FRANCIS *breaks loose from his hold*)

FRANCIS. I want to meet the wolf.

JOHN. The trouble is, he wants to meet *you!* Come on!

FRANCIS. No, I will stay.

JOHN. (*undergoes a terrible struggle, running to far Right and then running back to* FRANCIS, *unwilling to leave him . . . finally he drops to one knee and catches* FRANCIS' *hand, speaking in a choking voice*) All right, then. I'll die with you. The wolf can eat a double portion.

(*Enter the* WOLF OF GUBBIO, *Left, growling.* JOHN THE SIMPLE *groans loudly and crawls behind* FRANCIS, *pulling* FRANCIS' *robes out to hide himself. The* WOLF *advances toward* FRANCIS *slowly, and with beautiful grace he comes almost directly in front of him. He pauses as though for the spring.* FRANCIS *bends forward slightly and looks steadily at the* WOLF. *The* WOLF *growls again, but relaxes his taut position just a little.*)

FRANCIS. So this is our Brother Wolf! You are a very famous fellow. (*The* WOLF *retreats a step and growls.*) No, don't deny it, Brother Wolf. Everyone in Gubbio talks of nothing but you.

(WOLF *retreats another step, and* JOHN *peers out from behind* FRANCIS' *robes.*)

FRANCIS. Are you happy, Brother Wolf?

(*The* WOLF *lowers his head, then looks up at* FRANCIS *pleadingly. He lowers his head again and gives a loud groan.*)

FRANCIS. I knew it. (*He moves forward and places his hand on the* WOLF'S *head.*) You feel most wretched, Brother Wolf.

JOHN. (*following* FRANCIS, *on his knees, peers out from behind again*) It's probably indigestion.

(WOLF *growls at* JOHN, *and he hastily conceals himself again.*)

FRANCIS. Your heart is full of misery, my poor Brother Wolf.

WOLF. (*wiping right paw across his eyes*) Yes.

FRANCIS. Hate is too much misery for any heart to bear.

WOLF. But everyone hates me.

FRANCIS. No so! Not I!

WOLF. Why not? I am most hateable.

FRANCIS. I find you rather lovable!

WOLF. Me? I am the wolf of Gubbio. You have someone else in mind.

FRANCIS. (*pats* WOLF *on the head*) I know of whom I speak, my little Brother Wolf.

(WOLF *makes inarticulate, choking sounds.*)

JOHN. (*looking out*) What's he doing? Choking on someone's waistcoat button?

FRANCIS. Hush, Brother John! The wolf is weeping. (*The* WOLF *puts his head down on his front paws and continues weeping.* FRANCIS *reaches down to stroke the* WOLF'S *head.*) What is it, Brother Wolf?

WOLF. Oh, don't say that!

FRANCIS. Not ask you about your troubles?

WOLF. No, do not call me Brother. It is more than a murdering wolf can stand.

FRANCIS. Yes, I agree with you.

JOHN. (*looking out*) I thoroughly agree with you!

(WOLF *snarls at* JOHN *who retreats hastily.*)

FRANCIS. Do not be offended at Brother John. He loves you, too.

WOLF. Why?

FRANCIS. Because the good God made you. He cannot make anything evil. Evil is what men make.

WOLF. But I am evil. And you say God made me? No, man created me!

FRANCIS. No, my little brother, but man taught you to be evil. Sit down, Brother Wolf, and I will tell you a story. (FRANCIS *sits on the bench, and the wolf sits back on his hind legs.* JOHN *has lost his hiding place and stands nervously behind the bench.*) Once, many, many centuries ago, God made a garden. It was bigger than the whole town of Gubbio, much bigger. And there was everything in it to make a man glad and contented. All things good to eat and all things beautiful to look upon. God made all the animals and birds and fishes and they were happy together. And the first man and woman God ever created ruled over all of them.

WOLF. Were there wolves in that garden?

FRANCIS. Yes, little brother, there were wolves. And they loved the man named Adam and the woman named Eve, because Adam and Eve loved them. Those wolves were your first parents, just as Adam and Eve were mine.

WOLF. I don't take after them.

FRANCIS. You do! (*sadly*) And I take after mine.

WOLF. Is that not good? Why are you sad?

FRANCIS. Because things went terribly wrong in the garden after a while.

WOLF. How so? Was not everything there to satisfy the heart?

FRANCIS. Indeed yes, Brother Wolf. But then the devil came.

WOLF. I have been called that name a thousand times.

FRANCIS. It does not belong to you. The devil, Brother Wolf, is a great archangel.

WOLF. (*stands up on all four legs in astonishment*) You don't mean it? I supposed angels were a different species. Don't they do a very different type of work?

FRANCIS. Yes, my brother. But it was not always so. The devil's name was Lucifer, which means "the light-bearer." He was the most beautiful of all the angels and had a shining throne in Heaven.

JOHN. (*forgets his fear in his interest and leans over the bench*) He had a splendid throne, but he fell off it.

(WOLF *moves as though to spring at* JOHN, *growls, but then thinks better of it and settles back again on his hind legs.*)

FRANCIS. That's the way to act, Brother Wolf. (*pats him on the head*)

JOHN. Yes, that's *much* better!

FRANCIS. The archangel Lucifer grew proud, my little brother. He would no longer serve God. He did not wish to worship our most blessed Lord!

WOLF. What happened then?

FRANCIS. God gave him his choice: to submit or to be eternally punished.

WOLF. I have a feeling he didn't give in.

FRANCIS. (*voice of infinite sadness*) No, my little brother!

JOHN. (*raising fist to Heaven*) He said: I will not serve!

WOLF. (*springing up*) Where is he? I will finish him up!

FRANCIS. You could not kill him. He is an archangel.

WOLF. (*pacing about*) I still think I could handle him. Where *is* he?

FRANCIS. He is in hell.

JOHN. God made hell especially for him.

WOLF. I know that name. People are always telling me to go there.

FRANCIS. *You* will never go there. Let's hope *they* won't. (*standing*) Listen carefully now, Brother Wolf. God put the archangel Lucifer in hell because he would not obey. He would not serve the God Who made him. And because there is no light in hell, but only bitter darkness, Lucifer's name was changed to Satan. He is the father of darkness now. He is the devil.

WOLF. (*settling down*) The same one who came into that garden?

FRANCIS. The same.

JOHN. The very same.

FRANCIS. The devil cannot bear anyone to be happy and obedient. He wants everyone to be as miserable as himself. So he coaxed Adam and Eve to disobey God also.

WOLF. What! In that wonderful garden?

FRANCIS. Yes, Brother Wolf, in that beautiful garden.

JOHN. Right there.

FRANCIS. And God was so offended because the first man and woman disobeyed Him that He cursed them.

JOHN. A curse is a frightful thing!

WOLF. I hear curses all the time. In fact, that's how people greet me.

FRANCIS. This was different. God's curse was a prophecy that we are still fulfilling.

WOLF. (*sitting up close to* FRANCIS) What was this curse?

FRANCIS. It was the ending of perfection. The mind of man was darkened. The heart of woman became perverse. And perfect understanding left the earth and fled to Heaven where alone we shall ever find it now.

WOLF. Oh, what a mess!

JOHN. It still is.

FRANCIS. And will remain so. Ever since that day, men fear the beasts God made to serve them. Our little sisters the birds are frightened when a man comes near them. And each small creature fears each larger one. My Father Adam began to hate your Father Wolf because they no longer understood each other. The common language of love and trust was lost.

WOLF. If I may say so, you speak Wolf very well.

JOHN. Brother Francis is not like other men.

WOLF. So I observe.

FRANCIS. (*walking toward Left*) Come with me, Brother Wolf.

WOLF. (*fast trot after* FRANCIS) Oh, anywhere! To the ends of the earth!

FRANCIS. No, just to Gubbio.

WOLF. (*halts abruptly and sits down*) Not *there!*

FRANCIS. Yes, there.

WOLF. (*shakes his head sadly*) The place is too full of memories.

JOHN. And tombstones. (WOLF *jumps at* JOHN *and takes* JOHN's *wrist in his jaws.*) (*John drops the portfolio*) EE-yow!

FRANCIS. (*raising his hand*) My Brother Wolf! (*The* WOLF *looks from* JOHN *to* FRANCIS *several times, then drops* JOHN's *wrist, pauses, and finally licks his hand.*) And now, my Brother John!

(JOHN *looks uncertainly at* FRANCIS, *then pats the* WOLF *awkwardly on the head.*)

FRANCIS. That's the way to do it. That's the way God meant all things to be when He planned the world. And we shall go to Gubbio and show them all how God meant things to be before men spoiled them.

WOLF. (*dubious, he walks slowly toward* FRANCIS) Unless I eat the people as fast as I can, they will kill me.

FRANCIS. No! for I shall protect you. I will make them promise to give you food for the future,—a different kind. And you will beg the people to forgive you for your crimes.

WOLF. (*paces about for a few seconds*) They don't speak Wolf in Gubbio.

FRANCIS. Well, I will translate! Come, my brothers!

(*all three exit, Left*)

(*Enter* LUCHESIUS *and* BELLADONNA, *cautiously, Right.* BELLADONNA *still clutches the gilt box.* LUCHESIUS *looks around, picks up a piece of chewed paper and holds out his arms in a gesture of despair.*)

LUCHESIUS. Gone! He killed them both!

BELLADONNA. Why didn't they run, the fools?

LUCHESIUS. Brother Francis never runs from anyone,—not even from such as us.

BELLADONNA. What do you mean?

LUCHESIUS. (*slowly*) I mean that small-souled men with unctious smiles and cheating hands must be harder company for Francis than the wolves.

BELLADONNA. Indeed! Well, now he's dead. Devoured. The two of them.

LUCHESIUS. (*sinks down on the bench*) This was the wolf's most heinous sin,—to kill a man and leave a million insects still alive.

BELLADONNA. (*kicks her train*) What insects?

LUCHESIUS. (*rising in a sudden anger*) You and me,—for two!

BELLADONNA. How dare you!

LUCHESIUS. I don't know! I only know while Francis lived, I could not quite face issues. Now that I have lost him, I have also lost something in myself I nearly found. (*advances toward* BELLADONNA *who retreats a few steps, awed and frightened*)

BELLADONNA. Don't you dare strike me! Are you mad, Luchesius?

LUCHESIUS. (*in measured tones*) No, my dear Belladonna, but I was almost sane for a while before Francis died. (*picks up the portfolio and takes out the two sticks which he sets reverently on the bench before sitting down again*) Do you see these sticks?

BELLADONNA. (*nervously*) Yes, ye-es, I do.

LUCHESIUS. Well, so do I. But Francis saw a fiddle. (*pause*) Do you see *me*? (*stands up abruptly and plants himself directly in front of* BELLADONNA, *uncomfortably close*)

BELLADONNA. (*really frightened now*) Yes, my lord Luchesius, I see you.

LUCHESIUS. And you see a sickening sight: your husband!— A man who loved your pretty face and loved his comforts and his pleasure. A man whose soul is like a dried-up pea. (*turns away*) But Francis saw a brother. He saw my soul as God had shaped it,—winging and beautiful and free. And for a while I nearly saw it, too. (*steps so close to* BELLADONNA *that she collapses onto bench*) You see that sky? (*pointing up*)

BELLADONNA. (*looks up and nods dumbly, beginning to cry a little*)

LUCHESIUS. Well, Francis didn't. He only saw a thin veil thrown across the face of God. (*drops beside her on bench, his anger as suddenly spent as it came*) I'll wager before he died, Francis even saw something of goodness and greatness in the wolf!

(*Enter* FRANCIS *and* JOHN THE SIMPLE, *with the wolf trotting happily between them.* LUCHESIUS *and* BELLADONNA *leap up, and* BELLADONNA *clings in terror to* LUCHESIUS *who puts his arms around her absentmindedly.*)

FRANCIS. (*smiling*) My Brother Luchesius!

JOHN. Our Brother Luchesius!

(*The* WOLF *inclines his head politely.*)

LUCHESIUS. (*teeth chattering*) Is it you, Brother Francis?

FRANCIS. (*briskly*). No other. My brother John you already know. And this (*pats the* WOLF *on the head*) is Brother Wolf.

(LUCHESIUS *drops his arms and steps forward dazedly.* BELLADONNA *screams, drops her gilt box and runs off, Right.* LUCHESIUS *looks after her, then back at the trio.*)

FRANCIS. She will come back.

JOHN. (*nodding sagely*) She will come back. She seems a little nervous, doesn't she?

LUCHESIUS. (*dazedly*) Are you alive?

FRANCIS. Positively.

JOHN. And never more so.

LUCHESIUS. (*drops back on the bench*) I don't understand. (*The* WOLF *trots over and puts his head on* LUCHESIUS' *lap.* LUCHESIUS *is still too dazed to be frightened. He is not even sure the* WOLF *is really there.*)

WOLF. Neither did I, at first,—till I met Brother Francis.

LUCHESIUS. But what has happened? Are we *all* dead? But no! I would not end up in the same place as Francis!

JOHN. (*loud whisper*) Pat the wolf's head, Brother Luchesius! He's very sensitive. (LUCHESIUS *pats the* WOLF *like a man in a dream.* BELLADONNA'S *head appears at the Right. She sees* LUCHESIUS *patting the wolf and screams again.* WOLF *trots over to the edge of the stage, gets* BELLADONNA'S *skirt in his teeth and pulls her over to the bench. She collapses on it, sobbing with fright.*)

BELLADONNA. Go on, devour me! I'm sick and tired of living, anyway. Everyone has gone mad.

WOLF. No, everyone's gone sane as Brother Francis. It's wonderful! (*crouches at her feet*) He told me my forefathers used to sit like this once in a garden at the feet of Eve. I wish you would look into her history, — I mean, before she ate that apple.

BELLADONNA. (*sobbing wildly*) Take him away!

FRANCIS. Don't hurt his feelings, my Sister Belladonna!

WOLF. (*trots over to* FRANCIS *and licks his hand*) It's quite all right. I understand. She feels a bit upset. I usually do not move in social circles. (*trots back to* BELLADONNA *and picks up her gilt box in his teeth, dropping it on her lap*) No hard feelings. Maybe you would like to change your earrings. I'm going back to Gubbio. I've made a lot of friends there.

(*Exit the* WOLF, *Left, at a brisk trot.* BELLADONNA *stares after the* WOLF, *as do the others. She then suddenly takes the gilt box and flings it on the ground.*)

LUCHESIUS. (*gradually recovering himself*) Why, Belladonna! What's the matter, sweet? Are you tired of those earrings?

BELLADONNA. (*rising*) I'm tired of all earrings. (*takes the two from her ears, starts to throw them away, too, then walks over to* JOHN *and puts them in his hand*) (*to* JOHN) There, take them. Take the box, too. Go buy bread for the poor that are always following him. (*gestures toward* FRANCIS; *wheels back on* LUCHESIUS) And furthermore, I'm not your sweet! You know I've been your *bitter* for many a long month now,—since you met *him.* (*points at* FRANCIS) And as for what's the matter,—*he's* the matter!

FRANCIS. I beg your pardon, for what I've done wrong. Won't you forgive me?

BELLADONNA. No, no, I won't! I never shall!

JOHN. Come now, forgive him!

LUCHESIUS. (*angry again*) For *what*, I'd like to know? What was his crime?

BELLADONNA. (*crying softly now*) It was to call me "sister." He called me "Sister Belladonna." You all heard him.

LUCHESIUS. He meant it well.

BELLADONNA. I know, I know. So why should I forgive him?

LUCHESIUS. (*understands at last, and puts his arms around* BELLADONNA) Ah, Belladonna!

JOHN. Sister Belladonna!

FRANCIS. No, Sister *Bona*donna! John, my brother, I think it's time for music!

JOHN. (*runs for the portfolio, finds it empty, looks around and spies the sticks on the bench. He snatches them up and holds them in fiddle position.*) I'm ready!

FRANCIS. (*jumps up on the bench*) Now, listen!

> No man is quite so wicked as he hoped he was.
> No woman ever is so lost as she swore she was.
> (*John begins to fiddle*)
> There is a goodness in our hearts we never will believe
> Until it tricks us into love, until it tricks us into love
> And makes us free as fools!
>
> (BELLADONNA *and* LUCHESIUS *begin to tap their toes as* FRANCIS *and* JOHN *repeat the tune. Gradually they swirl into a dance, circling Offstage, Left, as* FRANCIS *and* JOHN *go on singing the little refrain.* FRANCIS *leaps down from the bench and looks after* LUCHESIUS *and* BELLADONNA.*)

FRANCIS. They will be happy now. They will be saints.

JOHN. Are saints fools, Brother Francis? Or is it that fools are saints?

FRANCIS. (*Turning and smiling*) It all depends on how you look at it. This I can tell you: the true saints must think the wise men foolish. And this remember, Brother John: the fools of God are never foolish.

JOHN. (*closing his eyes in the effort to memorize it exactly*) The fools of God are never foolish.

FRANCIS. (*turns to the right and points offstage*) We have work to do. Come, Brother John!

JOHN. (*picks up the portfolio*) Shall I bring the fiddle?

FRANCIS. (*slowly and thoughtfully*) No, my brother. For when we need a fiddle again, the good God will send it. (*begins to move off, Right*)

JOHN. What is this next work we have to do?

FRANCIS. I do not know. I only wait to do it.

(*Exeunt, Right*)

The End

Some Are Fools for Money's Sake

Words: Mother M. Francis

Music: Rev. Joseph Roff

Bright and zesty (♩ = 108)

Some are fools for mon-ey's sake, and some are fools

for power's sake. Many are the fools of fear, but

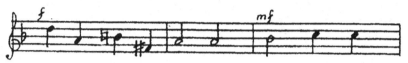

few the fools for God's sake! Come, learn, my

Brothers in my school A very few and simple

rules: Money and power are spent in an hour, but

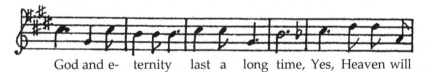

God and e- ternity last a long time, Yes, Heaven will

last for quite a long time, Heaven will last for

quite a long time, and nobody gains it but God's fools.

Heaven will last for quite a long time, and nobody

gains it but God's fools!

No Man is Quite so Wicked

Words: Mother M. Francis   Music: Rev. Joseph Roff

With joy and simplicity

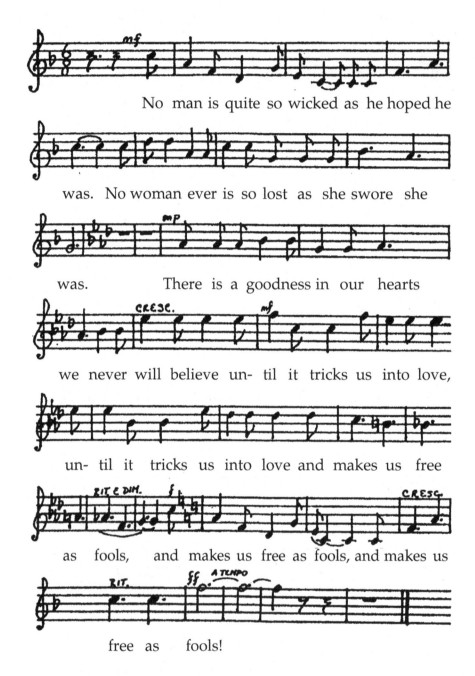

No man is quite so wicked as he hoped he

was. No woman ever is so lost as she swore she

was.   There is a goodness in our hearts

we never will believe un- til it tricks us into love,

un- til it tricks us into love and makes us free

as fools,   and makes us free as fools, and makes us

free as fools!

The Road to Emmaus

A Drama in One Act

© 1962, 1990 The Community of Poor Clares of New Mexico, Inc.

To

FATHER VARIN SLACKE, O.F.M.

Imprimatur: Edwin V. Byrne, D.D.
                 Archbishop of Sante Fe

Nihil Obstat: Rt. Rev. Francis Tournier
                 Censor Deputatus

                 July 7, 1962

Cast of Characters

In Order of Appearance

REUBEN . . . . disciple of JESUS, a heavy-set man, about forty, wears a long grey tunic and cloak, a short veil caught about his head with a band, sandals on bare feet.

DANIEL . . . . a boy of about nine, small for his years, wears a bright red short tunic reaching just below his knees, bareheaded, sandals on bare feet.

CLEOPHAS . . . . . . disciple of JESUS, tall and slender, about thirty, dressed like REUBEN.

BEGGAR . . . . scrawny-looking fellow of no particular age, dressed in rags, barefoot, has matted hair, is toothless.

SARA . . . . a pretty Jewish girl, about thirty, dark-haired, shy of manner, wears a long mauve-colored tunic and mantle, a long mauve veil over her hair and falling over her shoulders, sandals on bare feet.

JACOB . . . . her husband, about the same age, medium height, lean, eager and boyish in manner, dressed like REUBEN.

RACHEL . . . . his grandmother, about eighty, stooped and frail, piercing intelligent eyes, wears a dark blue tunic, cloak, and veil, sandals with stockings.

THE STRANGER . . . tall and strongly built, dark-haired, beautiful grace in every motion, wears a white linen tunic, a white woolen cloak, sandals on bare feet, is bareheaded.

Story of the Play

Scarcely a Gospel incident surpasses in freshness and poignancy the Emmaus vignette. Two weary and disillusioned men, suddenly bereft of the Figure about whom they had come to build their lives, trudge heavily along the road from Jerusalem to Emmaus. The flame of faith has gone down to a final weak sputter. Hope has dwindled to black depression. Everything is over. And then He is there, there beside them. The crucified Christ, risen and glorious, but still the complete and perfect Man, full of a loving and gentle raillery for their despondency. "Ought not Christ to have suffered these things?" That sorrow and defeat must always dung the field for joy to bloom is the message learned by two depressed men on the road to Emmaus.

The Road to Emmaus

SCENE. *A rough road outside Jerusalem. There are pieces of felled logs here and there on the side of the road, a profusion of small stones on the road itself. At the far Left, one fig tree is putting out green buds. It alone abstracts from the bleakness of the scene. Close by the fig tree are more pieces of log, one large piece turned upright so that it appears like a small table.*

TIME. *The year 33 A.D., April.*

AT RISE. *Enter* REUBEN, *Right. He is a heavy-set man of about forty. He has a pack slung over his shoulder and walks with a pilgrim's staff. He wears a long grey tunic and cloak, and the customary Oriental short veil caught with a band on his head. He looks sullen and defeated. He comes Downstage, kicks a small stone viciously out of his way and turns back, Right.*

REUBEN. (*Calling Offstage, Right.*) Cleophas! (*No answer—louder.*) Cleophas! Hurry up, man. We'll never get to Emmaus this night.

(*Enter a small* BOY *of about nine, Left, with a basket of loaves which he carries by a double handle.*)

DANIEL. Barley loaves! Fresh barley loaves! Who wants hot barley loaves? (*Comes up to* REUBEN.) Barley loaves, master?

REUBEN. (*Surly.*) No. Get along boy.

DANIEL. (*Peers at him.*) You look tired, master. I think you must be hungry. I think you need bread. (*Uncovers basket.*) I have—

REUBEN. You have a lot of nerve, that's what you have. I told you—no!

(*Enter* CLEOPHAS, *Right. He is a tall, slender man of about thirty with a sad, sensitive face. He is dressed like* REUBEN *and has a waterskin slung from his girdle. He is limping, and carrying one sandal in his hand. He looks around and seats himself on a piece of log, examining the sandal.*)

CLEOPHAS. Broken! (*Examines foot.*) Bleeding! Look at that.

REUBEN. Now what?

CLEOPHAS. A stone in my foot.

REUBEN. By heaven!—another delay!

DANIEL. Are you in a hurry, master?

REUBEN. Yes.

DANIEL. Why?

REUBEN. (*Startled.*) We have to get to Emmaus.

CLEOPHAS. (*Softly.*) We have to get away from Jerusalem, is what he means.

DANIEL. That's too bad.

REUBEN. What do you mean, too bad? Who asked your opinion, boy?

DANIEL. (*Grinning.*) Nobody, master. Barley loaves I sell. Opinions I give away. (REUBEN *gives* DANIEL *a cuff on the ear.*)

CLEOPHAS. Reuben! Churl! (*Rubs his own bleeding foot.*)

REUBEN. (*Embarrassed at his outbreak of anger, he ruffles the boy's hair.*) I am not in the best of humor today, lad. Go along, now.

CLEOPHAS. (*Frowns at* DANIEL.) What *did* you mean?—too bad? Who are you?

DANIEL. I'm Daniel, master. And I meant it is too bad you are hurrying away from somewhere, because it is much nicer to be hurrying to get somewhere. (*Props one foot on* CLEOPHAS' *log and balances basket.*) And it is a lot worse when you are two friends together, master, and one is hurrying to leave and one is hurrying to arrive.

REUBEN. That's enough out of you, Solomon. (*Gives him a light push.*) Go on now, you little loafer, and mind your own business.

DANIEL. (*Roars with delight.*) Loafer! Oh, master, there's a fine good joke! (*Laughs again.*) I'm Daniel the Loafer, seller of loaves! (*Hitches basket back to position and starts moving off, Right, calling his wares.*) Barley loaves! Fresh barley loaves! Buy your loaves from Daniel the Loafer! (*His laugh trails off. Exit* DANIEL, *Right.*)

CLEOPHAS. (*Laughs a little, then looks at sandal.*) I'll have to mend it.

REUBEN. (*Sitting down beside him.*) How do you keep a taste for laughter, Cleophas? (*Rests his face against his hand, elbow propped on knee.*)

CLEOPHAS. I think I have no more tears left, Reuben. (*Dangles sandal.*) A broken sandal. A broken dream . . . (*Takes a knife from under his tunic and cuts a piece of leather from his girdle, measuring it against the sandal.*) You can mend the sandal. How can you mend the dream?

REUBEN. (*Leans forward and eases pouch on his shoulder, clasps hands together on his knees.*) That was our mistake. It was *all* a dream. And dreaming is not for sensible men like us. Fishing is our business. We know the sea. Clouds are for fools.

CLEOPHAS. (*Softly.*) He never seemed a fool. Somehow, all the others seemed the fools when He was there.

REUBEN. Ay, ay, Cleophas! (*Straightens up.*) But now who is alive and who is dead? (*Stands up, suddenly impatient.*) The scribes are still writing, and the priests are still slaying the goats and taking in as good a fee as ever. (*Walks back and forth.*) The hawkers are still selling their pigeons, and the fishermen are hauling in their catch. But *He* is dead. (*Stops in front of* CLEOPHAS.) Dead as lashes and thorns and nails and a lance can make Him. (*Suddenly depleted of this burst of energy.*) It's the end of Him, Cleophas. That much, at least, is clear.

CLEOPHAS. (*Lets the sandal dangle and stands up to catch* REUBEN's *sleeve.*) Reuben! Did you see them spit at Him? Did you see Him squint their dirty spit out of His eyes? Did you see the way He looked at them when He wiped their filthy spit out of His eyes? (*Face working.*) My God, Reuben—I think He loved them.

REUBEN. (*Pulls away, overcome.*) Shut up.

(*Enter a* BEGGAR, *Left.*)

BEGGAR. (*Whines.*) A penny, good master! A penny for a poor beggar! (CLEOPHAS *and* REUBEN *seem not to hear him. Singsong.*) God will give you a long life for your kindness to a poor beggar. A penny for a long life, master? It's a good bargain, master! (*Stretches out his hand.*)

REUBEN. (*Whirls on him.*) Who wants a long life?

BEGGAR. Eh?

CLEOPHAS. (*Gives* BEGGAR *a penny.*) A long life is a long dying, my friend.

BEGGAR. (*Grabs at penny.*) I'm no friend of yours. I'm a beggar, master. Ya two talk queer. (*Looks from one to the other.*) Both of ya's talk queer. (*Digs* REUBEN *in the ribs.*) I think maybe ya's had a bit too much. Hee, hee! (*The beggar has a thin high cackle of a laugh which intersperse all his talk. Pantomimes a stagger.*) Or maybe not enough. Both makes a man talk queer.

REUBEN. You good-for-nothing! Whom do you think you're talking to?

BEGGAR. (*Toothless grin.*) To friends, rabbi! (*Points to* CLEOPHAS.) Master there says we're friends. Hee, hee!

REUBEN. Oh, yes? Well, you're no friend of mine. (*Turns away, then swings back.*) And I'm no rabbi, do you understand? (*Paces back and forth, then goes over to the fig tree and angrily breaks off a small twig.*)

BEGGAR. (*Confidentially to* CLEOPHAS, *pointing after* REUBEN.) Master don't feel good, I think. Them up in Jerusalem are different. When I call them "rabbi," they always give me a penny. Hee, hee! They like it good enough—them with the long trains and the fringes. (*Prances up and down, drawing imaginary long garments around him and holding head very high.*) Ya's two are different. (*Shakes head.*) I never knew one of them big ones (*Jerks thumb in direction of Offstage, Right, indicating Jerusalem.*) that didn't like being called rabbi.

CLEOPHAS. (*As though to himself.*) We had a Friend who really *was* a rabbi. And He died. That is why my friend Reuben is upset.

BEGGAR. (*Compassionately.*) Oh, so that be the way of things. (*Reaches to scratch his back, and squirms to indicate vermin.*) Dying is bad. (*Shakes head.*) I be feared of dying, and not feared of dying, all at the same time. (REUBEN *drifts back.*) But it's bad. (*To* REUBEN.) Be you feared of dying, master? (REUBEN *withers him with a look—or tries.* BEGGAR *turns back to* CLEOPHAS *with a shrug.*) Be *you* feared of it?

CLEOPHAS. (*Studies sandal, fitting new strap.*) I don't know. I think I am only afraid to go on living while I am dead.

BEGGAR. Eh? (*Studies* CLEOPHAS.) Hee, hee! Oh, master, ya *do* talk queer!

REUBEN. (*Irritated.*) Hurry up, will you, Cleophas. It is getting toward evening.

BEGGAR. (*Scratches head vigorously and examines hand for findings, shrugs.*) Hee, hee! I never heard nothing like it. (*To* REUBEN. *Points at* CLEOPHAS.) Master there says he don't like to live while he is dead! Hee, hee!

REUBEN. (*Shakes* BEGGAR *by his shoulders, yelling.*) Shut up, you fool!

CLEOPHAS. (*Jumps up, pulls* REUBEN *away, speaks gently.*) Let him alone, Reuben. It is only what I said. (*To* BEGGAR.) You had better go on your way.

BEGGAR. (*Cocks head.*) I like ya's two. (*Looks toward* REUBEN, *addressing* CLEOPHAS *with motion of head toward* REUBEN.) Even him. Ya's two are not like them others. (*Gesture toward Offstage Jerusalem. Edges up between the two* DISCIPLES, *confidentially.*) There was One up there was different, though. (*Stops, suddenly thunderstruck by his discovery.*) Why—ya's remind me of Him a little bit. (*Studies* REUBEN *and then* CLEOPHAS, *turning back and forth.*) Ya's are not near so grand looking, I'll say that. But still—there's something.

CLEOPHAS. (*Fists clenched with emotion.*) Who—who is it you are talking about? (REUBEN *walks a little apart.*)

BEGGAR. (*Gestures toward Jerusalem.*) The good One up there. That One they made an end of. (*After* REUBEN, CLEOPHAS *on his heels,* BEGGAR *looks from one to the other.*) Only once I seen Him, but I don't never forget it, masters. He had a look on Him. (*Scratches head, wipes nose with back of hand and then wipes hand on his ragged garments.*) Beautiful is what ya'd want to say about Him, except it's no right word for a man. (*Pulls shoulders back and tries to stand imposingly.*) He—well—He had a look on Him.

CLEOPHAS. (*Turns away.*) Oh, my God! Be still!

REUBEN. (*Fascinated, his breath coming in little gasps.*) *Who?* Who is it you mean?

BEGGAR. (*Bites at fingernail, putting dirty finger far back in mouth, as there are no teeth in front.*) That One up there. (*Gestures toward Jerusalem.*) He cured a friend of mine. (*Spits out end of fingernail.*) Isaac is his name, my friend's name. Blind as midnight. (*Mimics groping about.*) Never could see nothing, Isaac couldn't. And one day he takes it in his head to ask that One— (*Gestures off Right.*) that One with the look on Him— (*Digs* REUBEN *in ribs for emphasis.*) which Isaac couldn't see, mind you, master, hee, hee!—He asks that One to make him see. Cool as that.

(REUBEN *and* CLEOPHAS *close in on the* BEGGAR, *each clutching at one of the beggar's arms.*)

CLEOPHAS. (*Almost a sob.*) And then what? (BEGGAR *tries to break loose, but cannot.*)

REUBEN. (*A real shout.*) And *then* what?

BEGGAR. (*Indignant.*) And then he sees, that's what! Leave me be. (*Shakes himself free of them.*) Ya's can take it or leave it, I don't care none. But Isaac can see, I'll tell ya's that much. That One up there (*The gesture.*) just looked at Isaac—never so much as touched him—never used no salve, understand? He never poured nothing in Isaac's eyes nor nothing. He just *looked* at Isaac and says to him (*Squints eyes shut in effort to summon up exact memory of words.*) "What do you want of me?" (*Opens eyes and then imitates Isaac with closed eyes, stretching out his arms.*) And Isaac says: "Lord, that I may see!" Mind you, Isaac called Him "Lord," though he never seen that look He had on Him, that grand One. There was that about Him, masters—that One up there— (*The gesture.*) that you knew He was a great One, even by His voice—or even just having Him near you.

CLEOPHAS. (*Scarcely above a whisper.*) Oh, I know!

BEGGAR. Eh? (*Scratches back, looks at hand, shrugs.*) Well, anyhow, so what do you think He says to Isaac? (*Draws himself up to imitate the Saviour.*) Just as grand as a king, He says. (*Holds out hand in command.*) "I will it. See!" (*Turns back and slumps to ordinary position, scratching the top of one bare foot with the sole of the other.*) And just like that,—Isaac *sees!* (CLEOPHAS *turns away, weeping. Puzzled, to* REUBEN.) What's wrong with him? (*Gesturing after* CLEOPHAS.) Don't he believe it?

REUBEN. (*The first time he has spoken in a gentle voice.*) Yes. Yes, he believes it.

BEGGAR. (*Immediately encouraged.*) Oh. Just got a jelly heart in him, I guess. (*Steps back.*) I tell ya's— (*Looks from one to the other.*) there *is* that in ya's both that makes me think of that One up there— (*The gesture.*) that One that had the look on him. (*Hands out, in gesture of futility.*) Too bad they finished Him up, I say for one. I could name ya's fifty of them with the fringes (*The gesture.*) that had better been finished up than the One with the look on Him.

REUBEN. (*Gruff again to hide his feelings.*) Who cares what you say, beggar! He is dead. The others are alive.

BEGGAR. (*Wipes nose with back of hand, scratches head.*) That's the pity of it. This other One—

REUBEN. (*Gives* BEGGAR *a shove.*) We've heard enough. (*Sounds almost angry.*) Listen, we knew Him. You don't have to tell us.

BEGGAR. (*Delighted.*) Ya's don't tell me! (*Edges in on* REUBEN.) Well, I guess ya's both feel bad they finished Him up. I'll be moving on. (*Back to first singsong.*) Only a penny for a poor beggar, master. (*Slyly.*) A penny in memory of that One— (*The gesture.*) that had the look on Him.

REUBEN. (*Face working, takes out a penny like a man in a dream,* BEGGAR *snatches it.*) Go. Please go.

BEGGAR. (*Reaches to scratch back, inspects hands.*) Ah! (*Drops louse and stomps on it.*) Thank you, master. Ya's are good men, though ya's do talk terrible queer. (*Moves off, Right, looking back.*) Remind me of that One that had the look on Him. (*Shakes head. Exit* BEGGAR, *Right.*)

(CLEOPHAS *comes limping back to the log and picks up his broken sandal absentmindedly.*)

REUBEN. (*Snatching sandal, eager to do something.*) Here, give it to me! You haven't even made a start. Wasting all this time!

CLEOPHAS. (*Sad, mocking smile.*) Can you tell me something better to do with time—*now?*

(*Rumbling of a* CART *is heard Offstage Left.*)

REUBEN. We have to go on living, Cleophas.

CLEOPHAS. I suppose. (RUMBLING *grows louder.*)

REUBEN. (*Fumbles in pocket of tunic for cord and holds it out for* CLEOPHAS *to cut off a length with his knife, threads cord into heavy needle.*) Good thing I always travel prepared. (*Takes* CLEOPHAS' *sandal.*) I'm always ready for anything.

(RUMBLING *very loud. Enter* JACOB, RACHEL, *and* SARA, *Left.* RACHEL *is very old and seated in an odd cart-like sedan which* JACOB *pulls along after him, holding it by two long side bars.* SARA, *Jacob's wife, walks beside the cart. They are about thirty,* RACHEL *about eighty.* JACOB *suddenly jerks the cart to one side violently as* REUBEN *and* CLEOPHAS *are staring at the little group.* RACHEL *lurches precariously over the side toward* REUBEN *who instinctively holds out his arms to protect the* OLD LADY. SARA *gives a little cry.*)

CLEOPHAS. (*Little smile at* RACHEL *in* REUBEN'S *arms.*) Ready for anything, eh, Reuben? (JACOB *is peering down into footlights.*)

SARA. Jacob!

JACOB. (*Jerks back.*) Oh, sirs, pardon me! I thought that little rabbit (*Gestures toward footlight, indicating other side of road.*) was just going to dart across the road. I was afraid I would kill it.

RACHEL. (SARA *helps her to sit upright, while* REUBEN *embarrassedly steps back.*) You weren't one bit afraid to kill your old grandmother, though!

JACOB. (*Sets bars of the cart down carefully and turns back to his* GRANDMOTHER.) Mother! (*Kisses the* OLD LADY *on the forehead.*) You lie as grandly and beautifully as you do everything else.

RACHEL. (*Smiles and gives him a little push away.*) Hush, boy. (CLEOPHAS *abstractedly runs his hand along bars of the cart.* REUBEN *clears his throat loudly.*)

SARA. (*Pulling at* JACOB'S *sleeve.*) I think we owe these friends an apology. Jacob. (*Timid smile at* REUBEN.)

JACOB. Oh, yes! Yes, indeed! Excuse me, sirs. It was the rabbit. (*Turns away.*) Somehow I cannot bear the thought of killing anything today. (*Turns back.*) We are going up to Jerusalem. A Friend of ours has just died there.

SARA. (*Softly.*) He was *killed* there.

JACOB. Yes. (*Little silence, then jerks back to reality.*) This is Rachel, my grandmother. This is my wife, Sara. (*Indicates each.*)

RACHEL. We are grateful for your help. My Jacob is a wild boy. (*Affectionate hand on his hair.*) And today we are all upset.

REUBEN. (*Tries to laugh, not succeeding very well.*) Well, the cart was upset. (*Toward* CLEOPHAS.) This is my friend, Cleophas. Reuben is my name.

(SARA *smiles and bows toward each, then drifts over to the fig tree and caresses its green leaves.* RACHEL *also inclines to each of the disciples.*)

JACOB. Are you going to Jerusalem? We could travel together. Sara made a lunch. I bought some barley loaves from a little lad.

REUBEN. No, we are going to Emmaus. The other way. (*Gestures off Left.*)

CLEOPHAS. We are going away from Jerusalem. I think we shall never go back to Jerusalem again.

JACOB. (*Looks from one to the other, surprised at* CLEOPHAS' *dramatic finality.*) No? But Jerusalem is the heart of the world.

CLEOPHAS. For us, Jerusalem is only a burial ground.

RACHEL. (*Leans out of cart and touches* CLEOPHAS' *sleeve.*) You have a sorrow upon you, my son. I see it. (SARA *drifts back, a little green leaf in her hand.*)

CLEOPHAS. (*Softly.*) I have lost my best Friend.

SARA. (*Loud whisper to* RACHEL.) And he has lost his sandal. (*Gestures toward* REUBEN, *still holding sandal and cord, and at* CLEOPHAS' *bare foot.*) I could mend it faster than the menfolk.

RACHEL. (*Looks from one to the other.*) Yes! Here, son—you, Reuben! (*Smiles and holds out her hand.*) Give me that. Sara will mend it for you.

REUBEN. Oh—I don't—

RACHEL. (*Taking sandal.*) Yes, you do, son. Now, sit down (*Points to log.*) and you, too, (*To* CLEOPHAS.) son. Sara! (*Points to the place beside her in the cart and* SARA *settles herself down with the sandal and cord.*)

(JACOB *sits down on the roadside, drawing his knees up under his chin and circling his arms around his knees on which he rests his chin. The* DISCIPLES *sit down stiffly on the log.* RACHEL *studies* CLEOPHAS *and then* REUBEN.)

RACHEL. (*To* REUBEN.) What are you running away from, son?

REUBEN. (*Awkward grin, shifts his heavy frame on the log.*) I am a little aged to be called son, good mother.

RACHEL. (*Little smile.*) I have four score of years, son. You are little children to me. (*Points to* JACOB *and* SARA.) Like these two. (*Nods head several times.*) Little children, all of you.

JACOB. Mother knew *Him* when *He* was a little child. (*Looks away.*) So did I, though. We were children together, He and I.

REUBEN. (*Springs up, seems strangely upset.*) *He? Who is He?*

CLEOPHAS. (*Pulls* REUBEN *back down on log.*) You know that we know. (REUBEN *sinks down.*)

RACHEL. (*Very gently.*) Is it the same One, then? The Friend we lost—He was your Friend, too?

REUBEN. (*Shifting around, miserable.*) How do I know, woman? You keep talking in riddles. There are millions of friends in the world, aren't there?

SARA. (*Looks up timidly from her task.*) But *this* one was *Jesus.*

REUBEN. (*Little groan, tries to change the subject, interjecting foolishly.*) We are going to Emmaus. (*Clears throat.*) We'll be much obliged for that sandal, woman. (*Holds out hand.*)

SARA. (*Smiles.*) Not quite. (*Stitches again.*) Almost, now.

JACOB. Did you know Him well?

CLEOPHAS. Very well.

JACOB. (*Eagerly but sadly, too.*) We used to live in the cottage next to Miriam and Joseph. I played with Him.

SARA. (*Looks up as she speaks, then quickly lowers her head again in shyness.*) I—I—used to watch Him. I watched Him all the time. Somehow you always wanted to keep on looking at Him.

JACOB. (*Stands up.*) He used to bring us curls of shavings for our play when we were very small.

SARA. (*Gathering courage.*) He used to have shavings clinging to his sandals, and sometimes in His hair.

(RACHEL *keeps looking musingly around the little group, nodding her head from time to time.*)

JACOB. His father had a carpenter shop.

CLEOPHAS. (*Jumps up.*) Why are you going back there? (*Faces the* THREE *aggressively.*) Why do you want to go back there?

RACHEL. (*Hand on* CLEOPHAS' *sleeve.*) We go to comfort Miriam. For Joseph is dead. And now her Boy is dead. She is alone.

CLEOPHAS. (*Comes Down Center, pulling away from* RACHEL.) But *everyone* is alone. Each one is alone. There is no company anywhere. (*Short steps back and forth.*) Grief is the knife that cuts all hearts apart. Cleaves all friends apart. No one can ever enter into another's grief. (SARA *stops stitching and stares at him, then exchanges a surprised glance with* JACOB. REUBEN *sulks.* RACHEL *watches* CLEOPHAS *intently.*) We stand in the vestibule of sorrow, but we cannot come in. We can enter the inner court of only one man's grief, and that is our own. And that one we cannot leave. Never. Never can we leave it.

(SARA *and* JACOB *stare at him.* REUBEN *turns away.* RACHEL *steps out of cart as* JACOB *abstractedly gives her a hand. She walks up to* CLEOPHAS.)

RACHEL. No, my son. Love is the key to every man's grief. And even when a man *refuses* to let us enter his sorrow, love will still turn the key on it. (*Hand on* CLEOPHAS' *shoulder.*) And love is the key that lets us out of our own grief. For we do not love unless we believe. And when we believe, we already hope.

REUBEN. (*Much embarrassed by this talk, comes up to them stiffly.*) It is all fantastic. All nonsense. We were fishermen, making a good enough living. Sensible men with no nonsense about us. Cleophas there—(*Flick of his hand.*) was one to talk wildly sometimes—to get excited at the way the sunlight hit the water and crazy things like that. But he was a good fisherman. We always got along. (*Paces irritably back and forth.*) Now we stand here, trying to talk like poets and prophets. We are *fools.* (RACHEL *smiles;* REUBEN *grows embarrassed over his faux pas and continues more gruffly.*) I mean—we—(*Jerks hand toward* CLEOPHAS.) we two are a pair of fools. And we must get on to Emmaus and stop talking like idiots. (*Back to cart.*) Is it finished, woman?

SARA. Yes, my lord. (*Hands him the sandal which he tosses to* CLEOPHAS.)

REUBEN. There! Let us be on our way, Cleophas. (*Back toward cart with awkward bow.*) And we are very much obliged to you. You are very kind.

(CLEOPHAS *absentmindedly puts on the sandal.*)

JACOB. Why don't you come back to Jerusalem with us?

REUBEN. (*Real yell.*) No! We are going to *Emmaus.* And we shall *never* return to Jerusalem.

RACHEL. (*Toddles up to him.*) I wonder. Here, give an old woman a hand, my son.

(REUBEN *embarrassedly helps* RACHEL *back into the cart.* SARA *steps down and motions to* JACOB. *They whisper together, and then* JACOB *takes a loaf from pouch in cart.*)

JACOB. Here, sirs, please take this loaf. You have yet a long walk to Emmaus. You will be hungry.

REUBEN. No, we don't need it.

SARA. Please take it.

REUBEN. (*Self-conscious.*) Oh—I—we— (*Grabs at the bread.*) Well, thank you. (*Hands the barley loaf to* CLEOPHAS *who puts it into a pouch he had carried, flattened down, in the folds of his garments.*)

CLEOPHAS. Thank you. (*Slaps waterskin at his side.*) Water and bread. It is enough.

RACHEL. (*Tenderly, to* CLEOPHAS.) Is it only water, then, in that waterskin, my son? Or, is it tears?

CLEOPHAS. (*Staring.*) What?

RACHEL. What does the psalm say, my son? (*Closes her eyes and tilts her face back slightly to the sky.*) "My tears are carried in His waterskin."

(CLEOPHAS *turns way.* REUBEN *hits the ground with his staff.*)

RACHEL. Come, Jacob, get into your harness! (*Smiles at the* DISCIPLES. JACOB *gets in position to pull the cart.*) He is my pack mule. He is a good boy. He always tried to be like Miriam's Son. (*Nods.*) He is a good boy.

SARA. (*Smiles shyly at the* DISCIPLES.) I hope God may ease your grief. He has eased ours.

CLEOPHAS. (*Desperately.*) How? I thought you were mourning Jesus.

RACHEL. We are. But we go to comfort Miriam. And something lies ahead.

REUBEN. (*Adjusting garments, squaring shoulders to finish journey.*) What?

RACHEL. We do not know what. But *something* lies ahead.

CLEOPHAS. (*Fastening on sandal.*) Death is death. End is end. Despair is despair.

RACHEL. Ah, ah, son!—Death! End! Despair! Look at the fig tree there (*Gestures, and all look.*) It was dead in the winter, we thought. And see—it lives!

REUBEN. (*Frowns, to* JACOB.) What is she talking about? Is she queer? (*Taps head significantly.*)

JACOB. Oh, no! Old mother is wise. I don't know what she means. But she is wise.

SARA. (*Nods.*) We *always* believe her.

CLEOPHAS. (*Standing up again.*) Do you understand her?

JACOB. No. Often we do not understand her. But we always believe her. Well—farewell, friends! (*Starts pulling cart off, Right.*)

(*The* DISCIPLES *stand staring after the trio. Exit* TRIO, *Right.*)

REUBEN. That's a queer trio, I'll say.

CLEOPHAS. What is not queer, Reuben? What is not strange? (*They move toward fig tree, then pause. Loudly.*) Oh, Reuben, I have no heart to go on to Emmaus!

(DISCIPLES *are looking off Left. Enter the* STRANGER, *Right. The* STRANGER *wears a pure white linen tunic, a white woolen cloak. He is tall and strongly built. He walks with beautiful grace.*)

REUBEN. (*Gruffly.*) Have you a heart for going back to Jerusalem?

CLEOPHAS. (*Miserable.*) No, never! What are we to do? How can we go on living? When we pull out into the water for our fishing, I shall see *Him* preaching from Peter's boat. (*The* STRANGER *comes closer.*) And when the sun slants through the treetops, I shall hear *Him* saying: "Blessed are the poor!"

REUBEN. Oh, stop it, will you! (*Turns on him irritably.*) He is *dead*, Cleophas. Defeated. Ruined. We have to pick up our lives where they were before we met Him. (*The* STRANGER *closes in, directly behind them.*) He is disgraced. Finished, I tell you. Jesus is finished.

THE STRANGER. Peace be to you.

(CLEOPHAS *and* REUBEN *start violently and whirl on the* STRANGER.)

REUBEN. How did you get there?

CLEOPHAS. Where did you come from?

THE STRANGER. I have been visiting friends. Many friends. Now I travel on.

REUBEN. (*Mystified.*) We did not hear your step.

CLEOPHAS. We heard nothing.

THE STRANGER. I heard you. I could not help it, could I? Tell me—what are these discourses you hold together? (*Looks from one to the other.*) And why are you sad?

CLEOPHAS. Who is *not* sad? Are you only a stranger in Jerusalem, that you do not know the things that have happened?

THE STRANGER. What things?

REUBEN. (*Exasperated.*) What things! Everyone talks of nothing else. Even the beggars, the old ladies, the young couples.

CLEOPHAS. The things that happened to Jesus of Nazareth.

THE STRANGER. Who is He?

REUBEN. Kind heaven!—Have you been slumbering under the earth, man? Who does not know about Jesus of Nazareth?

THE STRANGER. (*Evenly.*) Tell me about Him. (*Motions toward log where* DISCIPLES *had sat before.*)

CLEOPHAS. (*Exchanging puzzled glance with* REUBEN.) We are moving on to Emmaus.

THE STRANGER. I am going that way myself. But tell me first about this Jesus. (*Motions to log again, and* DISCIPLES *move toward it in a manner to indicate they are being impelled to obey. The* STRANGER *sits between them on the log.*)

CLEOPHAS. (*Flat voice.*) He was a prophet. He was mighty in His words and His works.

REUBEN. Mighty—yes, that is what He was. No man ever spoke as He spoke. And no one could resist His words.

CLEOPHAS. (*Softly.*) No one could resist His eyes, even. He had only to look at a man—and— (*Turns away.*)

REUBEN. (*Gruffly.*) And a man would make a fool of himself. A man would drop his fishing nets and run after Him.

CLEOPHAS. A man would leave his father and his mother, and go after Him. A man would die for Him.

THE STRANGER. Someone you knew died for Him?

REUBEN. No. *He* died.

CLEOPHAS. We could not believe it. We cannot believe it yet. But He died.

THE STRANGER. It was unexpected?

REUBEN. (*Uncalled for loudness. He jumps up.*) *Yes!* — Of course, it was unexpected. We always believed Him. We always thought He could not be defeated. We thought He would not even die. We always believed Him.

THE STRANGER. And did He tell you that He would not die?

REUBEN. Yes. That is—no. He—well—He,—well, not exactly.

THE STRANGER. What *did* He tell you? (*Indicates with a gentle motion of head that* REUBEN *should sit down again.* REUBEN *does.*)

REUBEN. (*Hands clasped on knees, looking out across the road.*) He told us such things as we never heard before. In fact, He told us just about the opposite of everything we had always heard before. (*Voice drifts off.*)

THE STRANGER. (*Gently urging.*) Yes?

CLEOPHAS. He had a way of turning truth inside out for you. He spoke so simply—about sparrows and flowers and—(*Gestures.*)—fig trees. Nothing unusual. Nothing extraordinary. Yet. . .

THE STRANGER. Yes?

CLEOPHAS. (*Looks directly at the* STRANGER *for a long moment.*) Yet, He made you feel you had never seen a sparrow or a flower or a fig tree in all your life before. He made you feel you had never seen yourself before. (*Very softly.*) And you knew you had never been really loved before.

REUBEN. (*Gently, for him.*) He was all for the poor. He didn't give that— (*Snap of his fingers.*) for the rich ones or the great ones just because they were rich or great. He never seemed to care what the big ones said about Him. (*Ghost of a smile.*) A couple of times, He even told the big ones quite a few fundamental facts about themselves. "Hypocrites!" He called them—the pharisees, mind you! Just as much as told them they stank to high Heaven. "Whitened sepulchres" was the way He put it. Told them they just had a good coat of paint over the stink inside them.

CLEOPHAS. (*Eagerly.*) But to the little people, He was always so gentle—the sick ones and the frightened ones, the womenfolk—even the bad ones. (*Little silence.*) Only, after He had been with them awhile, the sick ones got well. The frightened ones grew brave. The bad ones turned good. That is the way it went when He was around.

THE STRANGER. What did He do for you?

REUBEN. (*Stares at the* STRANGER *and then gets to his feet and looks down at Him.*) You ask a lot of questions. I can't imagine that you never met Him. *Everyone* knew about Jesus.

THE STRANGER. (*Enigmatic half-smile.*) Yes?

REUBEN. (*Gruffly, almost a rebuke.*) *Yes!*

CLEOPHAS. I'll tell you what He did for *me*. He gave me such faith that I thought—I really thought He was the — Messiah . . . the One we have hoped for, prayed for, waited for. The One our fathers and our fathers' fathers waited for . . .

REUBEN. (*Pacing up and down.*) It's true. We all thought He was the Redeemer of Israel. There was never anyone like Him. He looked right into you, and you did not care. Read your thoughts, that's what He did. (*Nods to himself for emphasis.*) And it made you feel happy, not afraid. (*A little embarrassed at his self-revelations, he stops in front of the* STRANGER.) —If you can figure that out.

THE STRANGER. Yes, I understand that.

CLEOPHAS. We thought He was going to establish a new kingdom. But in the end, it all came to nothing.

THE STRANGER. Why?

REUBEN. (*Sits down abruptly.*) Because the chief priests and the pharisees killed Him, that's why!

CLEOPHAS. They got even, all right. They won. In the end, they carried the day.

REUBEN. (*Staring into space, as if seeing painful past scenes.*) They beat Him.

CLEOPHAS. Spat on Him.

REUBEN. Hammered spikes into His head.

CLEOPHAS. And then—they crucified Him.

THE STRANGER. What did *He* do?

REUBEN. (*Anguished.*) Nothing! Just, absolutely—nothing!

CLEOPHAS. (*Walks over to fig tree, breaks off a twig which he keeps turning in his fingers.*) That is what we could not understand. We saw Him raise dead men off their biers . . . that boy in Naim. (REUBEN *nods vigorously.*) Even call dead men out of their tombs.

REUBEN. (*Another determined nod.*) Lazarus!

CLEOPHAS. (*Pacing up and down, stops in front of the* STRANGER.) We thought He could do anything. But in the end, He could not do a thing for Himself. He could not save himself.

THE STRANGER. Did He try?

(REUBEN *and* CLEOPHAS *start at the* STRANGER *in surprise.* CLEOPHAS *sits down, continuing to stare.*)

REUBEN. (*Clears throat and points a finger, in the manner of one making a discovery.*) I think maybe that was what made it worse, even. (*Slowly.*) He seemed not to care at all—just went along with everything like it was planned—almost like it *had* to be that way.

CLEOPHAS. (*Looks out into space again.*) And at the very end, He never even blamed those dirty hypocrites—(*Tightens lips and clenches fist over the twig, breaking it.*) those lying, cheating, stinking pharisees.

REUBEN. (*Jumps up, pointing finger excitedly down into the* STRANGER's *face.*) What do you suppose He said?—hanging there, mind you—(*Another shake of the finger.*) nailed up there, and the blood streaming out of Him, and those damnable spikes through His skull!—He said—He said—(*Sits down, unable to continue.*)

CLEOPHAS. (*Softly.*) He said: "Father, forgive them. They don't know what they are doing." (*Long silence.*)

REUBEN. (*Flatly.*) And then He died. That's the whole story.

CLEOPHAS. (*Up.*) Yes, except for the wild tales some of the womenfolk are telling.

(*The* STRANGER *is always calm and interested, looking from one to the other, sometimes half-smiling.*)

REUBEN. You know how women are. He was good to them. He treated them as though they were just as good as men. That was another of the queer things He did. Now that He's dead, the women won't believe it. They can't face facts like men can. You know how women are.

THE STRANGER. (*The half-smile.*) Yes, I know how women are.

CLEOPHAS. They are saying He is still alive.

REUBEN. (*Patronizingly.*) Meaning, of course, that they *wish* He were. He's *dead*.

THE STRANGER. Can the women not see the dead body in its grave?

CLEOPHAS. (*Frowning down at the* STRANGER.) That is the strangest part of all. (*Sits down and stares across the road.*) The body is gone.

THE STRANGER. (*Rises slowly and looks down lovingly at the* TWO.) O foolish and slow of heart to believe in all the things which the prophets have spoken. (*Moves forward and looks up at the sky.*) Ought not Christ to have suffered all these things, and *so* enter into His glory? (REUBEN *and* CLEOPHAS *stare at Him, fascinated. The* STRANGER *looks at them again.*) What did Isaias say of the Christ? Was it not that He would be led as a lamb to the slaughter? (*Silence. Insistent.*) Was it not that?

REUBEN. (*Almost gruffly.*) That is what is given in Isaias—yes.

THE STRANGER. (*Down toward footlights, looks afar off.*) And has he not also said: "I have given my body to the strikers; I have not turned away my face from them that spit upon me." (*Walks back and looks at the* DISCIPLES.)

CLEOPHAS. (*Sounds frightened.*) Some have thought so.

THE STRANGER. And this Jesus—did He Himself never speak of dying?

CLEOPHAS. (*Rises, comes up to Him, rather timid now.*) He said it was always like the grain of wheat sown in the earth . . . it had to die . . . (*Frowns.*) and then it would live.

REUBEN. (*Frowns, too.*) I remember now—He *did* say that. (*Up.*)

REUBEN. (*Next to the* STRANGER.) But that was nothing like what He said when He called Lazarus out of the tomb! (*Turns to* CLEOPHAS.) You remember! You know! We were both there. (CLEOPHAS *nods. Excited.*) He said that He *was* life. He said that He was resurrection from death. (*More excited.*) He said that the men who believed in Him—even if they were dead—(*Finger at the* STRANGER *for emphasis.*) Even if they were *dead*, He said—would come alive. (*Excitement dies, sadness comes back to his voice.*) We had never heard anything like it.

THE STRANGER. Did you believe that?

REUBEN. (*Offended.*) Certainly! We believed Him all the time. We believed every word He ever said.

THE STRANGER. Did you believe Him when He said He would be lifted up, and only then draw all men to Himself?

CLEOPHAS. (*Head to one side, frowning.*) We never understood that. Christ could not be lifted up—that means on a cross—like a criminal—like a low fellow. We thought He was a king.

THE STRANGER. And when He said He was going up to Jerusalem to be mocked and scourged and spit upon and crucified—did you believe Him?

REUBEN. (*Staring, drops back a few steps in a kind of fright.*) We—we thought He was really talking queer then. Peter tried to stop Him talking like that. (*Silence,* CLEOPHAS *nods.*) But Jesus kept it up. He spoke pretty strong to Peter, too—called him satan, as a matter of fact.

THE STRANGER. And when He said that if they would destroy the temple, He would build it up in three days—did you believe Him then? (*The* DISCIPLES *now stand frozen before Him.*) When He said to you plainly: "On the third day I shall rise again"—did you believe Him?

(REUBEN *and* CLEOPHAS *stare, fascinated and trembling.* REUBEN *twists his fingers.* CLEOPHAS *drops the broken piece of twig. The* STRANGER *lifts his arms and moves toward Left, as though departing, then pauses.*) You have not believed the Christ.

(REUBEN'S *and* CLEOPHAS' *eyes meet for a long moment, then both look at the* STRANGER *who now stands at extreme Left of stage.*)

REUBEN and **CLEOPHAS.** (*One voice.*) Wait! (*After* HIM.)

THE STRANGER. I must go on.

REUBEN. No! Wait! Stay with us, Master! (*The* STRANGER *smiles a little at the first use of this title.*)

CLEOPHAS. See, it is toward evening! (*Catches at the* STRANGER'S *sleeve.*) Stay with us. Tell us more.

REUBEN. (*Eagerly.*) We have bread—a barley loaf!

CLEOPHAS. And water! (*Takes off waterskin and throws down the pouch with bread on the upright log.*)

REUBEN. (*Like a delighted child, engagingly clumsy in his quick efforts to arrange everything.*) This will do for a table. (*Slaps upright log where* CLEOPHAS *set the bread.*) Oh, it is good, good, we took that loaf from Jacob! (*Almost running, like a big eager dog, as he drags other pieces of log into place to serve for seats.*)

THE STRANGER. (*The melting half-smile.*) I should travel on.

REUBEN. No! No! You must break bread with us first.

CLEOPHAS. You must tell us more—more of all this.

THE STRANGER. (*Looks at them for a long moment, and then at the loaf.*) Sit down, little children. (REUBEN *and* CLEOPHAS *start at the appellation, and* CLEOPHAS *instinctively extends his hands as at a familiar call. Then both sink down on the log benches, leaving the one at the extreme Left for the* STRANGER. *They never take their eyes from Him as He takes the loaf into His hands and looks toward Heaven.*) My Father, I give Thee thanks. (*He breaks the bread into three parts and reaches a portion first to* CLEOPHAS *and then to* REUBEN. *They stare at the bread and then at the* STRANGER, *half-rising, as though trying to re-join some half-forgotten links of memory. The* STRANGER *blesses them, and they lean across the log-table toward Him, their faces close to His. As by a common urge, they then draw back a little and stare at the bread again. They pick it up. The* STRANGER *stretches out both arms over the bent* DISCIPLES. *Exit the* STRANGER, *fading off Left.*)

(REUBEN *and* CLEOPHAS *remain looking dumbly at the bread.* BOTH *at last look up to find the* STRANGER *gone.*)

REUBEN. (*A great cry.*) He is *gone*! (*Both run to the edge of stage, Left, peering out, hands over eyes. They turn back. Almost a sob.*) Gone!

CLEOPHAS. (*Fingers tightening on* REUBEN'S *arm.*) Reuben! (*They look at each other, lips of both moving wordlessly. They nod.* CLEOPHAS *grips both* REUBEN'S *arms with his two hands.*) Was not our heart burning within us as He spoke to us?

REUBEN. (*Nods excitedly.*) Was it not He? (*Louder.*) Did we not know Him in the breaking of the bread?

(*Enter the* BEGGAR, *Right. The* BEGGAR *wears the same rags, but over them a fine brownish cloak.* REUBEN *sinks down on the log, buries his face in his hands on the log table and weeps.* BEGGAR *comes closer.*)

CLEOPHAS. (*Staring off, Left.*) The Lord! It is the Lord!

Beggar. (*Closing in.*) *Who* be it, master?

Cleophas. (*Whirls about and presses verminous beggar to his heart.*) The Lord! The Lord lives! (Beggar *squirms loose.*)

Beggar. (*Wide-eyed.*) Ya's know it! I come back all this way to tell ya's what they're saying up there—(*The gesture, Right.*) about the One that had the look on Him. They *all* call Him the Lord now—just like ya's do. Except the big ones with the fringes, that is. They be hopping mad, the ones with the fringes, hee, hee! Things never turned out like they figured, hee, hee! (*Sees* Reuben *for the first time.*) Master there is feeling worse than ever, eh? (*Points at* Reuben.)

Cleophas. (*Jubilant.*) No! No!

Reuben. (*Looks up, tears streaming down his craggy face which is luminous with joy—rises.*) The Lord lives!

Cleophas. (*Arms out in excess of joy, he takes the* Beggar *by the shoulders.*) The One with the look on Him!

Beggar. How do ya's know it? I come back because I got a heart in me for both of ya's. I took a liking to ya's. I wanted ya's to know that they are telling it up there—(*The gesture.*) That the One that made my friend, Isaac, see—the One that was finished up proper, mind you, and every drop of blood drained out of Him as everyone could see—well—(*Pause for dramatic effect of his message.*) They're telling it that He's up and around!

Reuben. (*Takes* Beggar's *arm.*) We have seen Him!

Cleophas. (*Like a child singing.*) We have seen the Lord!

Beggar. Ya's don't tell me? How did He get here so quick? Them up there— (*The gesture.*) are telling how *they* seen Him in Jerusalem. But I never seen Him on the road.

Reuben. (*Shakes* Beggar's *arm in his excessive joy.*) The Lord *lives*!

Beggar. (*Pulls away.*) I don't mind it none that master feels good again, but keep yourself clear of this cloak. (*Draws it proudly around his rags.*) I got it off a young fellow named John. (*Close to them, confidential.*) I ask him for a penny like I always do—a man has to make an honest living—(*Scratches one foot with the other.*) And he gives it to me, right off. Then this woman with him—Miriam, he calls her, John does—and she calls him, John. Well, anyway, she whispers to him—and don't he take off his cloak and put it on *me!* (*Walks up and down proudly in cloak, back to* Disciples.) The woman—this Miriam—smiles and says: "You look cold." And, quick as a flash, I answer: "That's the truth."

(*Enter* Daniel, *Right, dragging empty basket, rubbing eyes sleepily. It is getting very dark now.*)

Cleophas. (*Exchanges glances with* Reuben, *catches his breath with emotion.*) This Miriam? —Was she weeping?

Beggar. Weeping? Nah. (*Scratches head.*) But she had a queer look on her. (*Screws up mouth in effort to find a description of her.*) Ya's ever seen the sun come up quick, real quick, after it's been raining enough to drown ya's? (*Hunches shoulders.*) Well, that's as good as I can tell ya's . . . She looks like that.

Reuben. (*Voice trembling, to* Cleophas.) The Lord!

CLEOPHAS. (*Awed.*) She has seen the Lord.

BEGGAR. Eh?

DANIEL. (*He stumbles up to them. Tugs at* CLEOPHAS' *sleeve, yawns.*) I sold them all. (*Turns empty basket upside down.*)

REUBEN. (*Happily, smooths* DANIEL'S *hair.*) It is good bread!

DANIEL. (*Reproachfully.*) You did not buy any.

REUBEN. (*Swings* DANIEL *up in the air.*) But we had some! (*Sets him down.*)

DANIEL. (*Wide-eyed.*) Where did you get it, master?

REUBEN. From a friend.

CLEOPHAS. It is blessed bread.

REUBEN. Wonderful bread.

CLEOPHAS. The best bread in the world. (DANIEL *looks bewilderedly from one to the other.* BEGGAR *dusts off cloak examining material.* REUBEN *turns back to log table, snatches up his piece and begins to eat it.* CLEOPHAS, *after him, breaks his piece into three parts and gives pieces to* DANIEL *and the* BEGGAR. *They begin to munch it.*) It is blessed bread. Holy bread.

BEGGAR. (*Points at log table.*) There's another piece.

CLEOPHAS. (*Picks it up reverently and places it in his pouch.*) This is the most blessed of all. This we shall never eat.

DANIEL. It gets stale, master.

CLEOPHAS. (*Takes* DANIEL'S *hand.*) Nothing grows stale when the heart is fresh.

REUBEN. (*Loudly, energetically.*) We must go back to Jerusalem!

BEGGAR. Tonight? It's too late. That's a parcel of walking.

CLEOPHAS. (*Laughs.*) Oh, no! It is early. And we are not tired. It is only a bit of a walk!

BEGGAR. Ya's are all mixed up. It's—

CLEOPHAS. To us, now, it is only a bit of a walk. (*Laughs and looks up at the sky.*) Look! the stars are breaking through!

(DANIEL *yawns.* REUBEN *swings* DANIEL *up and sets him on his shoulder, hands basket to the* BEGGAR.)

REUBEN. Come on! We must go to Jerusalem, together—all of us friends.

BEGGAR. (*Shakes head.*) Ya's two are the queerest I ever met.

CLEOPHAS. Come along with us, friend.

BEGGAR. (*Shrugs.*) Oh—I guess. I did take a liking to ya's. (*Draws cloak about him, swings basket.*) Ya's remind me more than ever of that One that had the look on Him.

CLEOPHAS. (*Moves toward Right, cradling pouch with the bread, and strapping on the waterskin.*) The One that *has* the look on Him.

BEGGAR. (*Moving.*) Ya's really believe He *is* up and around?

REUBEN. (*Moving Right, with* DANIEL *perched on his shoulder.*) We *know* it.

DANIEL. (*Points down at waterskin.*) What's in there? —Water?

CLEOPHAS. No. —Tears.

DANIEL. Your tears?

CLEOPHAS. (*Now well off Center, Right.*) The tears of all who do not believe.

BEGGAR. (*Farther Right, moving.*) Myself, I'm a believer. And I don't lose no tears over things. (*Shrugs.*) What's the use? Hee, hee!—Them up there— (*The gesture.*) Them with the fringes, got plenty to cry about, if ya's ask me. Hee, hee! Thought they finished Him up proper. And now He's up and around, hee, hee! Me, I got nothing to cry about. I always thought good of Him. (*Nods emphatically, now at far Right with* CLEOPHAS.) Me, I'm a believer.

REUBEN. (*After them, holding* DANIEL *firmly on his shoulder with right hand, left hand on* BEGGAR'S *shoulder.*) And so am I, my friend.

(*Exit* CLEOPHAS *and* BEGGAR, *Right.* DANIEL's *head droops against* REUBEN'S. *The* LIGHTS *go down to almost darkness.*)

DANIEL. (*Half asleep.*) Barley loaves! Bread! Good, fresh bread! (*His head falls in sleep.* REUBEN *lifts him down from his shoulder and holds the sleeping* CHILD *in his arms. He looks up at the sky.* SPOTLIGHT *on* REUBEN *and* DANIEL.)

REUBEN. The Lord lives.

Slow CURTAIN.

The End

Road to Emmaus

Property Plot

Pack with shoulder strap — REUBEN.

Pilgrim staff — REUBEN.

Large wicker basket with double handle and napkin covering loaves — DANIEL.

Waterskin to hang from girdle — CLEOPHAS.

Broken sandal — CLEOPHAS.

Small knife — CLEOPHAS.

Pouch folded into tunic, later opened out — CLEOPHAS.

Penny coin — CLEOPHAS.

Penny coin — REUBEN.

Rough wooden cart on two wheels, with long front bars for drawing it along.

Barley loaf — in a pouch in the cart.

Fine brown-colored cloak — added to beggar's costume at end of the scene.

Fig tree, several pieces of broken logs, one standing upright, small stones strewn about.

Road to Emmaus

Scene Design

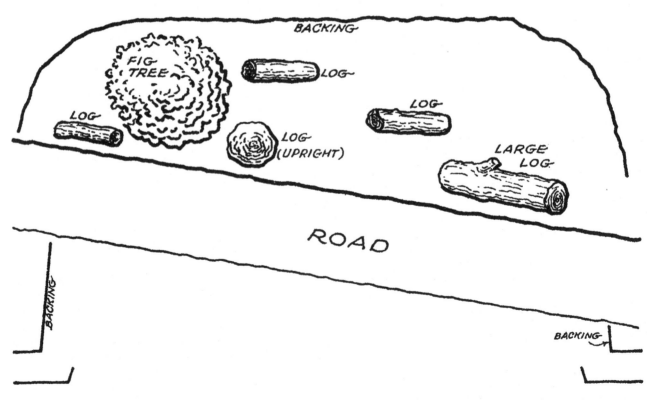

Christmas at Greccio

A Christmas Play in One Act

© 1959, 1987 The Community of Poor Clares of New Mexico, Inc.

To

CLARE ANN LOUIS

Imprimatur: Edwin V. Byrne, D.D.
Archbishop of Sante Fe

August 31, 1959

Cast of Characters

ST. FRANCIS OF ASSISI . . . . a slight man of 43, he wears a brown habit and white knotted cord, is barefoot

BROTHER JOHN THE SIMPLE . . . . . . about 30, he is dressed like ST. FRANCIS, also barefoot

SIR VELITA, LORD OF GRECCIO . . . . about 40, a large and imposing nobleman, somewhat haughty but devoted to Francis

LADY GIACOMA SETTESOLI . . . . about 40, an aristocrat, disciple of FRANCIS and called by him "Brother Jacoba"

PACIFICA . . . . a lovely girl of 18, niece of LORD VELITA

AMATA . . . . PACIFICA's little sister, about 11, a fairylike child whose wisdom is sometimes mistaken for fancy

ANTHONY SETTESOLI . . . . a handsome young nobleman, son of LADY GIACOMA, engaged to Pacifica

MARIANO . . . . a young highwayman of about 22

BEPPI . . . . MARIANO's companion, about the same age; both wear long, rough cloaks and small caps worn on the side of their heads; they carry knives slung from their belts

Story of the Play

St. Francis of Assisi is loved by many people on many accounts, but perhaps one of our greatest devotional debts to him is the origin of the Christmas Crib. Replicas of the manger of Bethlehem and the Holy Child now appear in every church and chapel, basilica and wayside shrine throughout the world. It was on Mt. Greccio in 1223, that the first popular Christmas Crib was set up by St. Francis who so loved to dramatize the Gospel. The world is still rejoicing that he did.

Christmas at Greccio

TIME. *December 24, 1223, the foot of Mt. Greccio on the estate of Lord Velita just outside Assisi, towards evening.*

SCENE. ANTHONY *and* LORD VELITA *are shovelling loose rocks and small debris away from the entrance of a cave-like opening near the foot of the mountain on a kind of rocky plateau, and tossing them into a large receptacle on one side. There is a very large bin of straw to one side and some pieces of wood are lying about.* BROTHER FRANCIS *stands to one side Downstage, finger on lip, speculating on the scene above him.* BROTHER JOHN THE SIMPLE *is on the plateau, with hands on hips, lustily singing: "Oh, Come, all ye Faithful!" At the words: "Oh, come ye, oh, come ye to GRECCIO!" he slips on a loose rock and slides off the low plateau, sitting down abruptly on the stage.* ALL *run to* JOHN, *who smiles unperturbedly.*

JOHN. I *came*, didn't I! Do you think anyone else will?

LORD VELITA. Well, I hope if they come they will stay on their feet, Brother John. (*Pulls* JOHN *to his feet, and* JOHN *dusts off his habit.*)

FRANCIS. My Lord Velita, I hope they will stay on their hearts. (*Jumps up onto the low plateau.*)

ANTHONY. (*Leans on shovel.*) What do you mean, Brother Francis?

FRANCIS. I mean that men fall off their hearts too often, Anthony.

JOHN. (*Nods.*) Happens every day.

FRANCIS. It's from trying to live by their heads alone.

JOHN. (*Looking up at them and then at* VELITA.) A risky business! (*Shakes head gravely.*)

FRANCIS. —and falling instead on their faces.

JOHN. Can't see anything then. (*Arms out in wide gesture of finality.* VELITA *laughs and goes back to shoveling rocks.*)

FRANCIS. Exactly, Brother John! (*Flings out his arms.*) And I want them to see! I want to see it myself,—the poor cold cave and the rude manger. (*Gestures from one side to the other.*) I want the dumb ox (*points*) and the little ass (*points*) and the straw and the singing shepherds! I will make another Bethlehem at Greccio! (*Takes some straw and begins strewing it in front of the cave.*)

JOHN. I'll be a shepherd! (*Begins singing again and walks about making motions of playing a shepherd's pipe.*)

VELITA. I might be the ox. I speak better when I am dumb!

ANTHONY. (*Strangely serious.*) I am surely the ass. (*Kicks a rock viciously and* JOHN THE SIMPLE *stops dead and comes up to peer at him.*)

JOHN. Are you in trouble, Brother Anthony? Tell me! I will fix it.

ANTHONY. (*Affectionately, to* JOHN.) You could never understand my troubles. You are John the Simple.

I am Anthony the Complicated.

FRANCIS. (*Hand on* ANTHONY'S *shoulder.*) We can all play Brother Ass very well, my son.

JOHN. (*Enthusiastically.*) There will be a great crowd of people coming here tonight, I'm sure of it. Let's have a whole herd of asses at the Crib! (*Wheels around and looks Offstage, Left.*) Look! Here come some now! People, I mean.

(*Enter the* LADY GIACOMA SETTESOLI *with* LORD VELITA'S *two nieces,* PACIFICA *and* AMATA, *Left.* PACIFICA *looks at the group with distaste.* GIACOMA *carries a large basket which* ANTHONY *hurries down to take from her, kissing her on the check. He then kisses* PACIFICA'S *hand.* AMATA *runs straight to* FRANCIS *on the plateau, throws her arms around him for a brief moment and then runs into the cave.*)

PACIFICA. Amata! Really! Uncle Velita, can't you scold her? She is too old to act like an infant.

VELITA. (*Gently, from plateau.*) May she never be too old to be a child of God's. Or you, Pacifica. (*He looks at* PACIFICA *gravely and she turns slightly away.*)

JOHN. (*Happily.*) Good evening! Good evening! (*Confidentially to* PACIFICA, *gesturing toward cave.*) Your little sister likes Brother Francis, I think.

FRANCIS. (*Smiles and looks after* AMATA, *then comes down to greet the ladies. Deep bow, eyes downcast.*) Lady Pacifica, may God give you joy! (*Looks into* LADY GIACOMA'S *face.*) Our Brother Jacoba! Welcome in the Lord!

PACIFICA. What is he calling her?

GIACOMA. (*Smiles.*) Brother Jacoba! It is my name—in the Order.

JOHN. (*Always acts like he and* PACIFICA *are intimate friends, to her annoyance.*) She is blessed beyond other women. She is a member of our brotherhood.

PACIFICA. Oh, Lord!

JOHN. I'm not sure Brother Francis will let *you* join. But pray!

VELITA. (*Props up shovel against cave and jumps down. To* GIACOMA.) Any trace of it yet?

JOHN. Trace of what?

GIACOMA. He means my gold cloak that was stolen yesterday.

JOHN. Oh. Is that all?

PACIFICA. (*Annoyed.*) That is quite enough! And just before Christmas! A person is not safe anywhere these days.

FRANCIS. (*Back up on plateau, spreading straw from the bin and laughing.*) We are very safe,—for we have nothing.

ANTHONY. (*Peering into his mother's basket.*) Well, here is something! (*Draws out bottle and folded napkins.*) Well done, Mother! Wine! And almond cakes!

GIACOMA. (*Happily.*) The kind you like, Brother Francis. I know you must be hungry after working here all afternoon.

VELITA. Excellent! Oh, this is excellent! (*Begins spreading the things out on a flat rock.*)

PACIFICA. Uncle Velita! Are you mad, too? Is this a place to have a picnic? On Mt. Greccio in the cold, on Christmas Eve? (*Begins to cry a little.*) Anthony, this is fantastic!

ANTHONY. (*Wiping his face with his handkerchief.*) It certainly is!

GIACOMA. Why, Anthony, you disappoint me.

ANTHONY. My darling mother, it is really fantastic,—for me to sweat, and in December. (*Wipes his face again and goes back to shovelling rocks.*)

GIACOMA. (*Laughs.*) That's better.

PACIFICA. (*Stomps her foot petulantly.*) No, it's worse!

VELITA. (*Pats her shoulder.*) It's all right, dear.

PACIFICA. I tell you, uncle, it's all wrong.

AMATA. (*Appearing in opening of cave.*) Oh! It *shines!* (ALL *look at her in surprise.*)

VELITA. What shines, Amata?

AMATA. In the cave!

FRANCIS. (*Peers in.*) Not yet, sweet child. But it will shine tonight. I am going to have it all, just as it was at Bethlehem. (*Gestures around.*) The little Infant and the ox and ass, the straw and singing shepherds—

AMATA. (*Shakes her head happily.*) No, Brother Francis, it is shining now.

FRANCIS. (*Strokes her hair gently.*) I think you see many splendors before we do.

JOHN. (*To all, sagely.*) She sees things faster than we do. (*Up on plateau again.*)

PACIFICA. You *know* she is slow. You *know* she never sees things as they are. Why do you indulge every silly notion that comes into her head?

AMATA. (*Jumps down from plateau and goes to pat* PACIFICA's *hand as though her sister were the injured party.*) I am slow, Pacifica. Yes, I am the slow one. Come, sister, let me show you how it shines! (*Pulls at* PACIFICA, *who jerks her hand away.*)

PACIFICA. Amata, please come home.

AMATA. Home? Yes, I am home. (*Goes to stand by* FRANCIS.) I am always home where it shines. What are you doing, Brother Francis? What are you making, Uncle Velita?

VELITA. I am making a manger for the Holy Child, my darling. (*Leaps back onto plateau.*) But first I have to clear the rocks away. (*Back to it.*)

FRANCIS. I am spreading straw for Him. (*Does.*)

AMATA. (*All interest.*) Is little Jesus coming here?

FRANCIS. Yes, tonight!

JOHN. This very night! (*Jumps down to play his imaginary flute again.*) I am going to be a shepherd.

ANTHONY. (*Back to plateau and rocks.*) I shall be the ass.

AMATA. What can I be?

FRANCIS. You shall be the star that led the wise ones of the earth.

JOHN. You can be the star, little girl. Shine! Shine!

AMATA. (*Points into cave.*) Oh, yes, it shines!

PACIFICA. Uncle Velita, I can't stand any more of this. If you want to spend Christmas Eve acting like a madman, you can't expect us to go off our heads, too.

JOHN. (*Delighted.*) Brother Francis was just explaining why men go off their heads. (*Confidentially.*) It's because they won't stay on their hearts.

PACIFICA. Who *are* you?

JOHN. (*Deep bow.*) Brother John the Simple—at your service. Come, my lady, you can be a shepherdess at the crib. (*Grabs up a stick.*) Here is a flute to play!

VELITA. (*Comes down and motions* JOHN *away. To* PACIFICA.) Sit down, dear, until we finish. Here, take an almond cake. (*Turns to get her one from rock.*)

PACIFICA. (*Really crying now.*) I won't sit down! I don't want cakes! Anthony, please take me home.

ANTHONY. (*Hesitantly.*) I'm not finished here, Pacifica.

PACIFICA. All right, then! Let your fiancée walk home alone in the dark. Maybe the robbers will kill me.

ANTHONY. But, Pacifica—

PACIFICA. I'm going. (*Exits Left.* ANTHONY *makes a helpless gesture toward* FRANCIS, *kicks angrily at the rocks, and then goes after her.*)

ANTHONY. (*As he goes.*) I guess the Child didn't want me at the crib in any case. (*Exits Left.*)

GIACOMA. Oh, dear, lovers' quarrels!

JOHN. Who named her Pacifica?

AMATA. What are lovers?

GIACOMA. They are people who want to spend all their lives together—and—and, be happy together—and— (*Looks after the young couple.*)

AMATA. (*With finality.*) Anthony and Pacifica are not lovers then.

VELITA. Be still, darling.

AMATA. (*Shakes head.*) No lovers where there is no love. It never shines where they are. (*Singsong.*) But in the cave it shines.

VELITA. (*A little desperately, catching her hand.*) Come on, we'll see if we can make them happy. (*Apologetically to* FRANCIS.) I'm very sorry, but it's Christmas Eve—and—my niece—you understand. (*Hurries off, Left, with* AMATA.)

JOHN. Now we have no ox, no star. And all the asses are leaving. (*Sits down on a rock, miserable, chin on fist.*)

GIACOMA. (*Laughs lightly.*) Not all of them! Come, Brother Francis, take some wine and warm yourself. Those children always quarrel. No use to worry.

FRANCIS. (*Walks slowly toward the little repast.*) Yes, worry is a waste, a hindrance.

JOHN. (*Shakes head.*) No sense in it. Gets you nowhere. (*Little pause — after him.*) Francis?

FRANCIS. Yes, my brother?

JOHN. (*Rises.*) You said our mission is to bring God's peace.

FRANCIS. I did.

JOHN. Then why is everyone fighting?

FRANCIS. (*Smiling a little.*) Some find peace only after war. But peace will come. Peace will surely come this blessed night.

(*Great* NOISE *Offstage and sound of* HORSES *being reined in.*)

GIACOMA. (*Starts.*) Oh, what is that?

JOHN. It sounds like the ox and the ass.

(*Enter* MARIANO *and* BEPPI, *Right.*)

GIACOMA. (*Screams and falls back.*) The robbers! The thieves who stole my golden cloak!

MARIANO. (*Menacingly.*) Stop that screaming, if you want to live till Christmas.

JOHN. She does—take my word for it, brother. (*Bows.*) How do you do!

BEPPI. Shut your mouth, you simpleton.

JOHN. (*Pleased.*) He knows me! I must be famous. (*Back to* ROBBERS.) Yes, brothers, I am John the Simple, though some uneducated folk spell it simpleton. (*Realizes his blunder.*) I mean, you have got the general misspelling. And you are—?

MARIANO. (*Hard laugh.*) The wisest men in Assisi! Two men who know real values.

FRANCIS. Teach me, then, for I am only a poor unlettered fellow.

BEPPI. Another simpleton!

GIACOMA. (*Forgets her fright in her outrage.*) How dare you speak like that to Brother Francis! He's a saint.

MARIANO. Francis? Brother Francis? *He?* (*Scornful appraisal of* FRANCIS' *person.*) Is *he* the one the whole town's running after?

JOHN. The very man! You have found him. Merry Christmas, brothers!

BEPPI. Hold your tongue, you fool! (JOHN *does, and then lets go of it.*)

JOHN. (*To* BEPPI.) How long? (*Takes hold of his tongue again.* BEPPI *laughs despite himself, but* MARIANO *is angry.*)

MARIANO. Listen! What are you doing at this cave?

FRANCIS. I am building Bethlehem.

BEPPI. Eh?

FRANCIS. On Greccio. (*Jumps up on plateau.*) We shall celebrate Christmas as it really was! We shall have the straw and the poor dumb animals that breathed upon the Holy Child and warmed Him. (*Arms wide.*) I want all the people to come and see, and then they will forget their quarreling. They will only remember that God became a little Child and loves them.

MARIANO. You get away from that cave, I tell you!

FRANCIS. My brother, I regret to say I cannot.

JOHN. (*Lets go of his tongue and wipes his hand on his habit.*) He's here to stay. Why don't you stay, too? You can be the ox and the ass.

FRANCIS. No, they will be the wise men,—two of them, at least.

BEPPI. We are wise, all right. Now, move along, or we'll strip you of everything you own. (*Pulls out a knife and* GIACOMA *screams.*)

FRANCIS. (*Holds arms above his head and jumps off plateau.*) And welcome, my brothers! Only, I own nothing.

JOHN. He travels light.

MARIANO. Shut up, before I knife you, simpleton. (*Pulls knife.*)

JOHN. (*Links arms with* MARIANO.) My friends all call me John.

MARIANO. (*Drops knife.*) Good Lord, he's mad! (*Blesses himself.*)

JOHN. (*To* FRANCIS, *gesturing toward* MARIANO.) See, Brother Francis! He is a good and pious robber!

FRANCIS. (*Nods.*) Maybe better, maybe more of love within his heart than others I have seen.

MARIANO. (*With surprising bitterness.*) Don't mention love to me. I hate the very word like poison. (*Laughs.*) Maybe I love my trade, but nothing else.

FRANCIS. (*Lowers arms on sudden inspiration.*) Here! (*Goes to the flat rock.*) Look, here are wine and almond cakes. Our Brother Jacoba has made you a feast, my brothers. I think we were waiting for you to come.

GIACOMA. Oh, Brother Francis!

FRANCIS. Yes, hurry! It's all prepared. (*Takes* MARIANO *and* BEPPI *by the arms,* BEPPI's *knife hanging ridiculously from his right hand.* JOHN *picks up* MARIANO's *knife and runs the blade along his finger.*)

JOHN. Ye-ow! It's sharp! (*Thrusts knife into his cord and sucks blood from finger.*)

FRANCIS. (*Pushes* ROBBERS *down on the ground around the rock "table" as* JOHN *wanders over and smooths off a spot for* GIACOMA *on the low plateau just above and beckons to her, eyes to Heaven.*) Bless, O Lord, this feast prepared for Your friends who praise Your holy Name. (*Pours wine for the* ROBBERS *gaily.*) What are your names, my Brother Robbers?

MARIANO. (*Dazedly.*) Mariano. (*Takes the wine absently.*)

BEPPI. (*Staring.*) Beppi. (*Puts his knife down on the rock and takes his glass.*)

GIACOMA. (*Almost crying.*) Brother Francis, I brought those things for you! These brigands have my golden cloak, and you don't care. You even wine and dine them!

MARIANO. (*Jumps up.*) Clear out now, all of you!

FRANCIS. (*Sternly, to* GIACOMA.) Brother Jacoba, such discourteous words are not worthy of a member of our Brotherhood. Beg Brother Mariano's pardon!

GIACOMA. What!

JOHN. You heard him! Life in the Brotherhood is rugged, dear Jacoba. (*Takes a cake.*)

FRANCIS. Brother Jacoba!

GIACOMA. (*Swallows hard—to* MARIANO.) I'm sorry.

FRANCIS. (*Still stern.*) Our brother has a name.

GIACOMA. (*Mighty effort.*) I'm sorry, Brother Mariano.

BEPPI. Listen, Mariano, let's get out of here. (*Takes the* OTHER's *arm.*) These people make me nervous. (*Twitches his shoulders.*)

MARIANO. (*Almost shouting.*) You know as well as I do that we have business here. (*Shakes off* BEPPI's *hand.*) *They* leave! We *stay!*

JOHN. You hear, Brother Jacoba? They have business here at the Crib. They are converted! It's wonderful! (*Begins to dance around with his invisible flute again, humming.*)

MARIANO. Will you keep still, you idiot, or must I slit your throat? (*Looks around for his knife which* JOHN *still carries.*)

JOHN. (*Stops playing.*) Your knife? Here it is. (*Starts to hand it over and then pulls back.*) No, on second thought, your hand could slip. (*Feels his throat speculatively.*) You'd be surprised how sharp that thing is. (*Inspects his cut finger and turns to* FRANCIS.) You'd better keep this knife, Brother Francis. Brother Mariano might hurt himself. He gets excited.

FRANCIS. (*Comes and stands by* MARIANO.) Brother Mariano has already hurt himself.

MARIANO. (*Startled.*) What do you mean?

FRANCIS. You have great misery in your heart. I read it in your eyes.

JOHN. I guess he feels bad because we have nothing worth stealing. Listen, brother,—take an almond cake. (*Goes to get him one;* MARIANO *seems not to see or hear him and stares at* FRANCIS; JOHN *shrugs and starts to eat it himself.*)

FRANCIS. Why do men steal, my brother? Can you tell me?

MARIANO. (*Miserably.*) To get rich, I suppose.

JOHN. (*Mouth full.*) Don't you know for sure? (*Shakes head.*) A man ought to understand all the ins and outs of his profession.

GIACOMA. (*Indignantly.*) He took my gold cloak! Now he comes to tell us we cannot have our own cave on Greccio!

BEPPI. (*Nervous.*) You stay out of that cave, you hear me, lady? (*Raises his arm, threateningly.*)

GIACOMA. (*Jumps back.*) Brother Francis, save me!

(*Enter* LORD VELITA *and* AMATA, *Left.* VELITA *carries a lantern which he quickly sets down and rushes forward to grasp* BEPPI *by the wrists.*)

VELITA. What do you think you are doing, you ruffian! Get off my property! (*Drops* BEPPI's *arms and pushes him back, doubling his fist at him.*)

MARIANO. (*The hard laugh.*) Do you think that property means anything to us, old fool?

VELITA. Haven't I seen you before?

MARIANO. (*Steps back, as though struck.*) No, no, you haven't. (*Turns away.*)

AMATA. I have! Hello, Mariano!

VELITA. (*Puzzled.*) What are you calling him, Amata?

JOHN. His name. This is Beppi over here. Brothers, this is Sir Velita, lord of Greccio. (*To* VELITA.) Our brothers have business at the Crib. They like the cave.

AMATA. Yes, it shines inside.

BEPPI. Shut up, you little brat!

GIACOMA. (*Hands to forehead.*) Such language! I can't stand it.

(FRANCIS *calmly goes back up on plateau to his straw.*)

BEPPI. Lady, this is nothing. You take one step into that cave and I'll teach you a whole list of brand new words to use with your old gold cloak!

AMATA. She hasn't got it. Mariano— (*Reaches for the* ROBBER's *hand but he draws back as though afraid.*)

VELITA. How do you know this fellow's name, Amata?

AMATA. He used to whistle under Pacifica's window,—after you went to sleep.

JOHN. Well, what do you know! Then we're all old friends, more or less. Does Anthony know you, too, Brother Mariano?

GIACOMA. My son? Know robbers? How dare you, Brother John!

FRANCIS. (*Calmly spreading straw up on plateau, stands up and looks down at them all.*) Your son knows Lord Velita here. Velita is a robber.

JOHN. (*With respect.*) No! (*At* VELITA's *side.*) Listen, tell me about it. Only a sideline, I imagine.

VELITA. (*Astonished.*) What are you saying, Brother Francis?

FRANCIS. That there are richer goods to steal than cloaks and wallets.

VELITA. What have I stolen, tell me?

FRANCIS. Maybe a young girl's happiness. Perhaps her love for living.

MARIANO. (*Bitterly.*) For which respectable crimes no man is ever jailed.

AMATA. (*Jumps up onto the plateau and then leans down to squint at* MARIANO.) Mariano, how did you get so ugly? Pacifica used to say you were the handsomest man in the world.

GIACOMA. Amata!

VELITA. Amata!

MARIANO. (*Softly.*) Did she say that?

BEPPI. Who cares?

MARIANO. (*Swings on him—a real yell.*) I do!

BEPPI. (*Doubles his fists.*) Who do you think you are shouting at? Ladies' man!

AMATA. (*To* BEPPI.) My, now you are even uglier than he is!

BEPPI. Huh?

VELITA. (*Reaches up and lifts* AMATA *down.*) Darling, you had better look at me and leave these men alone. I'm not ugly, am I? (*Smiles as he sets her on the ground.*)

AMATA. Not mostly, but sometimes.

VELITA. What!

AMATA. (*Nods vigorously.*) When you say I am God's little dear, you look— (*Looks about.*) almost like Brother Francis. But when you tell Pacifica she has to marry Anthony, you look really horrid, Uncle, especially when you smile.

GIACOMA. (*Very nervous.*) I think we had better go home. (*Takes* AMATA's *hand. To* FRANCIS.) We can build your crib on Greccio next Christmas. Everything is quite insane today. The cave will still be here next year and maybe— (*Stiffly, toward the* ROBBERS.) conditions and the company will be somewhat improved.

AMATA. (*Excitedly, pointing up at* LADY GIACOMA.) See, now she looks ugly, too!

JOHN. Goodness, Brother Jacoba, are you losing your looks?

VELITA. Amata!—to insult the Lady Giacoma!

AMATA. What is an insult?

JOHN. It is the truth. But when you tell it to a person's face, it is an insult.

BEPPI. It's getting darker. Listen, Mariano, let's go home. These people give me the creeps.

FRANCIS. Where is home?

AMATA. (*Up on plateau again, takes* FRANCIS' *hand.*) Mine is where you are!

FRANCIS. No, home is where love is. Home is where the Child is. He is Love.

JOHN. Then, we all live here on Greccio. (*To* AMATA.) Say, where is your sister?

AMATA. Pacifica is where it doesn't shine.

GIACOMA. (*Worriedly.*) Where?

AMATA. With Anthony. You want to know where he is?

MARIANO. (*A bark.*) No!

AMATA. All right, I'll tell you. He is where it doesn't shine, too. With Pacifica.

VELITA. (*Sternly.*) Now, that will do, Amata. Were you spying on your sister?

AMATA. What is spying?

JOHN. (*Slips behind turn of the plateau and peeks out.*) It's like Hi Spy! Only not so interesting. (*Comes Downstage again.*)

BEPPI. I'm going. They're all crazy! (*Starts off, Right.*)

MARIANO. (*After him.*) Remember our business, Beppi!

BEPPI. (*Excitedly.*) *You* remember it! This place is bewitched, you take it from me. (*Almost Offstage, Right.*)

FRANCIS. (*Sprints after him.*) Wait, my brother! I think you have more business here than Brother Mariano knows. (*Starts drawing him back to the cave.*)

BEPPI. No! Listen! Let me go. I'm not myself here.

FRANCIS. Who is yourself?

BEPPI. Huh?

JOHN. He wants to know who you are. Where were you last seen, brother?

BEPPI. Lord, Mariano! Let's make a break for it! (*Grabs* MARIANO's *arm.*) Come on, the horses are waiting! We can get away before things get any worse.

(*Enter* PACIFICA *and* ANTHONY, *Left.* ANTHONY *carries a bundle in one arm and* PACIFICA *has a lantern. She stops short and gives a frightened exclamation when she sees* MARIANO, *and clutches* ANTHONY's *arm.*)

ANTHONY. (*Stares at* ROBBERS, *then turns to* VELITA.) Who are those men?

JOHN. (*Rushing up happily.*) Robbers! Friends of ours. They stopped by to celebrate Christmas with Brother Francis.

GIACOMA. (*Touch of hauteur.*) Maybe they would like to return my gold cloak while they are—celebrating Christmas!

ANTHONY. (*To his* MOTHER.) *These* are the thieves who took it?

GIACOMA. They are, my son.

ANTHONY. (*Hands his bundle to* PACIFICA *who takes it absently, setting down her lantern, eyes still on* MARIANO. *Advances toward* MARIANO.) Return that cloak to my mother or I'll break your jaw!

PACIFICA. Don't touch him!

ANTHONY. Don't be afraid, darling. I can handle him.

MARIANO. You call her darling again and I'll knock your teeth out.

(ANTHONY *and* MARIANO *confront each other like tigers before the spring.*)

GIACOMA. Oh, heaven help us!—and this is Christmas Eve! Why did we come here anyway!

FRANCIS. (*Forces his slight person between the* ROBBER *and the* YOUNG LORD.) We came because it is God's Birthday. And I want you to keep it as it was when He was born for all of us poor worms of sinners. But the Lord's guests must make merry for His coming! (*Steps forward a little.*) There is no Christmas anywhere for the heart is busy with hate. The narrow heart will never find the cave. I cannot make a Bethlehem on Greccio if you defile it with doubts or sadness or despair.

GIACOMA. You mean, because these robbers hate us, the Christ-Child will not come?

FRANCIS. Perhaps I mean He will not come because you think about gold cloaks, my poor Brother Jacoba, on this night when God was shivering in the cold. (GIACOMA *turns away.*)

AMATA. Oh, yes, it shines! (*Points to cave and then clasps her hands delightedly.*)

MARIANO. (*Roughly.*) Why did you go in there?

VELITA. What right have you to ask her? This is *my* mountain.

MARIANO. Yes! Sure. *Your* mountain. Your *world.* (*Mock bow.*) The little tin god of Greccio! That's you!

PACIFICA. (*In tears.*) Oh, Mariano, stop! (*She turns away.*)

ANTHONY. (*Looks amazedly at* PACIFICA *and then at* MARIANO.) Do you know him? (*Stiffens again.*) He robbed you, too? (*Doubles his fist.*)

PACIFICA. Yes, he did!

(ANTHONY *moves menacingly toward* MARIANO *again, but* FRANCIS *catches at his arm.*)

FRANCIS. I think our Sister Pacifica does not want what Brother Mariano stole from her returned.

ANTHONY. (*Confused.*) Is that right?

PACIFICA. (*Sobbing now.*) Yes, it's right. I only want him to keep it,—but he can't. (ANTHONY *shakes his head dazedly as though to clear it.*)

AMATA. (*Comes down and pats* MARIANO's *hand.*) I always find where it shines. That is why I went inside. Come on, I'll show you! (*Pulls him, but he jerks away.*)

PACIFICA. (*To* FRANCIS.) I'm going home. You said the Child will not come if there is sadness on Greccio.

ANTHONY. I am the one to go. I am a doubter. But how can I see God's purpose in the tangle of my life?

VELITA. (*Downstage, agitated.*) What tangle, boy? Your future is assured as the young lord of Greccio. Have I not pledged you my niece's hand—and since she was a child?

ANTHONY. (*Flatly.*) Quite so.

JOHN. He sounds like he doesn't want it.

BEPPI. (*Strangely embarrassed.*) Listen, I think you talk too much.

JOHN. (*Interested.*) Really? I had no idea! (*Takes* BEPPI *by the arm and walks him to extreme Right.*) Brother, you must admonish me. I'll depend on you.

BEPPI. Wait a minute. I only said—

JOHN. (*Pulling* BEPPI *Offstage, Right.*) If you would join our brotherhood, then anytime I started talking overtime, you could punch my head, and— (*Exeunt* JOHN *and* BEPPI, *Right.*)

FRANCIS. (*Forward more.*) My Lord Velita here is the real doubter.

VELITA. I? Why, I'm sure of everything!

FRANCIS. No, you have the greatest doubt of all, the one that shrinks the soul.

ANTHONY. A greater doubt than mine?

FRANCIS. Far greater. Lord Velita doubts that God can run the universe unaided.

VELITA. (*Stiffly.*) May I inquire what you mean?

(AMATA *is tired of this. She takes* VELITA's *lantern and jumps up on the plateau. She beckons* PACIFICA *to follow her and gives her a hand up onto the plateau.* PACIFICA *moves as though in a dream, still half crying. She sets down her bundle at the entrance of the cave and the* TWO SISTERS *disappear inside.*)

FRANCIS. Did you ever ask Pacifica if she wanted to marry Anthony?

VELITA. Of course not. Why? It is a perfect match. I made it.

FRANCIS. (*Smiles. To* GIACOMA.) Does Anthony seem happy?

GIACOMA. I—oh, you know young lovers always have their ups and downs.

FRANCIS. I have not observed any ups. Have you, my Brother Jacoba?

GIACOMA. I didn't really—notice. I was worried about my cloak. (*Ashamedly.*) Brother Francis, I do not want it back! (*To* MARIANO.) Keep it! For Christmas.

MARIANO. (*Solemnly, after a pause.*) I don't want it. I only stole it to forget my other business.

FRANCIS. The business of the heart?

MARIANO. Yes,—Brother Francis. (*To* GIACOMA.) Give the cloak to Beppi if you will. (*Turns aside miserably.*)

(*Enter* BEPPI *and* JOHN THE SIMPLE, *Right.* BEPPI *wears* JOHN'S *habit and cord, and* JOHN *has on* BEPPI'S *long rough cloak and small cocked hat.* BEPPI *is grinning sheepishly.*)

MARIANO. Beppi! Have you gone mad?

BEPPI. I guess so. It's very enjoyable. You ought to try it.

JOHN. (*To* FRANCIS.) I invited our brother to join our fraternity. And then I gave him my habit and cord to save him the trouble of stealing them.

FRANCIS. Brother John!

BEPPI. (*Grandly.*) It's all right, Brother. We understand each other.

JOHN. (*Holds out his hand as one does to feel raindrops.*) Dark! (*Grabs at* BEPPI'S *arm.*) Come on! We must finish the manger, or where shall we put the Child? Now, where are those knives? (*Looks about and finds them; he and* BEPPI *jump up onto the plateau and begin fitting the boards together for the manger, whittling off the ends with the knives.*) It's a good thing you brought these knives along.

FRANCIS. There is a purpose in everything. Nothing ever merely happens.

MARIANO. For me there is no purpose in anything.

FRANCIS. Why do you rob and steal, my brother? (*Broad gesture toward* GIACOMA *and* VELITA.) Tell them. Tell them both!

MARIANO. (*Gazes at* FRANCIS *and then replies in measured tones almost like one hypnotized.*) Because such people as the Lord Velita and the Lady Giacoma think there is no good in me, and I am strictly obliged to prove them right.

FRANCIS. (*Looks from* VELITA *to* GIACOMA.) Mariano is spending his life living down to your expectations.

VELITA. (*Suddenly.*) I know where I saw you before!

GIACOMA. (*A little peevish.*) I certainly know where *I* did! My cloak— (*Her voice trails off.*) I wish I had never had one. The trouble all started with it.

(BEPPI *sets the finished manger in the doorway of the cave, just to one side, and* JOHN *curiously picks up the bundle* PACIFICA *set there. He begins to unwrap it.*)

VELITA. (*To* MARIANO.) You used to come calling on my niece. And I sent you away.

FRANCIS. Why, my brother Velita?

VELITA. (*Oddly ashamed.*) I—he—had no station. And then I had arranged—Anthony—you understand. I thought he (*Jerk of his head toward* MARIANO.) would come to no good anyway. He always sang and laughed so much. I told him so.

FRANCIS. That he sang and laughed?

VELITA. (*Getting miserable.*) No,—that he would come to no good.

MARIANO. (*Short laugh.*) And I didn't.

ANTHONY. (*Moving in, curiously.*) What did you steal from Pacifica?

MARIANO. None of your business!

FRANCIS. It was her heart, I think.

(*A great shout from* JOHN. ALL *look up to the plateau.*)

JOHN. Look! The Bambino! He came to Greccio after all! (*Holds up a charming wood-carved Infant, its small arms stretched wide.*)

ANTHONY. (*Shyly.*) I brought it. It was for my mother's Christmas.

GIACOMA. (*At edge of plateau.*) And so it is!

JOHN. (*Rocking the little statue vigorously in his arm, he then hands it to* BEPPI.) Here, you hold Him! (BEPPI *holds the Infant awkwardly, but he is very pleased.* JOHN *quickly spreads straw in the manger.*)

MARIANO. Beppi! What will men say of you—a robber!

FRANCIS. (*Up on plateau.*) They will say that only a little love can work a great transformation.

JOHN. We have no swaddling clothes! (*Wrings his hands.*) Oh, what to do!

(PACIFICA *and* AMATA *emerge from the cave.* AMATA *holds up* GIACOMA's *gold cloak which shines in the light from* PACIFICA's *lantern. The stage is very dark now.*)

AMATA. You see! I told you it shines. It shines!

GIACOMA. My cloak! (*Looks at* MARIANO *and* BEPPI.) So *that's* why you didn't want us to go in the cave!

JOHN. (*Takes it.*) This will do nicely! (*Begins wrapping it awkwardly around the little Bambino and then stares out into the distance Offstage, Left.*) Lights! Torches! I think they are coming. (*Hands* FRANCIS *the Bambino and jumps off plateau to run to far Left. Strains of "Oh, Come, All Ye Faithful!" can be heard very softly in the distance and grow louder as the* CROWD *approaches.* FRANCIS *drapes the gold cloak carefully around the infant and lets the long shining folds hang down.*)

ANTHONY. (*Looking up at* PACIFICA.) Pacifica, now I know that I must tell you. There cannot be doubt on Greccio this night.

(JOHN *is enthusiastically waving the invisible crowd to come faster.*)

PACIFICA. Nor sadness. (*Sets down the torch and leans down, hands clasped.*) I must tell you something first. (*Little pause.*) Anthony, I don't love you.

ANTHONY. (*Stares at her dumbfounded, then gives a great shout.*) Oh, thank God! (*Takes hold of his*

MOTHER *and begins to dance around the stage with her.* AMATA *laughs delightedly and takes* PACIFICA'S *lantern, jumps down and follows the dancing pair around the stage.*)

GIACOMA. (*Trying to get her breath.*) Anthony! Are you insane?

BEPPI. He seems to enjoy it even more than I do. I'm sorry I ever took up thieving. (*Singing Offstage grows louder.*) I never did *thoroughly* enjoy it.

(JOHN *begins "conducting" the singing crowd with both hands.*)

ANTHONY. (*Wild with joy.*) She doesn't love me, Mother! Did you hear that? (*Hugs his MOTHER and then goes to kneel at edge of plateau.*) Oh, Brother Francis, will you have me in your brotherhood? It is all I ever wanted!

GIACOMA. My son!

BEPPI. Our brother!

ANTHONY. I thought I had to marry the Lady Pacifica because she wanted to marry me. I have played the ass all right!

FRANCIS. (*Smiling as he gently rocks the Infant.*) But now you are the ass at the Crib, and that's a different thing.

VELITA. (*Seeing light.*) Pacifica, child, what did he—(*Gestures toward MARIANO.*) steal from you?

PACIFICA. My heart!

MARIANO. (*New life.*) Pacifica! (*Jumps up on the plateau and takes PACIFICA'S hands in his.*)

JOHN. (*From far Left.*) Brother Beppi. (*Waves broadly.*) Come! We must lead the procession to the Crib! (BEPPI *jumps down from plateau and runs over to* JOHN *who tosses the little cap he took from* BEPPI *into the air and catches it.*) The Christ-Child has come to Greccio! (*Wheels around toward the cave.*) That means that there is love on Greccio, doesn't it, Brother Francis?

FRANCIS. (*Nods down into the face of the carven Infant in his arm.*) Yes, my Brother. And love is finding all the things that were lost.

AMATA. (*Dancing around the manger.*) I found the cloak! I told them all how it shines. But nobody ever believes me except you, Brother Francis.

FRANCIS. Yes, I believe you, child of God. (*Smiles at her.*) Now, where is the other loot?

AMATA. Pacifica's heart? Oh—I guess Mariano carries that around with him.

VELITA. (*Choking slightly.*) Then—I think—he ought to stay very near Pacifica. She might need it.

PACIFICA. Uncle Velita! (*She slips down off the plateau and* UNCLE VELITA *puts his arm around her.*)

MARIANO. (*Jumping down. Shyly.*) You don't mean that you will—?

VELITA. I mean that I resign from my position! I was never meant to be a deity and govern the world.

PACIFICA. Forgive me! (*Looks up to* FRANCIS *and around at the others.*) Forgive me, all of you. I could not let anyone be glad because I was always sad. (*Holds out her hands to* MARIANO.)

ANTHONY. (*Slowly, walking toward them.*) I know—(*Looks around.*) I doubted the goodness of God, and so I saw bitterness everywhere.

GIACOMA. (*Comes to put her hand on* ANTHONY'S *arm.*) Forgive me, son! I did God's planning for

Him, and so I nearly ruined everything.

AMATA. (*Looks from one to the other.*) Why, no one looks ugly any more! Everywhere is shining, shining! (*Reaches up and touches* FRANCIS' *cheek.*) See, how it shines!

FRANCIS. The Lord of Greccio has come!

(CROWD *with torches begins entering, Left.* JOHN *and* BEPPI *lead the way toward the manger as* FRANCIS *lays the small Figure in it. The gold cloak trails along the ground on either side of the manger.*)

GIACOMA. (*Kneeling at edge of plateau.*) Oh, Child, forgive me my poor gold cloak! It brought us all together. It was your instrument of peace.

(CROWD *has filled the stage now, holding torches high. Their singing dies away as* FRANCIS *turns to them.*)

FRANCIS. Welcome, my brothers, welcome to Greccio! (*Arms wide, he bends over the Crib.*) Sweet Child! Holy Child! Little Son of God! Make us all the instruments of Your peace. (*Turns to the* CROWD.) Where there is hatred— (*Left hand toward* BEPPI.) You—(*Right toward the Child.*) sow love. And where there is injury— (*Left toward* GIACOMA. *Right toward Child.*) pardon. (*Leans slightly toward* ANTHONY.) Where there is doubt, You bring us faith, and where there is despair— (*Toward* MARIANO.) You bring hope. Where there is darkness, little Child—(*Arm around* AMATA.) You come and bring the light. And where there is sadness— (*Toward* PACIFICA *and* VELITA.) You come with joy. (*Both arms wide over manger.*) Oh, little Son of God, grant us to know what Christmas is. And not to be understood, but to understand. Not so much to be loved, as to love. (*The* CROWD *kneels down, instinctively.*) For it is only in giving that we shall receive You. It is only in pardoning that You will pardon us. It is only when we have learned to die, that You will live in us.

AMATA. (*At edge of plateau, hands clasped over her heart.*) Oh, how it shines!

(CROWD *bursts out with refrain: "Come and behold Him, born the King of angels!" As they sing: "Oh, come let us adore Him!" three times, the* CURTAIN *slowly closes.*)

The End

Christmas at Greccio
Property Plot

Two shovels and quantities of small rocks

A bin of straw

A large receptacle for the rocks

A large wicker basket with a wine bottle and a few napkins and cakes

A gold cloak

Pieces of wood to be formed into a manger

Handkerchief for ANTHONY

A wood-carved figure of the Christ-Child, wrappings for it

Some sticks lying about

Two knives (like daggers)

Two lanterns

Torches for the crowd

Counted as Mine

The Story of
Our Lady of Guadalupe

© 1954, 1982 The Community of Poor Clares of New Mexico, Inc.

To

FATHER M. BEDE O'LEARY

Imprimatur: Edwin V. Byrne, D.D.
Archbishop of Sante Fe

In the Marian Year, February 2, 1954

Cast of Characters

In Order of Appearance

FRAY FERNANDO. . . . .⎫
FRAY SILVESTRO . . . .⎬ Franciscan Friars

JUAN DIEGO . . . . a Cuautitlan Indian

MARIA LUCIA . . . . his wife

INDIANS OF CUAUTITLAN AND THEIR WIVES

THE BLESSED VIRGIN MARY OF GUADALUPE

RICARDO. . . . .⎫
FRANCISCO . . . .⎬ servants in the Bishop's palace
ANTONIO. . . . .⎭

FRAY JUAN DE ZUMARRAGA. . . . . . first Bishop of Mexico

A SPANISH NAVAL OFFICER

THE MAJOR-DOMO . . . . servant of the Bishop

BERNARDINO . . . . uncle of Juan Diego, Standard-bearer

THE GREAT CHORUS

Story of the Play

Perhaps the tenderest of all the apparitions of Our Lady are those to Juan Diego, a humble Indian of Mexico in 1531. Actually, there were four apparitions, but all Our Lady's words are given in the two dramatized here. The Blessed Virgin did not hesitate to reveal her identity at the very outset to the little Indian whom she called, "least of my sons," giving him words of comfort and healing to bequeath to all hearts everywhere who love and trust her, and painting on the Indian's rough tilma the miraculous image of her own beautiful self which now stands crowned with precious stones in her Basilica in Mexico.

But when our Lady appeared to Juan Diego, Mexico did not have its present boundaries. There were no United States, no Canada. It was to AMERICA she came, and she is patroness of the Americas. It is Our Lady of Guadalupe whom Pope Pius XII has called THE HOPE OF AMERICA!

Counted as Mine

ACT ONE

SCENE I

SCENE. *The center of the Indian village of Cuautitlan in Mexico, October, 1530. About twelve INDIANS stand in two broken rows, arms akimbo, before two FRANCISCAN FRIARS. Nine or ten INDIAN WOMEN sit to the side, on the ground. The men wear loose and very coarse tunic-like garments reaching just below their knees, and straw sandals on their feet. The women wear full-skirted dresses and all have some rude, colorful jewelry; they are barefoot. They sit modestly with heads slightly inclined, but are obviously intent on what the friars are saying. FRAY SILVESTRO has a small tambour strapped about his neck, but the eyes of all are focused on FRAY FERNANDO who is standing on a rough box and obviously concluding some discourse.*

FRAY FERNANDO. (*He fingers the beads hanging from his cord.*)
> My children, not alone at Tlatelolco
> In shadows of the chapel, does God hear
> Your prayer; but under skies and out in weather,
> The Great Chief listens. Every thud of heartbeat
> Sounds against His shining golden tambour!
>
> He sees the flight of swallows, and He marks it
> If one small nameless sparrow falls to earth!
>
> No chief is wise like this brave God of glory
> Who keeps and measures every blade of wheat,
> And paints the peppers redder than the sunsets,
> And makes your corn as golden as the sun.
>
> The great white Father is the God of color
> And maker of the music of the spheres.
> They dance forever and ever in His palace;
> And all His braves sing: Holy! Holy! Holy!

(*The INDIANS exchange curt nods of pleasure, and a few of the WOMEN look up timidly to smile delightedly at one another. FRAY FERNANDO steps back and throws his arms upward in invitation.*)

> Come! dance to the lion-hearted Chief, and praise Him
> For this full harvest! Sing to the fearless Lord
> Who braved the thorns and whip and Cross to save you
> And build you golden huts in His bright city!
>
> Dance for the wounded brave and his beautiful mother.
> Sing praises to THE GOD OF THE TASSELLED CORN!

(*FRAY SILVESTRO begins to beat a rhythm on his tambour, and the INDIANS fall smartly into place. FRAY FERNANDO stands to the Right, clapping his hands three times as he says:*)

> Laudate!

(He then glances toward the WOMEN *who, at a nod from him, begin to hum.* FRAY FERNANDO *sings the first two lines of the dance-chant he has composed, and then gestures toward the* WOMEN *who repeat the lines and continue the chant. The* FRIAR *energetically directs both the dancing* MEN *and the chanting* WOMEN*. He intones the first line of each new strophe alone, and the* WOMEN *continue it in chorus. The* WOMEN *beat out the rhythm of the dance with the flat of their hands on their knees, alternating the rise and fall of either hand. Occasionally, this gentle thudding rhythm is changed as* FRAY FERNANDO *directs his chorus to clap the rhythm. For this, they stretch their arms high above their heads, giving the loud clap on each accented syllable and soft handclaps on the unaccented syllables. The sixth Gregorian psalm tone may ideally be used for this dance-chant.)*

THE DANCE: GOD OF THE TASSELLED CORN

FRAY FERNANDO. Praise the great white Father in the heavens
        Who holds a golden torch to light the day!

THE WOMEN. Praise the great white Father in the heavens
        Who holds a golden torch to light the day,
        And strikes off flinty stars just after twilight,
        Lest any Cuautitlanan lose his way.

        We have a great white Father in the heavens;
        We wait His golden torch at break of day.

FRAY FERNANDO. Our God can make the prickly-pear, but also,

THE WOMEN. He sews the petals into every rose,
        And pours a perfume down the throats of flowers
        More humble than the fine Castilian rose.

        If God makes jests with prickly-pears, He also
        Drapes royal robes on a Castilian rose.

FRAY FERNANDO. Praise the chief of every tribe and village!

THE WOMEN. The lion-hearted Brave Who tossed the seas
        Like fine spray from His hands, and flung the oceans
        Between their granite banks with utmost ease.
        He is the Chief of every tribe and village
        And lion-hearted Master of the seas!

FRAY FERNANDO. Our God paints the peppers scarlet, makes wheat amber!

THE WOMEN. He is the beautiful God of the tasselled corn.
        Only this great Brave knows the vast secret
        That brings our seed to harvest a summery morn.

        He paints the peppers red, but likes wheat amber,
        Our brave and beautiful God of the tasselled corn!

FRAY FERNANDO. Praise the fearless Hunter in the skyland!

THE WOMEN. He owns the land and every man upon it.
        He brings our souls like stags down in the evening,
        Arching His bow and flinging bright love from it!

The great and fearless Hunter in the Skyland
Has pierced the land with Love, and all men on it!

FRAY FERNANDO. Our God has lightning in His eyes, and thunder

THE WOMEN. Is common talk of His! His bow and arrow
Can empty clouds of rain upon our planting
And fill the thirsting seed locked in the furrow.

Our God has lightning eyes and talks like thunder;
But only to work our good, lets fly His arrow.

FRAY FERNANDO. Praise the Son; and praise the great-winged Spirit

THE WOMEN. Whose breath blows favor on us from the sky,
And warms us in the bitter cold of sorrow,
And folds his wings across us when we die.

The Father and the Son and great-winged Spirit
Watch us by day, and guard us when we die!

FRAY FERNANDO. Our God composed all songs that birds go singing

THE WOMEN. Under the clouds and on the boughs of trees.
The Father made the birds; the Son released them
In flight, the Spirit taught them tones and keys.

God favors music; every bird declares it,
Singing His praises from the tallest trees!

FRAY FERNANDO. Praise the little Maid who bore our Savior,

THE WOMEN. For she is fair as wheat-sheaves in the breeze.
Her lips are bright poinsettias in the winter;
Most gracious little queen of hills and leas!

Sing to the sweetest Mother of our Savior!
She smiles like morning dews upon the leas.

FRAY FERNANDO. Our little Queen likes Indians to honor

THE WOMEN. Her tall, brave Son with songs, and pray to Him.
She walks like gentle winds, and talks like water,
And never in her life did any sin.

The Holy Virgin Mary is our Mother,
And never in her life did any sin.

(There is a little silence. FRAY FERNANDO claps his hands three times; and the INDIANS drop to their knees, bending slightly forward with inclined heads and touching the ground with their fingertips. The WOMEN, too, rise to a kneeling position, but cover their hands in the folds of their shawls. They obviously await something. FRAY FERNANDO looks upward to the open sky and then, extending his arms over the group, blesses them with great love and respect. FRAY SILVESTRO, too, traces the Sign of the Cross over them, his tambour still suspended from his shoulders.)

FRAY FERNANDO. The God of Planting bless you: great white Father.
   The God of Harvest bless you: brave Chief-Son.
   The God of Increase bless you: the great-winged Spirit,
   Strong and holy God of land and sky!

(*The* INDIANS *make the Sign of the Cross and break up into small chattering groups, gradually drifting Offstage, Right, each woman going in turn to follow her husband. They move at a leisurely pace with the air of those reluctant to end a joyous hour. The last two* INDIANS, *unaccompanied by wives, engage in earnest conversation at Backstage Right with* FRAY FERNANDO; *they are the last to exit,* FRAY FERNANDO *pointing Offstage to something he would show them. Meanwhile, one* INDIAN, *smaller than the rest and of very humble bearing, comes shyly up to* FRAY SILVESTRO *at the Left. He is* JUAN DIEGO, *accompanied by his wife,* MARIA LUCIA, *who stands timidly behind him.* FRAY SILVESTRO, *who has been earnestly examining his tambour, looks up and smiles at them.*)

FRAY SILVESTRO. You dance far better than many a fine young brave,
   My Juan Diego!

   (*He turns to* MARIA LUCIA.)

                  Is he made of rubber,
   Maria Lucia mia, that he leaps
   Like arrows? Your tortillas keep him young,
   I say! — no village woman makes them better!

(*They look pleased, and* MARIA LUCIA *shyly hangs her head.*)

JUAN DIEGO. I count no less than fifty-four bright summers
   On my old head, my Father. Soon, old Juan
   Will sit and watch the young braves at their dancing;
   And then I take my sleep in the deep earth.

(MARIA LUCIA *prods* JUAN *gently. When he hesitates, she herself speaks softly.*)

MARIA LUCIA. My Father, there is a thing that we would know.

   At evening, when the darkness comes like vapors
   Of herbs into our hut, there is a thing
   We talk of; and a sweetness comes upon us
   Like one held note upon a far-off flute.

(*Overcome with having made so long a speech,* MARIA LUCIA *hangs her head and blushes.* FRAY SILVESTRO *looks at them wonderingly and drops to a low bench, motioning them to be seated. The* INDIANS *seat themselves with graceful dignity upon the ground.*)

FRAY SILVESTRO. Perhaps I cannot answer this great question
   That troubles you so strangely, — like herb vapors,
   You say? Or yet like flutes? What is this thing?

(MARIA LUCIA *prods* JUAN *again, and he looks up trustingly.*)

JUAN DIEGO. Wisest of men, you surely can inform us,
   Good Father! You talk so often of our Savior
   And Chief in Heaven, bravest of them all.
   We think with pain upon His battle-stricken

Hands and feet, the great spear in His Heart.
We see Him in the lightning and the waters
And know His breath that blows the primrose pink.

(*He pauses.*)

But there is this other thing that we would know.

(*His voice trails off, and* FRAY SILVESTRO *looks at him intently.*)

MARIA LUCIA. (*Gently.*)

It is the little Mother, Padrecito!
We would know more about the Maiden Mother.

(FRAY SILVESTRO *smiles down at them, and at last* JUAN'S *tongue is loosed.*)

JUAN DIEGO. (*Eagerly.*)

The little Mother …. have you ever seen her,
My Father? Are her eyes like hidden waters?
Did she perhaps sing softly in the twilight,
And laugh when her brave Nino tried to walk
Before His time?

(*They look up at the priest like guileless children.*)

We know you are a holy
And learned man. We thought the little Maiden
Had sometime come to talk to you and tell you
The many things you know about her Son.

(FRAY SILVESTRO *looks strangely moved, and there is a little silence.*)

FRAY SILVESTRO. (*Very gently.*)

My children, never would such as I be worthy
To see that Maiden Mother. Who could look
Upon that loveliest of maids, and bear it!

(*He looks away.*)

No, never have I seen her; but my heart
Is like a locket closed about her face.

(*He glances at* JUAN.)

One day, one day, we hope to see that Maiden
When *all* of us have slept in the deep earth
And risen, cleansed and fortified to meet her;

But surely not on earth could man be worthy
To look upon her face, and see again
The dullness of the world that mourns her leaving
Still, in the whisper of dove and willow-branch.

(*His voice trails away, and he places his hand on* JUAN DIEGO'S *shoulder.*)

CURTAIN

ACT ONE

SCENE II

SCENE. *The foot of the mountainous range of Tepeyac, December 9,1531. The curtain opens on an empty stage; the inner curtain is three-quarters open.* JUAN DIEGO *enters from the Right and trudges slowly to the foot of a small hillock. Midstage, he pauses, looks dispiritedly about him, and sighs deeply. Clenching his fists against his heart, he begins his lament for his dead wife,* MARIA LUCIA.

JUAN DIEGO. Because my swallow has cut
One long, last valley through the air,
I cannot forgive the days
That come to walk my heart on soft-clawed feet.

If the night falls like her black hair upon me,
I'll dread the night, and blame the strike of birdnote
For memories of gilt bracelets and chains.

(He drops his hands and turns toward the rise of Tepeyac.)

At least, at least the roses will not bloom
To taunt my grey December. Here's my pity
On those unflowering wastes of Tepeyac!
Here is my compassion in this dumbstruck
And colorless bed of silence.

My swallow flew
Away, and beauty in her trail, and joy,
All of my joy. Shall any hue of green
Or gold or scarlet live where she has died?

(He sighs and fingers his rough tilma.)

Here is my bent old life, a twist of face
And hunch of body in this fitting frame
Of Tepeyac, bleak and flowerless. I blame
The night that swings down on me like her hair!

(He turns away from the hill and speaks with deepest sorrow.)

Now they will count my lonely, "one!" for Mass
When the great God of tasselled corn comes down,
Discovering old Juan without his sole
Claim on the nobleness of song and shade,
Forgiving if I blame the glint of sunlight
For memories of gilt bracelets and chains.

(His head droops, and there is a moment of complete silence. Then the sound of flutes and violins is heard. JUAN'S *head jerks up and he looks about in all directions, great wonder and surprise on his face. The sound of violins ceases, and there is one very long-sustained flute-note;* JUAN *raises his hands and stands entranced. As the note finally dies, our* LADY'S *voice is heard.)*

THE VOICE. Juan! Juanito! Juan Dieguito!

(Each time our LADY *speaks, throughout this scene, there is a very soft sound of strings and winds.)*

JUAN DIEGO. My name was sturdy as my hut, and solid
        As skins against the wind, Why do I hear it
        Fragile as flute-notes on this winter dawn?

THE VOICE. Juanito! Juanito!

JUAN DIEGO. I never knew my name is like a star!
        My eyes are wakened by it, and my life
        Is shining like a thousand hunters' knives!
        I never knew . . . my name is like a star!

THE VOICE. Juan Dieguito!

JUAN DIEGO. Why, how is this? — My name is like perfume
        Spilling in rivers down my whole life's years,
        Soaking my thoughts! I cannot understand . . .
        My poor name smells like a Castilian rose!

THE VOICE. Juan! Juanito!

JUAN DIEGO. *(He looks about him wonderingly, as for something suddenly missed.)*
        I cannot find my fears!
        Where is my sorrow —
        Familiar friend of every winter dawn?

        My fears are hidden in a maze of music,
        My weariness is tangled up in stars.

        (He stands very erect, and his voice grows jubilant.)

        Now let the sun-dial crumple; let the sand-glass
        Splinter and scatter; let the corn meal stand
        Unneeded and untended! All my living
        Is sweetly tangled in a mesh of stars.

        (His voice falls back on the tone of wonder.)

        I never knew my rough name smells of roses.
        I never guessed my name is spelled with flutes.

(He begins to clamber up the small incline, and the inner curtain is fully opened to reveal the VIRGIN *standing atop the hillock. Her hands are folded very lightly together, only the fingertips actually touching, and her head is inclined a little forward and to the Right. Her dress is of rose-colored stuff embroidered in gold, and her mantle is blue-green. She smiles, and* JUAN *falls to his knees.)*

THE VIRGIN. Where are you going, least of my sons?

*(*JUAN *accepts her presence without self-consciousness, and answers simply.)*

JUAN DIEGO. I go to the church, gracious Lady,
        And into the Mass, sweetest Child.*

---

* *The term, "Child," used thus seems strange to us. However, it was the usual title used by the Indians in addressing their superiors or persons of rank and nobility. "My Child," "Little one," etc.*

The way is rough for my treading,
But not so rough as the road
My heart must take every hour
Of every day that dawns.

(*He gathers his tilma more closely about him.*)

And you, my Child and my Lady,
Does the cold wind give you sorrow?

(*Our* LADY *smiles, but makes no reply.*)

My spirit is cold past the blasting
Of any fierce wind. My Maria
Took with her to heaven my summers,
And now all my life is a winter
Of waiting the God of the Harvest
To reap my poor years He has sown
Like seeds in the rocks of Tepeyac.

(*He looks up at our* LADY *wonderingly.*)

I would you had seen my Maria!
She danced like the breezes in springtime.
And rainbows were born in the sun
When she patted the dough for tortillas.
And her earrings would shiver with color.

(*There is a little pause; then* JUAN *stands up and looks more closely at Our* LADY. *He speaks in the tone of one making a great discovery.*)

Yet this moment, my Child and my Lady,
I perceive you are lovelier far
Than even Maria Lucia!

(*He drops to his knees again, and holds his hands out with the irresistible gesture of a child.*)

Who are you? And whence have you come?

(*Our* LADY *holds her hands against her heart and looks heavenward. After a few moments she speaks.*)

THE VIRGIN. Know, then, and heed what I tell you,
Juanito, least of my sons.
I am Holy Mary the Virgin.
My name is: Mother of God.

(*There is a pause. The winds and strings come up louder and then dim again.*)

The Maker of earth and of Heaven,
The One Who created the world,
The true God and only, the Savior,
And God of the tasselled corn
And God of the swallows and starlight,
Calls me His Mother forever.

(JUAN *shows no real surprise, only delight. As our* LADY's *gaze returns to rest on him, he touches his forehead to the ground three times, and then kneels up with his hands clasped in a gesture of expectation.*)

THE VIRGIN. I am graced with many cathedrals
That witness my bright exaltation.
Turrets and towers proclaim me
In majesty loaned from my Son,
And spandrels of doorways enclose me
For bright benedictions on men.

But here, my Juanito, I tell you,
I urgently wish that a temple
Shall stand to proclaim my compassion,
My succor, my shield and my love.

(*She pauses, and the music swells and diminishes as before.* JUAN's *gaze never leaves her face. Her eyes return Heavenward.*)

For I am a merciful Mother
To you, Dieguito, and all
Who love me and trust me, and call me
When darkness of sorrow is on them.

(*She smiles very faintly, her gaze coming back to* JUAN.)

I listen, Juanito, whenever
A man's lamentation makes bruises
Upon my own love and compassion.
I listen and solace and heal.

(*Her eyes return Heavenward once more.*)

All men must know this compassion.
A temple must rise to proclaim it.

(*She looks about her.*)

My little son, here, in this valley,
I desire men to build me a temple.
My mercy shall dwell in it always
That men may discover my love.

(JUAN *gazes into her face and nods happily.*)

JUAN DIEGO. Be it so, my Child and my Lady!
You must tell this desire of your heart
To men of wisdom and riches
Who are fitted to hear your command.

(*Our* LADY *smiles and extends one lovely olive hand out slightly over him.*)

THE VIRGIN. Least of my sons, Dieguito,
It is *you* I entrust with my wish.

(JUAN *throws up both hands in shocked surprise.*)

You will go to the bishop and tell him
All you have seen and admired.
Word for word, you must tell him, Juanito,
All which I have confided to you.

(*She clasps her hands lightly together again.*)

Be assured that I shall be grateful
And give you a mighty reward.

(*She looks on* JUAN *with great tenderness.*)

I will make your life brighter and gladder
Than ever it was when Lucia
Danced like the breezes, and sunlight
Slanted along her heels.
The great and mighty Chieftain,
The God of the tasselled corn,
Is still my own Nino. He gladdens
All hearts, as I ask Him, forever.

(*The music grows louder. Our* LADY *smiles.*)

I shall make my Juanito worthy
Of all the trouble I give him!

My bidding is plain. Pray you, do it
With courtesy, least of my sons.

(JUAN *bows his forehead to the ground and then, rising, sweeps our* LADY *a broad and graceful bow. He gathers his tilma about him and going down again upon one knee, looks up at her.*)

JUAN DIEGO. Your humble servant, my Lady!
I go now to do your wish.

(*The winds and strings come up to full power.*)

CURTAIN

ACT TWO

SCENE I

SCENE. *An anteroom in the palace of the Bishop of Mexico,* FRAY JUAN DE ZUMARRAGA, *later the same day.* JUAN DIEGO *stands humbly but determinedly at the far end of the room.* TWO SERVANTS *sit on scarlet-cushioned chairs opposite. They are laughing heartily at some jest when a* THIRD SERVANT *enters from the Left. He glances at* JUAN *with light contempt, and then addresses himself to the other two.*

RICARDO. What, does the knave still linger!
Must we suffer two holes in the Bishop's rug
From the man's great feet?

(ANTONIO *laughs, but the second servant,* FRANCISCO, *looks reprovingly at* RICARDO.)

FRANCISCO.　　　　He has patience
　　　　Enough to make five saints set in a row!

(JUAN *shows no interest in their conversation. He is absorbed in his thoughts, and from time to time his lips move as though he were memorizing something important.*)

ANTONIO. Patience, you say! Ha! Francisco,
　　　　Were it not for your own, I had shown
　　　　Our stubborn caller the exit hours ago!

RICARDO. He wearies *me* with his waiting!
　　　　And what can he have to say
　　　　To such as his Grace, I wonder?
　　　　The man is clearly a fool
　　　　To trouble the Bishop with nonsense.

ANTONIO. (*Laughing.*)
　　　　　　　　Thunder upon you, Francisco,
　　　　If you gain the knave admittance
　　　　To tire his Grace with some jabber
　　　　Of wild recounts and requests!

FRANCISCO. (*Smiling.*)
　　　　　　　　Let thunders clap on me! I wonder,
　　　　If maybe the sun bursts instead;
　　　　And you mistake the explosion
　　　　By reason of noise in your heads!

(*All three laugh good-naturedly. There is a sound of scraping chairs within the* BISHOP'S *private room, and the heightened murmur of voices. All three* SERVANTS *spring to attention, and* FRANCISCO *steps over to the door.* JUAN *looks up, and* FRANCISCO *turns toward him kindly.*)

　　　　I mean to solicit his lordship,
　　　　The Bishop, to hear you just now.

(JUAN *draws himself up with dignity and bows gratefully, but says nothing.* FRANCISCO *turns to the other two and speaks in a low tone.*)

　　　　There is a something, I tell you,
　　　　Within the Indian's eyes
　　　　That makes me think of sunlight
　　　　After long weeks of rain.
　　　　Where he has been I wonder,
　　　　Or what he has ever seen,
　　　　That he stands there wrapped in that tilma
　　　　As though he possessed all Spain!

(ANTONIO *shrugs, and* RICARDO *waves his hand carelessly. The door opens and the* BISHOP'S *caller, a Spaniard wearing Naval insignia, bows himself out. He looks curiously at* JUAN *who seems not to notice him, as* FRANCISCO *slips inside.* ANTONIO *and* RICARDO *bow smartly to the caller who nods to them and passes through the outer door which* RICARDO *opens for him with a grand gesture.*

FRANCISCO *reappears almost immediately and beckons* JUAN *to enter. The inner door opens to reveal* FRAY JUAN DE ZUMARRAGA *seated behind a massive mahogany desk. The outer curtain is simultaneously drawn part way to conceal the* SERVANTS. JUAN *drops to his knees just inside the door, and the* BISHOP *eyes him wonderingly. At last,* ZUMARRAGA *rises and beckons* JUAN *to approach and kiss his ring.* FRAY JUAN DE ZUMARRAGA *is a tall spare man with the fine features of an ascetic and marvelously beautiful hands. He fingers the heavy Cross suspended from a chain about his neck. After* JUAN'S *salute, the* BISHOP *sits down again, motioning* JUAN *to do likewise; but the* INDIAN *seems unaware of the gesture. Remaining on his knees, he looks up into the* BISHOP'S *eyes imploringly.)*

ZUMARRAGA. What is it, my son, that brings you
        So far from your village this day?

JUAN DIEGO. *(Clasping his hands before him, he plunges into his tale without preamble.)*
        The little Mother has sent me
        To tell you her urgent wish.

ZUMARRAGA. *(Smiling.)*
              Your little Mother has sent you?
        She must be very old.

JUAN DIEGO. No, no! but young, my Father!
        She is young as the folded primrose
        And fair as the waving wheat.

        *(*ZUMARRAGA *raises surprised eyebrows.)*

        Her cheeks have the dawn upon them,
        And her eyes hold the hidden waters.

        (He smiles happily.)

        No, no, not old, great Father!—
        The little Maid is young!

ZUMARRAGA. What do you say, my son?
        Have you not told me,
        You bring a message from your little Mother?
        And now you tell me of some strange young maiden!

JUAN DIEGO. *(He looks at the* BISHOP *patiently.)*
        But it is all the same! Beloved Father
        So wise and kind, surely you understand
        What Fray Silvestro teaches in the village:
        How the brave Savior's Mother was a Maid!

*(*ZUMARRAGA *starts, and then a shade of impatience crosses his face.)*

ZUMARRAGA. Take hold upon yourself, my foolish son!
        Heed what a strange, wild gallop your tongue is taking!
        I give you audience to tell your message,
        But not to let your fancy ride us both.

        (He leans forward.)

Come, come now, I have other pressing business.
Say what has brought you here this winter morning.

(JUAN *shows no least offense, but looks directly into* BISHOP's *eyes and speaks calmly.*)

JUAN DIEGO. I saw a little Lady of marvelous beauty;
And when I asked her name, she said it was:

(*He closes his eyes with the effort of repeating the Virgin's words precisely.*)

Holy Mary the Virgin, Mother of God.

(ZUMARRAGA *frowns, and leans back in his chair, folding his arms before him.*)

She is lovely! I would I could tell you
How it is when she says my name!—
Like a bird and a flute together.

What a sound *your* name would be,
My Lord!—But perhaps you have seen her
And often talked with her?

(*The* BISHOP *searches* JUAN's *face for several seconds.*)

ZUMARRAGA. No, I have not seen the Virgin
Nor heard her say my name.
And you, my son, do you often
Talk with the Mother of God?

JUAN DIEGO. No, never before, my father.
Only this morning she came

(*He shakes his head anxiously*)

Because of this message I bring you.
She is very concerned with it.

I believe it will give her sorrow
If your lordship does not hasten
To do her will. I see plainly
Her mind is filled with this thing.
We must give her rest and comfort
In such an urgent need.

(*The* BISHOP's *eloquent eyebrows lift again, and he smiles faintly.*)

ZUMARRAGA. So? And what will the Virgin
Have me to do for her need?

JUAN DIEGO. (*Excitedly and joyously.*)
It is a temple, my Father!
She will have a house for herself
In the valley of old Tepeyac.
My lord, you must build her a house!

(*He looks up happily at the* BISHOP.)

ZUMARRAGA. (*Unimpressed.*)
                                    Our Lady has many temples.
          My son, I think you dream
          More in the day than the nighttime.

JUAN DIEGO. (*Hurriedly.*)
                                    No, no! She has told me clearly
          How none of the great cathedrals
          And turrets and towers ease her
          Enough, for this urgent wish
          In her heart for a temple of mercy
          And a house for her great compassion.

ZUMARRAGA. A temple of mercy? You tell me
          Strange words! And where did *you* hear
          Such talk and such terms, I wonder?

(JUAN *plainly misses the implication of the* BISHOP's *unbelief and answers ingenuously.*)

JUAN DIEGO. The little Maiden told me all of it!
          You must not fear my lord, because her message
          Falls strangely on your ears. This lovely Lady
          Has sweet concern to ease your sharp surprise,
          Because she bade me tell you very clearly
          And word for word, all I saw and admired.

(*The* BISHOP *looks somewhat nonplussed at* JUAN's *naïveté.*)

JUAN DIEGO. (*Eagerly.*)
          She said that, to all men who love and trust her,
          She is a merciful Mother, and she hears
          The lamentations of all hearts in sorrow
          That cry to her. She solaces and heals.

          (*He extends his hands, as if to indicate to the* BISHOP *how very simple this all is.*)

          Now she will have this temple in the valley
          That all men may be healed of all their sorrows.
          It is your lordship who must build her house.

          (*He frowns a little.*)

          I fear the little Maid will have no comfort
          Till this is done. The matter troubles her.

          Could we begin today to build this temple
          Her heart is set upon, that she may rest
          Soundly tonight, my Father? Juan Diego
          Will drag the stones for you! But give the word!

(*The* BISHOP *smiles despite himself.*)

ZUMARRAGA. My son, I am convinced your soul is limpid
          As waters. Yet I fear you are deceived.

          (*He pauses and looks away.*)

Sometimes a heart grown lonely past endurance
Paints its own solace, and builds strange monuments
Of dreams and fantasies to ease the pain.

(*He glances at* Juan *and then begins to gather papers together on his desk, in a gesture of dismissal.*)

JUAN DIEGO. I do not understand these words, my Father.
I am a rough, unlettered Indian
And build no monuments and paint no pictures.

(*Patiently, as though the* Bishop *had not grasped the facts.*)

It is your lordship who must build a temple!
Holy Mary the Virgin has told me so.

(*The* Bishop *rises and speaks kindly but in a tone of finality.*)

ZUMARRAGA. Go back to the village, my son, and pray our Savior
To guide both you and me to do His Will.
Return to me later, when I have more leisure;
And know I shall consider all you have said.

(*He extends his ring for* Juan *to kiss it and depart, but the Indian seems not to notice.*)

JUAN DIEGO. (*Anxiously.*)
But, Father, what shall I tell the little Maiden?
She will be waiting to hear the news I bring.
I cannot bear to disappoint this Lady
Or cause this lovely Mother suffering!

(*Compelled by his urgency, the* Bishop *withdraws his hand and looks intently at* Juan. *He speaks slowly.*)

ZUMARRAGA. Tell this Lady that your message gives me
No urgent reason for a sudden act.
Ask her to send some sign that I may truly
Know this is the Mother of Jesus Christ.

(*He extends his ring again, and this time* Juan *seizes his hand and kisses the ring reverently. He looks up happily into the* Bishop's *face.*)

JUAN DIEGO. Gladly, gladly, my Father! Surely the Maiden
Will send some sign from Heaven to give you comfort.

(Juan *rises and sweeps a bow to the* Bishop. *At the door, he turns back, smiling contentedly.*)

Gracias! And I shall give your greetings,
My lord, to this sweetest Lady. May it please
Her soon to give you solace with some token
From Heaven, from her Nino!

(*He bows again.*)

Gracias!

(Juan *goes out, leaving* Zumarraga *staring after him curiously.*)

CURTAIN

ACT TWO

SCENE II

SCENE. *Tepeyac, early in the morning two days later. Only the outer curtain is open. JUAN DIEGO enters from the Right and walks slowly to midstage. He looks very troubled and uncertain, starts to retract his steps, and then goes forward again. He has almost reached the far Left, casting frequent glances over his shoulder, when he halts, transfixed.*

THE VOICE. Juan! Juanito!

(*Music as in* ACT ONE, SCENE II.)

(*The inner curtain opens to reveal the Tepeyac scene. This time, our* LADY *is facing Left and has descended several steps down the hill as though coming to meet* JUAN. *He runs toward her and falls on his knees. He touches his forehead to the ground, then kneels up with hands clasped like a supplicating child.*)

THE VIRGIN. What is the matter, least of my sons?

(JUAN *looks distressed and deeply embarrassed.*)

JUAN DIEGO. Does the morning find you well, my Child?
How early you are about, my gracious Lady!

(*Our* LADY *looks at him steadily, without replying.*)

JUAN DIEGO. (*Wringing his hands excitedly.*)
Believe me, oh! believe me, sweetest Lady,
My heart desired to keep the tryst with you
Yesterday; but I must give you sorrow
And tell you that which well I know will pain
Your tender heart.

Your servant Bernardino,
My well-loved uncle, has a sickness on him
And waits for death in suffering and distress.

Oh, yesterday my soul was torn within me,
Wondering where my plainer duty lay:
In coming to keep tryst with you, my Lady,
Or nursing Bernardino in his pain!

Be not offended, little one most dear,
Because it seemed your servant, my poor uncle,
Needed your Juan Diego for the time.

(*He rises and bows.*)

And now, my most beloved, I must leave you;
Although my heart would willingly remain
And hear your words.

I hurry to the city
And church of Tlatelolco where the priest
Must know my uncle turns in pain, waiting
Anointing and the shriving of his sins.

For well you know, my Lady and my Sovereign,
We all to death and sin are sadly subject,
And not like you, sweet Child, without offense.

(*He bows again.*)

Have patience now a little, and await me.
Comfort yourself that I shall soon return,
Having dispatched this business. And I shall give you
A clear report of what the Bishop said.

(*Our* LADY *smiles a little; then she stretches both hands out over him.*)

THE VIRGIN. Hear, my little son, what I now tell you:
Let nothing ever trouble or afflict you.
Fear neither pain nor sickness nor the things
That seem most grievous accidents to men.

(*She folds her hands on her breast; and* JUAN *falls slowly to his knees again, as though already forgetting his worry.*)

Am I not here? And am I not your Mother?
Am I not life itself and truest health?
You are beneath my shadow and protection;
In my lap are you and COUNTED AS MINE.

(*The music swells and dies again, as our* LADY *pauses. She looks down at* JUAN *very tenderly.*)

Of what more have you need, Juan Dieguito?

(*She smiles again.*)

Have no more sorrow for your uncle's sickness.
Bernardino will not die of this attack;
But, even now, he is already well!

(JUAN *throws up his hands in joyous surprise; his face is bright with faith in her word.*)

JUAN DIEGO. My Lady and my Child, I know most clearly
That every word your lips have said is true.
I take it on your word: My uncle needs me
No longer, for his sickness now is healed.

(*He touches his forehead to the ground. Raising up, he sighs deeply and relievedly.*)

As I am free now of this grievous worry,
We can get on with business of our own,
My little one most dear, and make an ending
To what I see is weight upon your heart.

Now I must tell you how his lordship heard me.
Most kind he was, my Lady and my Queen;
But I perceived he cannot yet believe me.

(*A shade of sorrow crosses his face.*)

I would that you could understand, sweet Child,
That you would fare far better by the choosing
Of someone great and noble for your work.
To me it is most clear, a lowly peasant
Like Juan Diego is not one for you.

Twice I have seen the Bishop, both times failed you.
His Lordship thinks I dream, or am deceived.
He asks a sign from you; but I must warn you,
I fear the servants will not give me leave
To bring it, even should you deign to give it.

Thus, I beseech you, little one most dear,
To find yourself an influential person
Worthy to bear your sign to this wise Father.

THE VIRGIN. Hear me now, much-loved son, and understand me.
I have no lack of servants I might send.
Many would willingly find employment with me
And gladly do what I might order them.

But it is entirely fitting that Juanito
Should do this thing for me, because I wish it.

By your means and no other, I will have it
So to be that a temple rises here.

(*She looks about her and then her gaze returns to* JUAN.)

JUAN DIEGO. Pardon, O Queen, my boldness. Well you know it,
Sweetest of Ladies, that my heart is set
Upon your wish. If you will have no better
Than Juan Diego, then, behold!—your servant!

(*He inclines deeply, remaining on his knees.*)

Send me again to see the Bishop; only
Give me the sign he wishes, sweetest Child,
That I may be believed, and you find comfort
For this great wish of yours that gives you trouble.

THE VIRGIN. (*She glances upward, turning slightly sideways.*)
Go up, my little son most loved and cherished,
Up to the very summit of the hill
Where first you saw me and I called your name.

There you will find a great supply of flowers.
Gather them in your tilma, and bring them here.
I shall then tell you what to do and say.

JUAN DIEGO. *(He frowns slightly.)*

> Gladly I do this for you, gracious Lady.
> I only hope your heart will not be pained
> if I should fail to find you any flowers.

> *(He looks up at her ingenuously.)*

> My Lady and my Child, I hate to tell you,—
> But nothing blooms here in the harsh December;
> only the barren rocks crown Tepeyac.

(Our LADY smiles but says nothing, only gesturing lightly with her hand again.)

> Forgive me, sweetest Child; I had thought only
> To spare you disappointment for your heart.

(He hurries up to the summit of the hill. Arrange this to be just out of curtain range if it is not feasible to play it on stage. Our LADY remains looking up after him, and smiles when his exclamation is heard. Offstage.)

JUAN DIEGO. Gracias a Dios! Gracias!

(There is a pause during which the music comes up to full power. After several minutes, it diminishes and JUAN comes hurrying down the slope, his tilma held out in front of him like an apron. It is full of Castilian roses, and JUAN's face is alight with joy. He falls on his knees before Our LADY, holding the tilma out for her to see the roses.)

> My Lady and my Child, how to explain it!
> Castilian roses bloom on Tepeyac
> In bleak December! See the dew upon them
> Like great pearls! There were more than I could bear
> Within my tilma! Will you have me gather
> Some others for you to take home with you?

(Our LADY smiles and begins to take the roses out of his tilma into her own arms.)

THE VIRGIN. No, my Juanito, little son most cherished;
> For I have roses always at my home.

(JUAN shows pleased surprise at this. Our LADY continues to lift the roses out as she speaks.)

> Here is the sign I give you for the Bishop.
> Tell him these roses gathered in December,
> At my word, from the rocks of Tepeyac,
> Will be his token that you speak most truly
> And that he set himself to do my wish
> As you have made it known.

> *(She pauses, her arms half full of roses, and looks at JUAN.)*

> > See, how I trust you
> And place my hope in you! Now, listen well
> To what I say: No one must see these roses

Until you come into the Bishop's presence.
Conceal them well, Juanito, that no eye
May feast upon their beauty till his lordship
Sees them and knows they come from Holy Mary.
Tell him what I have said, and thus dispose him
To build my temple here as I desire.

(*By now, Our* LADY *has taken all the roses out of his tilma. She begins to rearrange them in the tilma which* JUAN *continues to hold out to her, apron-wise. Let the music grow gradually louder with fuller orchestration being continuously introduced until the music has grown very dramatic. As Our* LADY *replaces the roses in the tilma, she smiles at* JUAN. *The music stops completely while she says her final word.*)

Go to the Bishop, Juanito, least of my sons!

(*The music comes in again immediately at full crescendo.* JUAN *draws the ends of his tilma up over his precious bundle, rises, sweeps Our* LADY *a bow, and hurries Offstage, Left. Our* LADY *stands gazing after him, her hands folded as we see her in the Miraculous Image.*)

CURTAIN

ACT THREE

SCENE I

SCENE. *The anteroom in the* BISHOP'S *palace, some hours later.* ANTONIO, FRANCISCO *and* RICARDO *are talking earnestly. The* BISHOP'S MAJOR-DOMO, *richly attired, stands erect and imperturbable at the entrance to the* BISHOP'S *room, his eyes fixed coldly on* JUAN *who stands with bent head at the far end of the room as before, the ends of his tilma held jealously up around his precious burden.*

FRANCISCO. Why do you trouble yourselves so mightily,
          My friends, to know the burden that he carries?
          Clearly, it is no least affair of ours.

          If his lordship wishes to receive him,
          Then let it be; and hold your souls in peace.

ANTONIO. You weary me, Francisco, with your speeches!
          Who does the knave and rascal think he is,
          That we are not permitted to examine
          His bundle for the Bishop? Peasant fool!

RICARDO. And so say I! Is he a lord or prince, so
          To issue orders freely out to us?

          (RICARDO *holds his hands up, mocking* JUAN'S *posture with the tilma, and imitating his voice.*)

          "I show the Bishop, but must show no other!"

          (ANTONIO *laughs.*)

We of the Bishop's household are not fit, then,
To see the trash an Indian brings in here?

FRANCISCO. (*Smiling wryly.*)
    It seems you think it altogether fitting
    To show a lavish interest, though, in trash!

(*This sets off the final flare of* RICARDO'S *angry curiosity. He looks darkly at* FRANCISCO *and then makes a sudden lunge at* JUAN. *The* MAJOR-DOMO *makes no attempt to intervene when* RICARDO *catches* JUAN'S *wrists and struggles to free the ends of the tilma from* JUAN'S *grasp. His tall figure towers over the little Indian who looks anxious but not resentful as he speaks calmly.*)

JUAN DIEGO. Beware, beware, most honored sir! Have caution
    Not to displease the Lady who has sent me
    To show my burden only to his lordship
    The Bishop. She may manifest displeasure
    If her desire is thwarted through your fault.

(FRANCISCO *makes a few quick strides and drags* RICARDO *away. The* MAJOR-DOMO *looks mildly amused, but* FRANCISCO'S *lips are tight with displeasure.*)

FRANCISCO. How shame should cover you, Ricardo!
    Never have I beheld you so ignoble. Well
    Indeed it is for you, his Grace is busy
    In the far rear and cannot hear you shout
    As wildly as a drunken scoundrel! Gather
    Yourself together, man; and cool your head!

(RICARDO *looks somewhat chagrined and glances apprehensively at the closed door of the* BISHOP'S *room. Meanwhile,* ANTONIO, *not at all abashed by the rebuke to* RICARDO, *takes advantage of* JUAN'S *gaze being fixed on* FRANCISCO'S *face, to thrust one of his own hands into the Indian's tilma. He leans over to peer inside; but* JUAN *quickly draws the tilma up closer, looking frightened.* FRANCISCO *wheels angrily on* ANTONIO, *but stops short as he notices the strange expression on* ANTONIO'S *face.*)

ANTONIO. (*He looks blankly about the room.*)
    Roses! Great Roses! Clearly I could see them!
    But when I touched their petals, my fingers closed
    Upon themselves; and I held nothing!

(*He stares down at his hands, repeating stupidly.*)

    Nothing!

FRANCISCO. (*He looks intently at* JUAN *and then back at* ANTONIO.)
    What do you mean, my friend, by talk of roses
    That find the eye, but will not meet the hand?

ANTONIO. (*He sounds confused and a little frightened.*)
    Just what I say! I tell you, there are roses
    There in the Indian's cloak such as no eye
    Has seen before, but yet I cannot touch them;

(*He opens and closes his fingers several times.*)

    My hands hold nothing when I reach for them!

FRANCISCO. I think you dream, Antonio, of roses!
Where would the little Indian have found them
In weather such as this!

(*He smiles.*)

I know your temper
Has painted things rose-red for you before!

(ANTONIO *seems not to hear him, and continues to stare at his hands. The* MAJOR-DOMO *looks a little bored.*)

RICARDO. I hold the man's a wizard! All this hiding
And secret talk! His Grace had well take caution
The Indian does not bewitch him yet!

(*The sound of a bell is heard, and the* MAJOR-DOMO *quickly steps forward. His voice is commanding.*)

THE MAJOR-DOMO. Enough of this circus now! Take your positions.

(*He motions to* FRANCISCO.)

Wait on his lordship.

(*Motions to the others.*)

Hold your busy tongues!

(FRANCISCO *disappears inside, and the* MAJOR-DOMO *glares warningly at* RICARDO *who keeps a sulky silence.* ANTONIO *seems absorbed in his thoughts, glancing at his hands from time to time.* JUAN'S *dark eyes dart anxiously about. Then he glances into his tilma, looks reassured, and fixes his glance on the door.* FRANCISCO *reappears very shortly and motions* JUAN *to enter. The outer curtain partly closes to conceal the* SERVANTS; *and the inner curtain opens to show* ZUMARRAGA *seated on a low throne, at the far wall. The great desk has been pushed to one side.* JUAN *bows deeply and, as* ZUMARRAGA *extends his ring, goes up to the throne. His face is happy now.*)

ZUMARRAGA. What is this thing you bring to me, my son,
And which Francisco says you guard as fiercely
As though you held your own soul in that tilma!

(*He smiles kindly.*)

JUAN DIEGO. My Father and my lord, I did exactly
As bidden by your word! I told this Lady,
Lovely as skies, how you would have a sign
To know her name indeed is: Holy Mary,
Mother of God, and Queen of earth and heaven;
And understand how she would have a temple,
And urgently desires that you should build it!

(JUAN *pauses, and* ZUMARRAGA *leans forward.*)

I told her, furthermore, that I promised
To bring you evidence of her desire
And witness of her name. This gracious Lady
Accepted your conditions and my vow.

(He hangs his head abashedly.)

Although I broke my tryst with her, attending
My Uncle Bernardino who had sickness
Upon him like the robe of death, she kindly
Forgave my lack of courtesy to her.

(He looks up joyously into the BISHOP's *face.)*

And even now, my uncle lives! and vigor
Is on his cheek and brightness in his eye!
This sweetest Maid from Heaven showed me plainly
How life and health go as she orders them!

*(*ZUMARRAGA *looks a little puzzled at all this, but asks no questions.)*

ZUMARRAGA. Yes, but the sign, my son? Where is the sign?

JUAN DIEGO. *(Unhurriedly.)*

I come just now to that point in the story!
She instantly complied with my petition
To give you comfort in your painful doubts,
And bade me gather roses from the summit
Of Tepeyac, — the place where first I saw her.

(The BISHOP *shows marked surprise, and* JUAN *nods energetically as though to show understanding.)*

I took great pains to tell the little Mother
That roses never bloom on Tepeyac,
And least of all in bleak and harsh December.

I warned her well, lest she should have a sorrow
Upon her heart to find no roses there;
But this sweet Maid took no alarm whatever!
I hurried, then, to do as she asked.

(His voice grows excited, and his face beams with joy.)

I reached the summit. Oh, could you have been there!
I thought myself in paradise to see it!
All flowers that the Savior made, abounded
In bright display among the barren rocks!

I gathered roses with bright dew upon them,
As much as I could bear within my tilma,
And hurried down to give her consolation
With sight and scent such as I never knew
In all my life before!

　　　　　She took them gladly
Out of my tilma into her own sweet hands
And then replaced them, saying I must bring them
To you, as sign from Holy Mary the Virgin!

(JUAN *rises with a sudden movement, dropping his tilma and releasing the Castilian roses which fall out in scarlet cascades on to the floor.* JUAN *looks down at them with exultant delight, and speaks without looking up.*)

Behold, the sign, my Father! Behold, the sign!

(ZUMARRAGA *rises from his throne and gazes in joyous amazement at the roses. He takes a step forward and then suddenly stops, transfixed, his beautiful hands outstretched and his lips moving soundlessly. He has seen the greater miracle, and for several seconds both men stand like this. Then* JUAN *turns his happy countenance upward and shows great confusion to notice the* BISHOP'S *eyes riveted, not on the roses, but upon himself.* JUAN *shakes his head slightly, as though to clear the mystery, turning slightly so that the miraculous painting on his tilma is now fully seen by the audience.* JUAN'S *eyes turn downward to find the focus of the* BISHOP'S *gaze, and he discovers the image of the* VIRGIN MARY *painted in glorious tones on his tilma. He flings his arms out wide, exclaiming reverently.*)

My Lady! My Child!

(*Meanwhile,* ZUMARRAGA *has stumbled down the two steps from the throne, his arms held out before him. He falls on his knees before* JUAN, *his eyes glistening with tears. His lips move silently again and again before the words come at last.*)

ZUMARRAGA. Holy Virgin Mary, Mother of God!

(*There are a few moments of complete silence; then the* VOICE OF THE MAJOR-DOMO *is heard at the door.*)

THE MAJOR-DOMO. Pardon my lord, but the hour is closing on us,
                    And . . .

(*He appears in the doorway and stops short. The three* SERVANTS, *alarmed, press in upon him, and they venture into the room. All four then stand rooted in their places until* FRANCISCO *drops to his knees and the others follow suit. At length* ZUMARRAGA *looks up at them, then back at the Image. Still on his knees, he speaks.*)

ZUMARRAGA. The Mother of God has visited this land.
                    Behold, the Virgin Mary! Behold, the Mother!

(*He rises from his knees and very reverently begins to untie the tilma knotted behind* JUAN'S *neck. The Indian's arms hang awkwardly at his sides as he watches the* BISHOP *with a kind of happy bewilderment. When* ZUMARRAGA *has loosened the tilma, he steps back, holding up the miraculous painting at full length.* JUAN *seems assured now, and falls to his knees, his hands clasped.*)

JUAN DIEGO. I have done all you bade me, my little Lady.
                    Behold me, Juan Diego, least of your sons!

CURTAIN

ACT THREE

SCENE II

SCENE. *Tepeyac, - twelve days later. A small shrine has been set up at the summit of the hill, and the barren place has been completely transformed. There are festooned arches all along the way, great masses of poinsettias everywhere; and Indians in bright head-dresses and beaded ornaments stand at attention. Their line reaches up the slope in two rows at either side of the shrine. Those on the level have their arms folded high in front of them; those on the slope hold bows and arrows. The sound of trumpets and beating of drums can be heard as the curtain opens. It grows louder and louder until the procession enters from the Right. BISHOP ZUMARRAGA walks at its head, followed by JUAN DIEGO and his UNCLE BERNARDINO bearing the Sacred Image on a standard. Behind them come the judges of the city, members of the Spanish nobility and the clergy, and a great mass of Spaniards and Indians. All of them sing (or chant) together the "Abatal" in honor of Our LADY.*

THE GREAT CHORUS. (*Many in the procession strew flower petals along the way.*)
> With joy, our eyes have watched the flowers open
> Their perfume for your presence, Holy Mary.
>
> We heard the Virgin sing beside still waters:
> "I am the precious plant with hidden buds.
> The One and Perfect God is He Who made me;
> And of His whole creation, I am Queen."
>
> We sing together from the book of anthems,
> And dance in perfect cadence here before you,
> Because you live again, most gracious Lady
> On earth of ours, in this most holy Image.
>
> God made you beautiful beyond the flowers
> And re-created you, O Holy Mary,
> In this most sacred painting in our land.
>
> With care, your face was painted on the tilma,
> So that your soul seems there for us to see.
> All things grow perfect and complete by gazing
> Upon you! Here, then, let us dwell forever!
>
> Come, oh! come after us, and scatter flowers
> Before the Holy Virgin! Kneel around her
> And sing all sweetest songs before her face!
>
> Until the little Maiden's wish is granted
> And her bright temple rises here, our souls
> Shall make no end of weeping and imploring;
> And this shall be the theme of all our songs!
>
> But when the Virgin's house stands in the morning,
> Our souls take rest and breathe the rare perfume
> That is her love; and songs shall praise forever
> The beautiful bloom that is her sacred face.

The flower of the cocoa spreads its fragrance;
The sweet pomoya perfumes every road
That leads to Holy Mary. Here, her singers
Will bring their hymns of joy for her to hear!

(*The great procession halts during the final strophes of the chant; and* ZUMARRAGA *seats himself on the throne prepared for him at the foot of the incline, his clergy around him.* JUAN *and* BERNARDINO *bear the Sacred Image up the slope and erect it atop the little shrine. A great hush falls upon the assembly as the miraculous Image stands alone in the sunlight.* BERNARDINO *drops to his knees, but* JUAN *stands enrapt before the Image, his hands clasped tightly before him. In the silence, his jubilant voice rings out.*)

JUAN DIEGO. Rest well, my sweetest Lady and my Mother;
          For all the land is yours, and all men know
          What you desire. Be well assured, your temple
          Will rise here, little noble Indian girl!

(*After a moment of silence, the trumpets sound again; and* JUAN *and* BERNARDINO *descend to the* BISHOP'S *throne. Both kneel before him, and* ZUMARRAGA *rises with tears shining in his eyes. He speaks in tones of greatest emotion. All fall on their knees when the* BISHOP *rises, except the trumpeters who lower their instruments and stand at attention.* ZUMARRAGA *looks tenderly on* JUAN, *and then his gaze returns to the Sacred Image. He extends his beautiful hands upward in supplication.*)

ZUMARRAGA. Our Lady of Guadalupe, Rose of Heaven,
          Make intercession for the Church of God!

          Protect the Sovereign Pontiff, and have pity
          On all who call to you in grief and need.

          Mother of God and ever-Virgin Mary,
          Win from your Son the grace that we keep faith
          And hope amid life's bitterness and sorrow.

          Make love burn brightly in our hearts all days
          Until you bring us safely to the vision
          Of your most holy Son, our God and Savior.

(BISHOP ZUMARRAGA *clasps his hands, and a great spontaneous cry goes up from the crowd.*)

THE GREAT CHORUS. Holy Virgin Mary! Amen! Amen!

(*As though a spring had been released, the kneeling populace springs up with one accord. The drummers and trumpeters begin their music, and Spaniards and Indians together fall into dance formations.* ZUMARRAGA *only smiles and settles back on his throne. His hands fall idly in his lap; and, as* JUAN DIEGO *seats himself like a happy child at the* BISHOP'S *feet,* ZUMARRAGA'S *face shows that his thoughts have left the earth.*)

CURTAIN

The End

The Smallest of All

*A Drama in Three Acts
about St. Bernadette of Lourdes*

© 1958, 1986 The Community of Poor Clares of New Mexico, Inc.

To

OUR LADY OF LOURDES

Imprimatur: Edwin V. Byrne, D.D.
                  Archbishop of Sante Fe

Nihil Obstat: M. J. Rodriguez, S.T.L., J.C.B.,
                  Censor Deputatus

                  August 27, 1957

Introduction

To anyone acquainted with Mother Mary Francis' previous writing it will come as no surprise that her most recent play, *Smallest of All*, is beautifully written and full of spiritual insight. What might come as a surprise is that this is a great play. For we never have a right to expect a great play from anyone. In the history of play writing there have been very few great plays. Objectively, *Smallest of All* is one of that very select company. If justice is done, it will come to be recognized as such.

The plot of *Smallest of All* is simply the story of what happened a century ago in the then insignificant little town of Lourdes. A young girl, Bernadette Soubirous, too unschooled to learn enough catechism to make her First Holy Communion, living in the direst poverty with her family in a condemned section of the town jail, was gathering faggots when a "beautiful Lady" appeared to her in a grotto along the River Gave. This was the first of many visions. News of these visions caused thousands to flock to the grotto. Both priest and police tried to break her story and to forbid the pious faithful access to the grotto. But no one could deny that a townsman had had his sight restored. And nothing could shake the disarming simplicity of Bernadette's story. Finally, her patent honesty and holiness win over her initially opposed pastor and cause even the chief of police to weep tears of redeeming contrition. Thus ends the play,—nothing about the worldwide effects of these visions, nothing about the further life of Bernadette, nothing about her future glory. The focus of attention is where Bernadette would want it to be,—upon "the Lady," upon her message and upon the meaning of these events.

One of the many things to marvel at in *Smallest of All* is that without changing the simple outlines of the story of Bernadette, Mother Mary Francis has written a play of flawless dramatic construction. From beginning to end, the play flows with the effortless grace of a bird on the wing. Intermingling scenes of dramatic tension, mystical exaltation, humor, pathos and suspense, the play moves swiftly through the last scene climax to its close. There is no denouement. For Mother Mary Francis has achieved the most daring ending possible in a play. She recognizes and portrays that the end of the play is not an end but only a beginning. It is the beginning of Wisdom, which is the living of Truth.

The interest in *Smallest of All* lies less in the external events that it portrays than in the meaning of those events. It searches out the enduring spiritual meaning of the fact that the Blessed Virgin Mary chose to appear to this poor, ignorant peasant girl; and the real significance of a miracle, especially of the greatest miracle, that God should permit us to love Him; it wrestles with the idea that "every miracle is a kind of crucifixion." *Smallest of All* does not tackle "current problems," only the eternal. But it does all this within the framework of authentic dramatic action that evolves out of predicated character.

It will be for its characters, perhaps, that the play will be most immediately loved. For it is rich in memorable acting roles. There are eight speaking parts, equally divided male and female. Bernadette is the young girl of fourteen whose lambent simplicity and undeviating faith move even the most difficult of all obstacles,—a cold, proud priest. Abbe Peyramale is an actor's dream-role, moving through aloof reserve to icy anger to warm love and dedication to the vision given him by the "smallest" of his spiritual daughters. Bernadette's younger sister, Toinette, is impulsively childish and disconcertingly blunt; while their slightly older girl friend, Jeanne Abadie, is a heedless chatterbox. Bernadette's father, Francois, is a delightful French version of Mr. Micawber—unreasonably optimistic and consistently uncomprehending. His harried wife, Louise, is a careworn but patient mother, eternally preoccupied by the practical necessities of keeping her family going. Francois' friend, Louis, is the snarling, bitter miller whose progressive blindness is the first public cure after the apparitions. Jacomet, chief of police, is a creation of nineteenth century secularistic bureaucracy that crumbles when it comes into contact with the spiritual truth that he had tried to smother beneath official forms. Over and above these principals, any number of townspeople for crowd scenes may be used. As happens in great plays, all of the main characters seem to breathe a life of their own with an easy, unpremeditated naturalness.

The staging of this play is uncomplicated, requiring only two alternating scenes—one interior and one exterior. These scenes can be as elaborate or as simple as one desires. They can easily be played before drapes. Costuming is equally simple. *St. Bernadette* by Leonard Von Matt and Francis Trochu (Henry Regnery Co., Chicago) is most helpful for authentic scenes and costumes. Its photographs are superb.

An unusual feature of *Smallest of All* is that it can be done by a great variety of age levels and with almost any conceivable facilities (or lack thereof). It does not depend on elaborate staging. It carries itself.

One of the most frequent remarks made by pilgrims to Lourdes is that the greatest miracles that occur there are the spiritual miracles and that one comes away with a greater spiritual strength than ever known in life before. *Smallest of All* is the play about this aspect of Lourdes—the aspect that remains undimmed and undiminished after a century of ever increasing devotion. This devotion cannot help but be increased and deepened by seeing *Smallest of All*. It is much more than a theatrical experience. It is a religious experience.

GERALD KERNAN, S.J.

Cast of Characters
In Order of Appearance

TOINETTE SOUBIROUS . . . . younger daughter, twelve years old

LOUISE SOUBIROUS . . . . mother, about thirty-two years old

BERNADETTE SOUBIROUS . . . . older daughter, fourteen years old

JEANNE ABADIE . . . . a neighbor, fifteen years old

FRANCOIS SOUBIROUS . . . . father, about fifty years old

LOUIS BOURIETTE . . . . the village miller, almost blind

ABBE PEYRAMALE . . . . the parish priest

JACOMET . . . . the chief of police

VILLAGERS . . . . men, women and children of Lourdes

Author's Note

This play is historical in that it tries to give a true picture of Bernadette and to show the effect of the apparitions and her own character on others. Events are sometimes telescoped for dramatic intensity, and the character of Louis Bouriette is speculative, as I think he may have been from what evidence we have of him. Other characterizations are precise, built on an exacter evidence.

It is important to remember that Bernadette was an unusual child, and the balance of wistfulness and vivacity, self-effacement and stubbornness, humility and sharp wit must be kept throughout, if the contradictory elements in her character are to have their full dramatic force.

Mother Mary Francis, P.C.C.

Smallest of All

ACT ONE

SCENE I

SCENE. *"Le Cachot," the abandoned jail in Lourdes which serves the Soubirous family for home, February 11, 1858. LOUISE SOUBIROUS sitting Left of table Down Center, pan in lap, a tired-looking woman of about 32, but looking much older, is languidly stirring a pan of maize. Her daughter BERNADETTE, small and frail for her 14 years, is mending a black stocking, Left Center. TOINETTE, her sister, 12, stands on a low stool, looking out, Right Center of the window whose bars she clasps with both hands. She suddenly turns.*

TOINETTE. Mama, when is our Lent?

LOUISE. It begins next Wednesday. You know well enough it does, Toinette.

TOINETTE. No, Mama, but *our* Lent. Next week will be other people's Lent.

BERNADETTE. (*Smiles, pausing in mending stocking.*) Do you want a special Lent just for the Soubirous, Toinette?

TOINETTE. Yes, Bernadette. This other is not for us.

BERNADETTE. Why not?

TOINETTE. (*Jumping off the stool, crosses Left to table, sticks finger in bowl; LOUISE gives it an absent-minded slap.*) Because Abbe Peyramale says that Lent is a time to make sacrifices. He told us we should give up sweetmeats and not spend our money for hair ribbons, but give it for the missions.

BERNADETTE. Well?

TOINETTE. (*Shakes her head mockingly, crosses Left to BERNADETTE.*) Well, yourself! The Abbe says Lent is for giving up things. (*Open gesture of her hands.*) We have nothing to give up. So this cannot be for us. Is there a different kind of Lent for the Soubirous, Mama? (*Crosses Right to Right of table.*)

LOUISE. (*Stops stirring and her lips quiver.*) For such as us, Toinette, it is always Lent. (*Looks off into space and the spoon falls into the pan.*)

BERNADETTE. (*Rises quickly, crosses Right to Left of table and puts her arm around her mother's shoulder.*) She didn't mean anything, Mama!

TOINETTE. I did, too! How can you give up sugar lumps if you don't have any?

BERNADETTE. Hush, Toinette.

TOINETTE. I won't, either. I'm almost as old as you, and stronger, too. Yes, and bigger! (*Runs over to stand beside BERNADETTE to show her superior height.*) You're just little, little, little! (*Singsong dancing up and down a bit.*)

LOUISE. (*Jerks back to reality.*) Toinette! For shame!

(BERNADETTE *winces and turns away Up Left. She starts to cough.* TOINETTE, *instantly sorry, runs to her, throwing both arms around her.*)

TOINETTE. Oh, but I'm sorry, Bernadette! I am mean, mean, mean. I guess maybe I'll go to Hell. (*Sudden happy inspiration. Turns to* LOUISE, *over* BERNADETTE'*s shoulder.*) It's warm in Hell, isn't it? That would be nice.

LOUISE. (*Hands to her head.*) Do hush, child!

BERNADETTE. (*Returns the embrace.*) It's not nice at all in Hell, Toinette.

TOINETTE. But it's hot?

BERNADETTE. Too hot. You will go to Heaven where the temperature is just right all the time. (*Coughs again.*)

TOINETTE. How will we get to Heaven if we do not give up things for Lent like the abbe said?

BERNADETTE. (*Down Left and picks up the stocking and sits down again.*) We'll get there by love and patience, Toinette.

TOINETTE. (*Down Right Center.*) What is patience, Mama?

LOUISE. (*Stirring again.*) It is not saying mean things when you feel mean. And not complaining when you have to go without things.

TOINETTE. Oh. We are very patient, aren't we? (*Rearranging things on table. Little silence.*) Mama, (*running her fingers through her hair*) did you ever have a ribbon for your hair?

(BERNADETTE *shakes her head warningly at* TOINETTE.)

LOUISE. Yes, darling. I had many ribbons for my hair,—blue ones and pink ones and yellow ones.

TOINETTE. (*Wide-eyed.*) And did you give them up for Lent?

LOUISE. I gave them up for life.

(*Rises abruptly and sets down the pan.* BERNADETTE *goes to her and takes her hands.*)

BERNADETTE. Your hands are cold, Mama. Here, let me warm them! (*Begins to rub them, coughing a little.*)

LOUISE. Save your strength, Bernadette! You have no warmth to give anyone. Coughing, coughing, all the time.

(*Loud* RAP *at the door.*) (*Loudly.*) Come in!

(*Enter* JEANNE ABADIE, *a large peasant girl of fifteen, who looks older; comes Down Right Center;* TOINETTE *to her.*)

JEANNE. Oh, but it's cold! My nose is frozen. Feel! Feel!

(TOINETTE *does and squeals.*)

LOUISE. Well, I hope you didn't expect to warm yourself here, Jeanne.

JEANNE. No, I want to gather sticks by the Gave. And I can't go alone. May Bernadette and Toinette come along?

LOUISE. Maybe Toinette, but certainly not Bernadette.

BERNADETTE. Mother, let me! Please let me go!

JEANNE. I bet there are lots and lots of sticks to pick up. Nobody else will go out in the cold, and we can gather big apronfuls.

BERNADETTE. Yes, Mama! And then we can have a fire and get warm and have a little hot maize. (*Hugs her mother.*) And you will feel happy when Papa comes home with good news.

LOUISE. Good news?

BERNADETTE. (*Smiling.*) Yes. I have prayed my rosary over and over today. And I feel so sure something wonderful is going to happen today.

TOINETTE. (*Crosses Left to* BERNADETTE.) You mean like having real bread to eat? Really, really enough, so that I won't have a pain in my stomach?

BERNADETTE. I guess so. I don't know. But something wonderful. I know it—in here. (*Clasps her hands over her heart.*)

(*Sound of men's* VOICES *Offstage—at which* TOINETTE *begins to drift Right.*)

JEANNE. (*Crosses to* BERNADETTE) How can you know things in there? You know things in your head. My, but you are a silly girl, Bernadette.

LOUISE. Hold your tongue, Jeanne Abadie.

JEANNE. (*Squeezes* BERNADETTE'S *hand and laughs good-naturedly.*) I never can! It's too long, my mother says.

TOINETTE. I hear Papa! (*Runs Right Center to the barred window.*) Oh, dear, Louis is with him. (*Back Left Center to table.*)

BERNADETTE. I'm glad he is. See you be kind to him now, Toinette.

TOINETTE. But he's always so cross.

BERNADETTE. Maybe you would be cross, too, if you were nearly blind.

(LOUISE *crosses toward door. Enter* FRANCOISE SOUBIROUS *and* LOUIS, FRANCOIS *kisses* LOUISE *on the cheek and holds out his hands to* TOINETTE *and* BERNADETTE.)

FRANCOIS. A good afternoon to you, Jeanne Abadie.

JEANNE. Not so good, sir. Unless you like being frozen.

LOUISE. (*Eagerly.*) Francois! You have good news for us?

FRANCOIS. Eh? Well, I'm home. There is good news for a devoted wife. And I've brought a guest besides. (*Pushes the bench, Right Center toward* LOUIS *Down Right and gives him a gentle shove onto it.*)

LOUIS. (*Flat, dull voice.*) What good news is there for such as we are?

LOUISE. I thought maybe you had got some work, Francois.

FRANCOIS. (*A little embarrassed.*) Not yet. (*Crosses Left, taking off hat and coat and hanging on wall Left.*) But something will turn up soon. Something is bound to turn up. We have to be patient. (*Looks vainly for food on table Up Left.*)

TOINETTE. (*Singsong.*) Patience is not to be mean when you feel like being mean, and not to complain when you have to do without things!

LOUIS. Well, one can get a free sermon here, if nothing else.

TOINETTE. (*Towards* LOUIS.) Is that a sermon? Mama made it up. Mama's a preacher, like Abbe Peyramale. Mama makes sermons! (*Crosses to* JEANNE.) Jeanne, you hear that?

LOUISE. Hush up, Toinette. (*Crosses Right.*) How are you feeling, Louis? (*Hands on his shoulders.*)

LOUIS. (*Dull laugh; shrugging off hands.*) I'm feeling more and more, and seeing less and less. Soon I'll do nothing but feel. And you can't run a mill by the feeling.

(FRANCOIS *sits by the cold fireplace.*)

TOINETTE. (*Squints her eyes close and goes through motions of turning, sifting, etc.*) I bet I could!

JEANNE. (*Gives* TOINETTE *a push.*) Get your cloak, Toinette. We'll never get started.

(TOINETTE *crosses Left.*)

FRANCOIS. Started on what?

BERNADETTE. (*Crosses to* FRANCOIS.) We want to gather sticks by the Gave, Papa. Jeanne says there will be lots of them. Can't I go along?

FRANCOIS. Yes, go along, by all means. We could use a fire in here.

LOUISE. (*Crosses to* FRANCOIS.) It's too cold for her, Francois. She's coughing all the time.

FRANCOIS. Oh, fresh air is good. Nothing like it. She'll be better in the spring. Things always get better in the spring,—people, too.

LOUISE. (*Turns back to the maize with a little sigh.*) Well, put on your capulet, too, Bernadette, and your stockings.

(BERNADETTE *Down Left to stool;* LOUISE *up to* FRANCOIS.)

Bernadette said you would have good news, Francois. I don't know why I listen to that child's chatter.

BERNADETTE. (*Down Left, drawing on her stockings.*) No, Mama. I said I was sure something good was going to happen. I just thought Papa might know of it.

JEANNE. (*Crosses Right, rubbing her hands and nose again.*) Listen to that! She knows all about something wonderful, but she doesn't know what it is!

TOINETTE. (*Crosses to* JEANNE.) Maybe she means lots and lots of sticks for a fire.

BERNADETTE. (*Stands up and takes her capulet from the hook and hands* TOINETTE *her cloak.*) No, better than that! Much better! (*Crosses Right.*)

FRANCOIS. What, then?

BERNADETTE. I don't know, Papa.

LOUIS. Good God, what nonsense your girl talks, Francois!

FRANCOIS. (*Laughs.*) She's all right, Louis.

LOUIS. Everything is always all right according to you, Francois. Even if we freeze and starve, it's all right. Even if I am nine-tenths blind, it's all right, I guess.

BERNADETTE. (BERNADETTE *goes and lays her hand gently on Louis' arm.*) Monsieur, maybe our Lord makes you blind because He loves you very much and wants you to see only Him.

LOUIS. (*Jerks his arm away.*) I don't care for pretty speeches, girl. They don't run a mill. They don't fill a man's stomach or warm his house.

FRANCOIS. Let her alone, Louis. (*Arises, goes Down Center, puts arm around* BERNADETTE.) Bernadette is studying her catechism day and night so she can make her First Communion in the spring. That's why she is so handy with the sermons. She's a great one for prayer, aren't you, Bernadette? Always has her beads in her hands.

LOUIS. Prayer? Where does that get you?

BERNADETTE. (*Half way Down Right to* LOUIS.) It gets you to Heaven, Monsieur.

LOUIS. So? And who says there is a Heaven?

LOUISE. (*Shocked.*) Louis!

TOINETTE. Abbe Peyramale says so. And he knows everything.

LOUIS. Does he know how to make a man see?

(*Awkward little silence.*)

BERNADETTE. (*Half step towards* LOUIS.) God knows how, Monsieur. I will pray for you that God will help you.

LOUIS. Save your prayers for the butterflies. Blind men need something more substantial than women's cant.

TOINETTE. (*Takes* BERNADETTE's *hand.*) Let's go. I like it better outside.

JEANNE. Yes, let's go before we all get cross as sticks! (*Laughs and begins to chant as she shepherds* BERNADETTE *and* TOINETTE *before her;* LOUISE *makes as if to stop her;* FRANCOIS *restrains her.*)

> If you're cross as sticks,
> Go, gather sticks
> By the banks of the Gave
> And then behave!

(TOINETTE *laughs delightedly and squeezes* JEANNE *around the waist. They repeat the rhyme together in singsong, while* BERNADETTE *smiles and follows after them.*)

JEANNE.
TOINETTE. {
> If you're cross as sticks,
> Go, gather sticks
> By the banks of the Gave
> And then behave!

(*Exeunt* BERNADETTE, TOINETTE *and* JEANNE, *Right.*)

FRANCOIS. (*Crosses to* LOUIS.) Cheer up, Louis. Things could be worse.

LOUIS. I don't know why I came home with you, Francois. That girl of yours always gets me into a rage.

LOUISE. (*Crosses Right.*) Bernadette? Why, Louis, no one is ever kinder to you than she is. Why do you dislike her so?

LOUIS. Oh, she gets under my skin. Coughing all the time, and so damned patient when I know she's nearly starved and half-frozen. Lord, doesn't she ever complain about things like a normal human being!

FRANCOIS. (*Suddenly thoughtful and backing Up Center behind table.*) No, she never does, Louis. She's not much good for anything, but at least she doesn't fuss about things.

LOUISE. As I do?

FRANCOIS. I didn't say that.

LOUISE. You implied it.

FRANCOIS. No such thing.

LOUIS. (*Leans his forehead on his hand.*) Oh God, now I've got you two quarreling! You see, Francois, it's as I told you—I bring gloom along with me wherever I go. I—

(*Loud* RAP *at the door.*)

FRANCOIS. Who is that? (*Crosses to door.*)

LOUISE. How can I tell? Who would want to visit us? (FRANCOIS *goes to the door and admits a large man of middle-age, buttoned up to the nose in a heavy soutane and cape.*)

Abbe Peyramale! Whatever brings you to the cachot?

ABBE. (*Advancing a few steps.*) I'm not welcome, then? (*His slow smile.*)

LOUISE. Oh, yes, yes. But (*Flustered.*)—it is a little chilly here today. We accidentally ran out of firewood, and Francois had to send the children out to buy some wood. Please sit down. I would offer you a hot drink, if only we had not let the wood supply run out. It was very careless of me.

(ABBE *looks at her and around the pitiable room with respectful compassion and accepts the chair* FRANCOIS *brings forward.*)

ABBE. It is all right, my friends. I am quite comfortable. I had not expected to see you here also, Louis.

LOUIS. (*Surly.*) No? Well, I no longer expect to see anyone anywhere.

ABBE. I am praying for you, my friend.

LOUIS. Thanks. But don't waste your time.

LOUISE. Louis!

ABBE. You think prayer is waste of time?

LOUIS. For me, yes. Better go pray for someone God has some interest in.

FRANCOIS. Snap out of it, Louis. Things will all work out.

LOUIS. (*Rising.*) Sure, oh, sure. The mill will stop turning. My children will starve. And I'll be one more blind beggar. (*Stumbles against stool.*) God will have it all worked out in no time. (*He starts to move falteringly toward the door.*)

ABBE. (*Up to* LOUIS.) It has been many a Sunday since I saw you at Mass, Louis.

LOUIS. (*Short laugh.*) That's right.

ABBE. Why should God take an interest in you when you take no interest in Him?

LOUIS. Save it for the pulpit, Abbe.

LOUISE. He is upset, Abbe. He forgets himself.

LOUIS. (*At the door, bitterly.*) I wish I *could* forget myself. I wish I could forget everything. I'd be better off in the River Gave.

FRANCOIS. (*Crosses to Louis, patting him on shoulder.*) Now, Louis, don't talk nonsense. Just take things easy. Do you want me to go along home with you?

LOUIS. No, thanks. I'll find my way like any other cat or dog does. Stay and entertain the Abbe here. Good-day, my friends. (*Exits Right.*)

LOUISE. (*Down Center to* ABBE.) He is almost in despair, Abbe. I wish we could help him.

ABBE. No one can help a man who won't let himself be helped, Madame. (*Glance at* FRANCOIS.)

FRANCOIS. (*Towards* ABBE, *embarrassed.*) The trouble with Louis is, he worries too much. A man ought to trust in God and let things be.

ABBE. (*Crosses Left to chair.*) A man can trust in God and still get things moving, my friend. You can't expect the Creator to carry you around on His back.

FRANCOIS. Ha! That's good, Abbe. You've got the quick tongue, all right.

ABBE. (*Sees it is useless and turns to* LOUISE.) I came to see you about Bernadette. (Sits.)

LOUISE. Bernadette? (*A step towards* ABBE.) What has she done?

ABBE. Nothing, Madame, nothing. I only wish she could do a little something.

LOUISE. She's a sickly child. But she has a good heart.

FRANCOIS. (*Towards* ABBE.) She's as pious as they come, Abbe. Got her beads worn to a shine.

ABBE. I believe it. But she'll have to know more than her Hail Mary before I can give her her First Communion.

LOUISE. (*Closer to* ABBE.) Oh, Abbe! You won't put her off! She talks of it day and night.

ABBE. I'm sorry, my friends. But Bernadette isn't ready. The child can't read her catechism. Her answers are a jumble.

LOUISE. (*Steps back; proud lift of her head.*) She's not stupid.

ABBE. I never said she was. But she's had no education. Can't even understand the French text of her catechism.

FRANCOIS. What does she need to know French for? Patois is our tongue.

ABBE. (*Impatient now.*) Man, stir yourself, for the love of God! You can't learn your catechism with Patois. (*Rises.*) And until Bernadette learns she can't make her First Communion. That's that.

LOUISE. (*Almost crying.*) What can I do, Abbe? I can't send her to school.

ABBE. (*Pointed look at* FRANCOIS.) She'll *have* to go to school. She can't just skid through life,—like some others.

(LOUISE *begins to cry softly.*)

FRANCOIS. (*Abruptly crosses to* LOUISE.) There's nothing to cry about, woman! The abbe says Bernadette must go to school. All right! She'll go. I am going to see about a job I was promised.

LOUISE. (*Toward* FRANCOIS, *wide-eyed.*) Oh, Francois! Really?

FRANCOIS. (*Gay now, enjoying himself as the rescuing hero.*) Certainly, really. What do you think,—make-believe? (*Smashes his cap down on his head and gathers his threadbare coat around him.*) I'll be back later. See you have a good hot supper, Louise. (*Nod to the* ABBE.) It was good to see you, Abbe. Drop in again. Any time. (*Begins to whistle. Exits Right.*)

LOUISE. (*Staring after him and then crosses Right toward door.*) What has come over him? Why, he's a changed man.

ABBE. (*Up Center to* LOUISE, *pityingly.*) Don't get your hopes too high, Louise. He was anxious to get away from me, that's all.

LOUISE. (*Turns away and Down Right to front of stool.*) I get so discouraged, Abbe. What is to become of us? (*She is too weary for more pretenses now.*)

ABBE. (*Towards* LOUISE.) Pray to our Lady. She will help you.

LOUISE. She will have to work a miracle, I think.

ABBE. Well? What is a miracle to the Mother of God? Pray to the Virgin of La Salette. It's a strange thing, but sometimes Bernadette makes me think of the little shepherds of La Salette. I picture them with eyes like hers.

LOUISE. (*Not much interested.*) How am I going to tell her she can't make her First Communion? She'll be heartbroken.

ABBE. (*Towards door.*) Life is a heartbreaking business for all of us sometimes, my friend. I'd like to let her come, but I can't. She simply has to study and learn.

LOUISE. (*Anguished.*) Mother of God, what am I to do? (*Crosses to rear of table.*)

ABBE. If you can't do any more, then the Mother of God will do the rest.

LOUISE. Pray for us, Abbe!

ABBE. (*At the door.*) I do, I do. Maybe Francois really will get some work. Maybe if Bernadette gets better food, she will be able to study and learn. Anyway, she's a good, pure girl with plenty of faith. Think of Louis, Madame. There is a man worth your worry.

LOUISE. Louis? (*Distracted.*)

ABBE. Yes, Louis. Tell Bernadette to offer up her disappointment for that poor wretch.

LOUISE. He doesn't like her.

ABBE. No? Well, that's his loss. And maybe Bernadette's sorrow will be his gain. (*Turns back, just as he is about to step through the door.*) Pierre made too much soup today. I'd be much obliged if you could send Toinette over to fetch it this evening and help us finish it. (*Begins exit.*)

LOUISE. (*Grateful, with sweet dignity.*) Thank you. Yes, I guess we can help you with it. (*Crosses to door and closes it; crosses back toward Center.*) Oh, dear God, how can I disappoint Bernadette again? (LOUISE *sits down at the little table and reaches under her apron, drawing out a small rosary from the pocket of her dress. She fingers it absently for a few moments.*) Mother of God, help her! Teach her,—teach her yourself. Mother of God, you must understand Patois as well as French. (*She puts her head down in her hands on the table and begins to cry.*)

CURTAIN

ACT ONE
SCENE II

SCENE. *The far end of a field adjoining the Grotto of Massabielle.* TOINETTE *and* JEANNE *are toiling along, looking cold and miserable. They have no sticks yet.*

JEANNE. (*Entering Up Right, calling Offstage, Right.*) Come on, Bernadette! You couldn't win a race with a snail!

TOINETTE. (*Entering, clapping her cold hands together.*) Where are all those sticks, Jeanne? You said there would be lots.

JEANNE. (*Going Down Center.*) Well, what if I did? I can't make the wind die, can I? They're all blown along. But I just bet we'll find them across the stream. Sticks catch against the rocks there. (*Gesturing and looking off Left.*)

TOINETTE. (*Following.*) All right. (*Calling back.*) Aren't you coming, Bernadette? (*Continues to Center.*)

JEANNE. (*Turning back again.*) Snail, snail! Drag your tail!

BERNADETTE. (BERNADETTE *appears onstage, Right, her little round face very white, and her shoulders drooping. She smiles tiredly. Looking gratefully at a little stump Right of Down Center.*) Let's sit down a few minutes. I get so tired.

JEANNE. (*To* BERNADETTE.) Why don't you run? (*To* TOINETTE.) That warms you up, doesn't it, Toinette?

TOINETTE. Uh—huh. But she can't run. It makes her cough.

JEANNE. Well, I'm not going to sit here in the cold like a silly goose. Come on, let's take off our sabots and wade the stream.

TOINETTE. Ugh! I bet the water's cold like ice.

JEANNE. (*Pulls off her sabots and runs off Left.*) 'Fraidy cat! I'll try first.

TOINETTE. (*Dropping down with* BERNADETTE.) You want to go home, Bernadette?

BERNADETTE. Yes, but we can't go back to Mama without any firewood.

TOINETTE. Then we'll have to freeze out here. There aren't any sticks at all. And you said we'd find lots and lots.

BERNADETTE. Toinette! I never did!

TOINETTE. Well, you said something wonderful was going to happen. Aren't lots of sticks wonderful?

(*Loud* SQUEALS *from Offstage, and* TOINETTE *runs to the extreme end of the stage, Left.*)

What's wrong, Jeanne?

JEANNE. (JEANNE *appears, jumping up and down on her cold feet.*) Oh, but it's cold in the stream! But I can see some sticks across the way. Come on! We'll splash across as fast as lightning. Hurry up!—take off your sabots.

TOINETTE. All right. (*Takes her sabots off.*)

BERNADETTE. I'm afraid I'll catch cold, Jeanne, and make lots of work and worry for Mama. (*Timidly.*) Do you think you could carry me across the stream on your shoulders?

JEANNE. (*Arms akimbo and toward* BERNADETTE.) Well, of all the nerve! I should think not, you little coward! You get across yourself, and hurry up about it. Snails get frozen, but lightning never does! (*Laughs and catches* TOINETTE's *hand.*) Come on, Toinette! Let's show this little custard how to cross a stream!

(TOINETTE *looks uncertainly back at* BERNADETTE, *but* JEANNE *gives her a wrench of the arm, and the two run off Left.* BERNADETTE *slowly rises and begins to remove one sabot when she suddenly stops, hearing a great* NOISE *like the sound of a sudden storm.*)

BERNADETTE. (*Hastily makes the Sign of the Cross.*) Virgin Mary, protect us!

(*The* NOISE *subsides; and after some anxious glances at the sky and terrain,* BERNADETTE *again starts to remove her sabot and stocking. Immediately the rushing* NOISE *is heard again and the girl stands still in fright.*)

(*Starting now to the Left.*) Jeanne! Toinette! Jeanne, come back! There's a fierce storm coming! Toinette! (*There is no answer, and* BERNADETTE *steps back a pace or two.*) Oh, dear! What shall I do? I wish I were home. (*She reaches in her pocket for her rosary.*) Holy Mary, Mother of God, pray for us sinners *now!*

(SOUND *out fast.*)

(BERNADETTE *looks about again worriedly and then seems transfixed, as she looks Offstage Down Left.*) Is it a cloud I see, dearest Lord? But all golden! Do You make golden clouds, Lord, at Massabielle? (*Frowns a little.*) How very quiet it is! And warm! (*Looks at her roughened hands.*) I'm not cold any more! (*Lays a hand against her cheek wonderingly.*) Maybe I am dying! Papa said you feel warm just before you freeze to death. But all alone! Shall I die all alone? (*She takes a few running steps to the Left.*) Jeanne! Toinette! Come and help me! (*She stops suddenly again, and her slow smile spreads over her face.*) No, I'm not alone! (*Holds the little rosary before her again and drops to her knees.*) Holy Mary, Mother of God, pray for us sinners now, AT THE HOUR OF OUR DEATH. (*She looks up and gives a little gasp, stretching out both arms.*) Oh, lovely! (*Makes a deep inclination, still kneeling.*) How do you do, Mademoiselle! I am happy to see you. (*Turns her head slightly to the side, smiling happily.*) I am Bernadette Soubirous, daughter of the miller. (*Little pause.*) I live at the cachot in Lourdes. Are you from Lourdes? (*After a moment, she draws up her thin shoulders slightly.*) Excuse me, Mademoiselle. I ask too many questions. Mama always says I do. (*A sudden happy inspiration lights her face.*) Would you like to say the Rosary, Mademoiselle? (BERNADETTE *starts to make the Sign of the Cross, and finds her arm is paralyzed.*) Mademoiselle! My lovely lady! Something is wrong with my arm! Help me! (*She fixes her gaze on the Virgin, and slowly smiles again and nods. She looks at her hands and slowly moves her arm.*) Ah, now it goes again! (*Makes the Sign of the Cross. She stops and gazes raptly at the vision for a few moments.*) You look so very happy, Mademoiselle. (*Cocks her head to one side.*) I guess you have made your First Communion already?—Maybe years ago? I am fourteen, you know. Old enough. But I am thick in the head, they say. (*Lowers her gaze an instant.*) I guess you would not know about that. You must have been very bright in school. (*Looks up again.*) I don't usually talk about it, but I feel that I have known you for a long time—Isn't that strange? (*Pause.*) Why are you smiling? Oh! I think you want to get on with the Rosary, don't you? All right. But will you pray for me, Mademoiselle? I want to make my First Communion. I want it more than anything else in the world.

(*She remains for some moments more, her lips moving in prayer and the beads slipping through her hands.* JEANNE *and* TOINETTE *appear at the Up Left.*)

JEANNE. Well, look at that! You are one lazy girl, Bernadette Soubirous, leaving us to gather all the sticks!

(*Down Center to Right of* BERNADETTE *who remains kneeling, seeming not to hear.*)

TOINETTE. (*Runs over and peers directly into* BERNADETTE'S *face.*) What are you doing, Bernadette?

JEANNE. She's doing nothing,—as usual.

TOINETTE. She looks funny, Jeanne. Maybe she's in—a—a—what is that word Mama said?—in a coda?

JEANNE. (*Laughs.*) Coma, goose! She's not in any coma. They're for important people that are sick.

(*Goes over and shakes* BERNADETTE *by the shoulders and* BERNADETTE *slowly rises and smiles at her.*) There's another bundle of sticks across the stream, lazybones. At least you can pick that up. Toinette and I will sit down and have *our* coma. (*Laughs and drops down on the stump Right, putting her bundle of sticks beside her. Business of pulling on socks and sabots during following.*)

TOINETTE. (*Crosses to Center.*) Are you all right, Bernadette?

BERNADETTE. Yes! Yes, I am! I feel so well.

JEANNE. I guess you do!—letting us do all the work while you take it easy.

TOINETTE. She was kneeling, Jeanne.

JEANNE. What were you doing?

BERNADETTE. (*Simply.*) Praying my rosary.

JEANNE. Well, you could pick a better time for your devotions, if you ask me.

BERNADETTE. (*To* JEANNE, *hesitantly.*) Did,—did you hear anything?

TOINETTE. What kind of a thing?

BERNADETTE. (*To* TOINETTE.) Oh,—just anything.

JEANNE. (*A little snort.*) We heard the water splash and we heard the sticks break when we tied them up. And we heard the sparrows scolding about the cold. What else did you expect us to hear?

BERNADETTE. (*To* JEANNE.) Nothing,—I guess. Did—did you *see* something?

TOINETTE. What?

BERNADETTE. Well,—something lovely? Something, very, very beautiful?

JEANNE. Who ever saw anything beautiful at Massabielle in February? Do hurry up and get that other bundle of sticks, you silly girl, or I'll tell your mother you are getting sick in your head.

(BERNADETTE *hesitates, and then moves away obediently, removing her stockings and sabots. Exits Left.*)

TOINETTE. I didn't see anything lovely, did you, Jeanne?

JEANNE. Of course not.

TOINETTE. But Bernadette did!

JEANNE. I don't believe it.

TOINETTE. (*Toward* JEANNE.) Bernadette never, never told a lie. And once when I told just a little one, she slapped me—right here. (*Hand on her mouth; crosses Left to stump and puts on stockings and sabots.*)

JEANNE. (*Laughs approvingly.*) She's got a good temper, that little snail has!

TOINETTE. What do you think she heard?

JEANNE. Her brains rattling in her skull! A little brain in a big head makes a lot of noise. (*She is pleased with her joke.*)

TOINETTE. You're a mean girl sometimes, Jeanne Abadie! Bernadette never says mean things about you. She never tells Mama,—even when you push her.

JEANNE. (*Her face softens.*) I know it. She never says anything mean about anybody,—not even that cross old Louis.

BERNADETTE. (BERNADETTE *appears at the Left with the third bundle of sticks. She dries her feet on her apron. Smiling.*) Why did you tease me? The water wasn't cold at all!

TOINETTE. (*Jumping up.*) Not cold? In the stream?

BERNADETTE. (*At Center.*) Why no! It's as warm as the water for washing the plates and cups.

JEANNE. Well, how do you like that!? She expects me to carry her across on my shoulders like a sack of flour, and then fibs about the water.

BERNADETTE. I'm not fibbing, Jeanne. Feel my feet! They're warm! (*Lifts one bare foot a little.*)

TOINETTE. (*Feeling.*) She *is* warm, Jeanne!

JEANNE. (*Feeling too.*) Huh! I like that all right! She's the strongest one of us all, that's what. And pretending to be sick! Come on, I'm going home. (*Picks up her bundle.*) And don't be lagging behind and pretending you are tired again, Bernadette. The nerve! Warm as toast and us half-frozen! (*She disappears off Right.*)

(BERNADETTE *puts on her stockings and sabots at stump Right.*)

TOINETTE. Bernadette, what did you hear?

BERNADETTE. (*Straightens up.*) Something like a big, strong wind. (*Sits down on the stump.*)

TOINETTE. There wasn't any big, strong wind. The sticks aren't blowing along any more.

BERNADETTE. I know it. Nothing was moving. But it was like the great wind that comes sometimes in the spring. You know, Toinette! (*Jumps up in her excited eagerness to explain.*)—When the bars dance in the casements at the cachot (*Trembling gesture with her hands.*) and the trees scream e-e-e-e-e-e, and the little sheep cry: baaa, baaa, baaa, in the pen.

TOINETTE. But, Bernadette, we would have heard it, Jeanne and I.

BERNADETTE. (*Puzzled.*) Yes. I don't understand.

TOINETTE. (*Pulls* BERNADETTE *down beside her on the stump again.*) Well, what happened?

BERNADETTE. It got quiet, Toinette. Still as still, like the night the baby died and nobody said anything and Mama just kept looking at Papa. I could hear my heart beating today just like I heard it that night,—loud like Papa's boots on the cobblestones, when Papa used to have boots. Remember?

TOINETTE. Uh-huh. I never heard *my* heart beat that loud, though.

BERNADETTE. And then a little golden cloud came out of the grotto across the stream, Toinette.

TOINETTE. A *what*?

BERNADETTE. (*Jumps up again and toward Down Left, looking out Left.*) A little cloud, Toinette, no bigger than this (*Measures with wide arms.*) but all golden. It was so pretty I wanted to catch it.

TOINETTE. You can't catch a cloud, silly.

BERNADETTE. No, I guess not.

TOINETTE. And clouds don't come out of rocks. They ride up in the sky. (*Up and to* BERNADETTE.) What's the matter with you, Bernadette?

BERNADETTE. Oh,—nothing. Never mind. (*She turns away and starts to put on sabots at Right.*)

TOINETTE. (*Pulls her down again and down herself.*) There's more, I know there is! Don't be angry, Bernadette! Tell me!

BERNADETTE. I'm not angry, Toinette. But—well, I don't understand it very well myself.

TOINETTE. The cloud?

BERNADETTE. N-no. Our Lord can make a golden cloud if He feels like it, I guess. It's not the cloud I mean—

TOINETTE. What else?

BERNADETTE. (*Stands up and looks down fixedly at* TOINETTE.) Toinette, I saw the loveliest, loveliest lady that ever was.

TOINETTE. You mean Mme. Gerau?

BERNADETTE. (*Laughs.*) Oh, no!

TOINETTE. Well, she's the prettiest lady in Lourdes isn't she?

BERNADETTE. I suppose. But this lady was a hundred-thousand times that pretty!

TOINETTE. (*Wide-eyed.*) Who *was* she?

BERNADETTE. I don't know.

TOINETTE. What did she say to you?

BERNADETTE. Nothing.

TOINETTE. Well, what did she want?

BERNADETTE. I didn't ask her.

TOINETTE. Didn't you speak to her?

BERNADETTE. Oh, yes, yes I did! But she just smiled (*Imitates posture of the Virgin with folded hands.*) and she didn't answer.

TOINETTE. Maybe she can't understand Patois if she's a stranger around here.

BERNADETTE. She's not a stranger.

TOINETTE. But you never saw her before!

BERNADETTE. No.

TOINETTE. Then of course she's a stranger. We know everybody in Lourdes.

BERNADETTE. She's not from Lourdes, Toinette, but she's not a stranger, either. I guess she's not from anywhere.

TOINETTE. What?

BERNADETTE. I mean I think she's from everywhere. Oh, Toinette, I don't know how to tell you, but when she came out of the grotto, everything looked like it belonged to her,—(*Gestures freely.*) the rocks and the cloud and the trees and the sky and *me*—everything!

TOINETTE. How could *you* belong to a lady you never saw before, Bernadette?

BERNADETTE. I don't know, Toinette. But listen! I didn't know what to say to her, but I didn't want her to go away, either. So I asked her to pray the rosary with me.

TOINETTE. Did she?

BERNADETTE. In a way. But wait! When I started to make the Sign of the Cross, I couldn't make my arm go. (*Demonstrates.*) It stayed right where it was and wouldn't go up like I wanted.

TOINETTE. What was wrong?

BERNADETTE. I don't think anything was wrong. I think it was to make me understand that I belong to the Lady, too.

TOINETTE. Because your arm was broken? You mean her arm was broken, too?

BERNADETTE. (*Laughs.*) Oh, no! I mean I was so frightened. For a little while I was like this (*Demonstrates, with her arm held out stiffly before her, Up and Down Center*) with my arm sort of frozen. And then the lady smiled and made the Sign of the Cross herself. And then my arm wasn't broken or frozen or anything. It worked again, Toinette. See! (*Makes the Sign of the Cross three or four times.*) She had to sign herself first, Toinette, like it was a permission for my arm to go, too. See?

TOINETTE. (*Up.*) I don't know. It's kind of mixed up. What did she look like?

BERNADETTE. (*Clasps her hands over her heart.*) Oh, Toinette, if you could see her! She wore a white dress, so soft and pretty and graceful. (*Demonstrates how the robes fell.*) And there was a blue ribbon around her waist that came all the way down her skirt like this. (*Demonstrates.*) She had a lovely white veil on her hair, too.

TOINETTE. What color was her hair?

BERNADETTE. Dark, I think. You could see just a little, little bit of it, because the veil hung like this, (*Pulls off her capulet and tries to drape the straight folds around her own head like a veil.*) and away down to her waist in back,—like this! She didn't have any sabots on, or any stockings, either.

TOINETTE. Wasn't she cold?

BERNADETTE. She didn't look cold.

TOINETTE. Maybe she's too poor to buy stockings.

BERNADETTE. (*Dubious.*) I don't know. She didn't seem to be poor at all. Kind of like an empress,—but young, too. Maybe like a princess. And oh, yes! There was a yellow rose on each of her feet.

TOINETTE. Oh, go on!

BERNADETTE. (*Eagerly.*) There was! There was! A *real* rose. Two of them. She stood like this with a white rosary hanging on her right arm (*Demonstrates.*) and when she slipped the beads along, the chain of the rosary shone out all golden like the roses on her feet.

TOINETTE. I thought she didn't say the rosary or anything.

BERNADETTE. She didn't know the Aves, I guess. But she said every Gloria Patri with me, right out loud.

TOINETTE. (*Gesture of disbelief off Left.*) You mean you heard her voice from across the stream?

BERNADETTE. Yes, I did.

TOINETTE. You couldn't.

BERNADETTE. But I did. (*Enter* JEANNE, *Right.*) I heard it in here, Toinette. (*Hands over her heart.*) It was like a bird, Toinette, singing with a violin.

JEANNE. (*Mockingly.*) A bird singing with a violin!

(TOINETTE *and* BERNADETTE *start violently;* JEANNE *Down Right of Center.*)

You crazy Bernadette Soubirous! Here you are, right where I left you! I come back all this way because I thought you must have fallen, and I find you talking worse nonsense than ever! (*Makes gesture of playing a violin and chirps, moving across the stage.*) Tweet! Tweet! (*She stops suddenly and faces them, arms akimbo.*) It's no wonder you are such a dunce at your catechism, Bernadette.

(BERNADETTE *winces and turns away.*)

TOINETTE. (*Going Up Left, throws her arms around* BERNADETTE.) You mean girl, Jeanne Abadie! She's smarter than you are. Yaa! Yaa! (*Puts out her tongue at* JEANNE.)

BERNADETTE. (*Shakes off* TOINETTE'S *embrace.*) Hush up, Toinette! I *am* a dunce, I guess. And you were good to worry about us, Jeanne. Where's your bundle of sticks? I'll carry it for you with mine.

JEANNE. (*Just a trifle mollified.*) I set it down over there. (*Gestures Offstage, Right.*) What were you doing all this time?

BERNADETTE. Oh,—nothing much.

JEANNE. Yes, you were! You're up to something!

TOINETTE. Yes, and you could never guess! Three guesses, Jeanne! Forty-three guesses! A hundred and three! Go on and try!

BERNADETTE. Shhh, Toinette!

JEANNE. You tell me what's going on.

BERNADETTE. I have nothing to tell you, Jeanne.

JEANNE. All right. Just wait! Just wait until we get back to the cachot! I'll tell your mother on you. Come on, both of you, before I box your ears! (*Takes hold of both* GIRLS *by their arms and marshals them before her.*) I'll get to the bottom of this. (*She gives them a push forward and gives a last look around.*) Birds! Violins! You'll hear a different tune when you get home!

(*Exeunt Right.*)

CURTAIN

ACT TWO

SCENE. *Le Cachot, ten days later.* LOUISE *seated and* FRANCOIS SOUBIROUS *pacing, are talking heatedly.*

LOUISE. You've got to do something, Francois.

FRANCOIS. What do you want me to do, woman? I can't see what you are in such a froth about.

LOUISE. (*Holding bowl and gesturing with spoon.*) Oh my God! Bernadette gone sick in her head and lying like the devil himself! The whole town buzzing with gossip about us. Abbe Peyramale in a cold fury. And now the police stepping in. And he asks what I am upset about!

FRANCOIS. Calm down, Louise. Bernadette has just got a young girl's romantic notions, that's all. She dreams about the way she would like to dress and look herself, and then tells a few fibs about it. Let her alone. (*Sits.*) It will blow over in a month or two. Next it will be a handsome prince on a golden cloud and a yellow rose behind his ear. (*He laughs and takes out his pipe.*)

LOUISE. Yes, you can laugh, Francois Soubirous! You go out in the morning and I am left to answer the door to every curious man, woman and child in Lourdes.

FRANCOIS. Well, you always like company, Louise.

LOUISE. (LOUISE *rises angrily and turns away just as a* RAP *is heard at the door. She whirls back on* FRANCOIS.) There! Some other busybody! Now you see how you like the company, Francois!

FRANCOIS. All right. (*Going to door.*) You watch me now and see what a case you are making out of nothing. (*Admits* LOUIS.) Well, man, come in! It's good to see you. (*Claps* LOUIS *on the back.*)

LOUIS. (*Startled.*) What the hell is the matter with you, Francois Soubirous? Are you tippling again?

LOUISE. Hello, Louis. No, he's sober enough. He's just giving me an object lesson, that's all.

LOUIS. In what?—Backslapping?

(*He reaches out for a chair which* FRANCOIS *shoves forward for him, during the following.*)

FRANCOIS. Louise has got herself all worked up to a fever because Bernadette has made up a pretty story. I'm trying to make her be reasonable. She probably built plenty of her own air castles when she was fourteen, but if Bernadette wants to dream about a lady in a white dress and blue sash, she's got to get into a fit over it.

LOUIS. The trouble is, people in Lourdes don't think Bernadette is dreaming, Francois.

LOUISE. You see!

FRANCOIS. Well, they've got no business calling her a liar. Every young girl is entitled to talk like a fool. I'm going to see my girl has her rights. (*Laughs and sits down Left, getting a light for his pipe.*)

LOUIS. They don't all say she's a liar. A lot of them say she's a saint.

LOUISE. (*To* LOUIS.) Saint! She's nothing but a sickly child with an imagination like a wild horse. And it's up to you, Francois Soubirous, to break that horse.

LOUIS. (*Slyly.*) Why don't you make the horse pay off?

FRANCOIS. What?

LOUIS. Use your head, man.

FRANCOIS. I don't get you, Louis.

LOUIS. No, you never get anything, Francois. You are always waiting for your ship to come in and now you can't even see that it's putting down anchor right here—and loaded with bags of gold!

LOUISE. (*Crosses and puts hand on* LOUIS' *head.*) You're feeling worse, Louis? The pain in your eyes,—is that it?

LOUIS. (*Impatient and shoving her hand away.*) How I feel doesn't matter to anybody but me. But I see a lot more with half an eye than you two do with four! Why don't you make this frenzy pay off?

(*Stands up in his excitement;* LOUISE *backs Up Left.*)

Everybody in Lourdes wants to see Bernadette, doesn't he? All right! Get some pictures of her, and sell them for a couple of sous each.

LOUISE. (*Thoroughly puzzled.*) Who would want a picture of Bernadette? They can see her everyday. She's no celebrity.

LOUIS. (*Pounds the table with his fist.*) Exactly! But she *could* be if you would use a little sense. Most of the people think there is really something in all this talk of a lady in white. Help them along, then! They all want to hear Bernadette tell the story, don't they?

LOUISE. Oh, if you knew! One after another, all day long! And now they are coming from out of town.

LOUIS. Fine! Fine! Don't let her talk to each one. Have regular sessions. One franc admission to hear Bernadette tell about the lady from Heaven! And for two sous more, you get an autographed picture of the saintly young seer to take along home.

LOUISE. Oh, Louis!

FRANCOIS. What kind of a stinking idea is that, man?

LOUIS. It's a smarter idea than any you ever had, Soubirous! And I'm giving it to you out of the goodness of my heart, for just a small settlement. Let's say ten per cent of the admission fees and five per cent commission on the pictures.

(LOUISE *looks at* FRANCOIS *and then taps her head significantly with a glance at* LOUIS.)

LOUIS. (*Shakes his finger in her face.*) Remember I have a little sight left, Louise Soubirous! Don't think you are putting anything over on me. I've got a better head on my shoulders than your man, anyday. Here you are, cold and hungry most of the time, bringing up your children in a jail that isn't good enough for thieves and cutthroats to be held in. And here I am, with half an eye left to me and my mill ready to close down anyday. Then fate sends us a golden opportunity to make a good pile of money with no harm done to anybody. (*Sits.*) And you start getting squeamish.

FRANCOIS. But it's like a fraud, Louis.

LOUIS. How do you figure? The people want to hear Bernadette's story. Let them put down their money, then. They want a souvenir. All right. Give them an autographed picture of your girl.

LOUISE. (*Weakly.*) She can't write very well.

LOUIS. Let her kiss the pictures, then. That will go over big.

FRANCOIS. I don't like it. It makes me sick.

LOUIS. (*Stands up again.*) And you make *me* sick, Soubirous. That girl of yours has never been good for anything. Now she can really be a breadwinner. (*Eagerly.*) What we need is a big sign. (*Squints his eyes closed and traces the lettering in the air.*) Something like this: HEAR BERNADETTE SOUBIROUS TELL ABOUT HER VISIONS! TWO SESSIONS DAILY, 10 AND 4. TAKE HOME A PICTURE OF BERNADETTE SOUBIROUS, SAINT AND SEER.

BERNADETTE. (BERNADETTE *enters in the middle of all this, unnoticed. Halts, transfixed when she hears* LOUIS' *words.*) Monsieur, what are you saying?

(LOUIS *whirls around to face* BERNADETTE *and* LOUISE *and* FRANCOIS *start.*)

LOUIS. (*All graciousness.*) Come on in, Bernadette child. We have something wonderful to tell you.

BERNADETTE. (*Dubious.*) What is it?

LOUIS. You want to help your poor parents, Bernadette? You want to get all the white bread that Toinette and the little ones can eat?

BERNADETTE. I,—I guess so.

LOUIS. (*Warmly.*) Of course, you do. And I'll tell you how. You just go right on telling the people about your beautiful lady with the blue dress. Only we will have them come in groups and give a little something at the door.

BERNADETTE. Money? Money to hear about the lady? And her dress is white, Monsieur, not blue.

LOUIS. That's right, money. (*To* FRANCOIS.) She's a smart girl. Quick as a flash.

BERNADETTE. No, Monsieur. I can't do that.

LOUIS. (*Instantly angry.*) You can! And you will!

FRANCOIS. Shut up, Louis. This is *my* house.

LOUIS. Your *jail*! And do you want to die in it?

FRANCOIS. Something will turn up soon. We won't always be here.

LOUIS. Something *has* turned up, you fool!

BERNADETTE. (*Gently.*) Monsieur, I couldn't take people's money just for telling them about the lady.

LOUIS. Why not?

BERNADETTE. Well, she came to me free. And she spoke to me even though I am the smallest and stupidest of all. (*Her face, relaxes into her lovely smile.*) It is all beautiful, Monsieur, and lovely. Money is not beautiful. It would insult the lady. She,—well, she is beyond price.

TOINETTE. (*The door is flung open and* TOINETTE *bursts into the room panting.*) Guess who's coming? (*Quickly over to* LOUISE, *Left.*)

LOUISE. (*A great sigh and going to window Right.*) I can't. I thought everyone in Lourdes had already been here today.

TOINETTE. Uh-uh, Mama! Not Abbe Peyramale!

LOUISE. Oh, my goodness! (*Looking out the barred window.*) It *is*, Francois! It *is* the abbe.

(FRANCOIS *to her Right Center.*)

BERNADETTE. (*Timidly touches* LOUIS' *sleeve while* FRANCOIS *joins* LOUISE *at the window.*) Do you understand, Monsieur? I know you mean well. But—it is all wrong. (*Smiles.*) It's not worth two sous to listen to me. And the lady is worth more than all the gold in the world. So it would be wrong any way you look at it.

LOUIS. (*Shaking off her hand.*) Keep your paws off me! You're your father's daughter all right, girl. No head for business at all. (*He starts toward the door.*) I'm going. I'm in no state of mind for one of the abbe's homilies. You think over what I said, Louise. Louise!

(LOUISE *turns from the window at this.*)

You've got the best head in this house. I said, you think over my proposition. (*Exit* LOUIS, *slamming the door.*)

TOINETTE. What is everybody fussing about?

LOUISE. (*Crosses Left.*) Be quiet, Toinette. Go cover up those dirty dishes. (*Gestures toward a dishpan set on the stove.*) The abbe is coming!

TOINETTE. (*Moving along.*) Sure. I told you.

FRANCOIS. (FRANCOIS *goes to the door and admits* ABBE PEYRAMALE.) Why, Abbe! Your Reverence! Come right in! To what do we owe this privilege?

(ABBE PEYRAMALE *looks around, tight-lipped, as* LOUISE *hustles forward with a chair and* TOINETTE *and* BERNADETTE *curtsey. His manner is entirely altered from his first visit.*)

ABBE. I believe your daughter knows why I am here. (*Towards* BERNADETTE *Center.*)

LOUISE. (*Trying to be calm; arm around* BERNADETTE.) You mean about her First Communion, Abbe? I have told Bernadette. Bernadette will make the sacrifice if you think she should wait.

ABBE. There are a number of things I think Bernadette should do. And I am not referring to her First Communion—which is certainly out of the question—*now*.

BERNADETTE. (*Quick curtsey again.*) I am studying every evening, Your Reverence.

ABBE. Indeed? I thought you wrote fiction every evening.

TOINETTE. (*Loud whisper.*) What is fiction, Papa?

FRANCOIS. (*Slowly.*) Something that isn't true, child.

TOINETTE. Like a lie?

LOUISE. Hush, Toinette.

ABBE. Yes, young lady, it *can* be exactly like a lie.

TOINETTE. Oh. Well, then, Bernadette doesn't write it, Your Reverence. She never even tells lies, so why would she take the time to write them?

LOUISE. Toinette, run over to Jeanne's house. She was asking for you before.

TOINETTE. (*Reluctant.*) I'd like to stay here, Mama.

LOUISE. Toinette!

TOINETTE. Ye-es, Mama. (*Goes slowly to the door, giving one last look back over her shoulder.*) Good-day, Your Reverence. (*Bobs a curtsey.*)

(*The* ABBE *nods curtly; exit* TOINETTE.)

LOUISE. She didn't mean to be bold, Abbe. She is so devoted to Bernadette.

ABBE. It seems Bernadette has a considerable number of devotees in Lourdes.

LOUISE. (*Crosses Down Left Center.*) Please have a chair, Abbe. (*Pushes it forward for him and he slowly seats himself.*)

ABBE. Now look here, my friends! I do not wish to be harsh. I have tried to be a friend and a father to you, haven't I?

LOUISE. Yes, oh, yes, Your Reverence.

ABBE. But I can't let affairs go on like this. Your daughter is bringing discredit on the church,—on Lourdes,—on the abbe of Lourdes.

FRANCOIS. What's that? How so, Your Reverence?

ABBE. (*His voice is always gruffer when he speaks to* FRANCOIS.) By telling fables that light-headed people believe as though they were part of the Creed! God knows religion is little enough respected these days. Now Bernadette (*A gesture toward her.*) is making our holy Religion a regular laughing-stock to outsiders. And she is *not* going to continue, do you understand me?

LOUISE. My husband and I are very sorry, Abbe. All this excitement! My poor child is not well at all. It is the asthma. She gets confused in her mind.

(BERNADETTE *looks anxiously from one to the other.*)

FRANCOIS. Now, Louise! (*He sits down, as does* LOUISE, *leaving* BERNADETTE *standing alone.*) Our little girl has made up a pretty story, Abbe. What of it? What's the difference?

(BERNADETTE *steps backward during the following until she is almost flattened against the back wall.*)

ABBE. My dear Soubirous, I'm very well aware that you are not the man to concern yourself with present realities, but even you must know that this "pretty story" is growing into a cult. (*His voice rises.*) Good, level-headed people going completely off their heads over your daughter's wild tales. Sensible folk running out to that old grotto of Massabielle to gape at your girl talking to the rocks, instead of attending to their devotions in the church.

LOUISE. (*Begins to cry.*) You see, Francois! We are a scandal in Lourdes! Abbe, you try to reason with her. (*Sits by fireplace and sobs.*) She won't listen to her mother any longer.

BERNADETTE. (*Her eyes fill with tears, crosses to* LOUISE.) Mama, Mama, I do! But I cannot say I am lying when I tell the truth.

FRANCOIS. Now look here! (*He rises and goes back to put an arm around* BERNADETTE.) I know you aren't really lying, child. It's quite a good story, that's all. I'd like to see a lady like that myself. But just tell the abbe here that it is only a story, and then he'll feel better.

BERNADETTE. (*Steps away.*) It *isn't* a story. It's true.

LOUISE. (*Both hands out in a gesture of despair.*) You see? It's useless, Abbe.

FRANCOIS. (*Crosses Down Center to his chair.*) Got a lot of spunk, hasn't she, Abbe? Not afraid to stick to her guns.

LOUISE. (*Stands up, desperate.*) Oh, Francois! I'm going! (*Draws her shawl around her.*) I'm going over to Abadie's. You'll make your jokes when I am in the madhouse. (*Turns back at the door and breaks into a sob.*) I'm sorry, Abbe. But I just can't stand any more. (*Exits.*)

ABBE. Well, Soubirous? Do you see what a state your wife is in?

(BERNADETTE *goes to the barred window and watches her mother disappearing down the street.*)

FRANCOIS. Louise is high strung. Loses her head. She's a good woman, though. Sound type, Abbe, sound. (*Start to light pipe.*)

ABBE. (*Steel.*) She would have to be to survive the cachot,—and her companions.

FRANCOIS. What's that? Oh, sure, Abbe. Yes, there is plenty of work for the mother of a family. Her companions? That's right, Abbe. Bernadette here is getting to be a real young lady. Good companion for her mother. Lots of help, too. (*Rises, going Left.*) Well, I hate to go when we have such a distinguished visitor as yourself, Abbe, but I have to see a certain party about a business deal we have on. You give Bernadette here a little boost with her catechism, won't you, Abbe? Louise will be back soon. She'll fix some lunch.

ABBE. (*Icily.*) I have lunched, thank you.

FRANCOIS. (*Puts on his cap.*) You don't say. (*Crosses Right.*) Well, have a nice visit. Watch your manners now, Bernadette. Bernadette! (*She turns back slowly from the window.*) It's a privilege to talk to the abbe here. You show him you appreciate it. (*At the door, raising his cap.*) Tell His Reverence about the lady and those yellow roses. Good-day, Abbe. It's quite a story she has there. Get her to tell you the whole thing. (*Exits.*)

ABBE. (*Sternly.*) Sit down.

BERNADETTE. (*Frightened.*) Shall I get Mama? (*Steps toward door.*)

ABBE. No. Can't you see she is ill?

BERNADETTE. (*Miserable.*) Yes, Your Reverence. (*Sits.*)

ABBE. And all because of your lies, your pride.

BERNADETTE. No, no, Your Reverence!

ABBE. Don't contradict me. You are a victim of delusion, Bernadette Soubirous. Do you realize that?

BERNADETTE. I don't know, Your Reverence. What does it mean? (*She starts to cough.*)

ABBE. (*A little startled.*) It means that the devil is whispering lies to you so often that you believe them yourself and tell them to others to deceive them, too.

BERNADETTE. Oh. Then it is not so, Your Reverence. I do not talk to the devil.

ABBE. (*Leans forward.*) How do you know? The devil can take any form he wishes. (*Slowly.*) How do you know that lady among the rocks isn't the devil? The *devil*, Bernadette Soubirous!

BERNADETTE. (*Smiles.*) Oh, never, Your Reverence.

ABBE. (*Angry again.*) And how would such a one as you know it is not the devil?

BERNADETTE. (*Calmly.*) The devil could never be that pretty, Your Reverence.

ABBE. (*A little shaken, he speaks more gruffly.*) And so now a young lady too thick-headed to learn the answers in the catechism is going to teach me theology! You are simply mad with pride, Bernadette Soubirous. I recognize pride when I see it. You think you know everything.

BERNADETTE. I know almost nothing, Your Reverence. I am the least of all.

ABBE. Ah, yes! And you are tired of it. So you decide you will make yourself the first of all, the greatest of all! You will make a name for yourself. People will never call you a student or a beauty, so you want them to call you—a saint. (*Looks at her closely.*) Isn't that it?

BERNADETTE. (*Same calm voice.*) If they would call me a saint, Your Reverence, they would make themselves out for fools.

ABBE. Whereas you prefer to make fools of them yourself?

BERNADETTE. (*Puzzled.*) What is it you mean, Your Reverence?

ABBE. Just this: you cannot bear to be contradicted. You cannot bow your head and admit you have made a bad mistake, that you have done wrong. Pride!

BERNADETTE. That is pride?

ABBE. (*Unexpected pause, and he looks away as he replies.*) Yes, that is pride. The most hateful of sins. That which God holds off from Himself like an evil odor. (*Back to* BERNADETTE.) Do you want God to hold you at arm's length, Bernadette, instead of against His heart?

BERNADETTE. No, Your Reverence.

ABBE. (*He seems strangely excited.*) Then, admit your pride! Renounce it!

BERNADETTE. All right, Your Reverence.

ABBE. (*Rises.*) So! You will confess your mistakes?

BERNADETTE. Yes, Your Reverence.

ABBE. You will admit you have done wrong?

BERNADETTE. (*Also rises and looks up at him.*) Yes, Your Reverence.

ABBE. Very well. Tomorrow you will come to the public square after Mass and tell all the people you have invented this story about a lady at the grotto.

BERNADETTE. (*Her jaw drops.*) No, no, Your Reverence. That is not true!

ABBE. (*Bends down toward her.*) You said you would confess your mistakes.

BERNADETTE. But the lady is no mistake.

ABBE. (*Enraged.*) You promised to admit your wrongdoing.

BERNADETTE. (*Kneels down and looks directly up into his face.*) But *this* is no wrongdoing. The lady has done it. And it is done right. (*Pause.*) Your Reverence, I am not good for anything. I cannot make you understand. But I will ask the lady to do it.

ABBE. (*Angrily.*) You are going to stop making people turn against me because I don't believe the tales of a foolish young girl!

BERNADETTE. (*Smiles up at him and clasps her hands together.*) I will ask the lady to make you understand. And then you will not be angry any longer. You will be so happy, Your Reverence! You will not care if the whole world turns against you.

(RAP *at the door; the* ABBE *stares down at her for several moments, not hearing the knock. The rap is repeated, and he suddenly jerks back to attention.*)

ABBE. Enter!

JACOMET. (*Enter* M. JACOMET, *chief of the Lourdes police force. He looks at the pair in surprise.*) Well, well, Your Reverence. This is a pleasant surprise! And where are the Soubirous?

ABBE. Away on business. And what business has the chief of police with them?

JACOMET. (*Suavely.*) Oh, no business with *them*, really. I spoke to them yesterday. My business today is with this young lady right here.

(*Gestures toward* BERNADETTE *who rises timidly and shrinks back.*)

BERNADETTE. How do you do, Monsieur? I think I had better get my mother. (*Towards door.*)

JACOMET. No, never mind that. I just happened to be passing by. May I sit down?

(BERNADETTE *remains motionless, and* JACOMET *looks at the* ABBE *who gives a slight nod. Both* MEN *sit down.*)

ABBE. Do you know who this gentleman is, Bernadette?

BERNADETTE. A—a—policeman, I think, Your Reverence. (*Coughs.*)

JACOMET. (*Laughing.*) That's right. But I'm just here on a friendly call. I'm hearing all kinds of things, about the grotto of Massabielle, little girl. Ladies and rose-bushes and windstorms! Well, young lady, I just want to get it all straight. (*Winks at the* ABBE.) So I know what to tell the mayor.

ABBE. Does the mayor know you are here?

JACOMET. His honor sent me, Your Reverence. He's a bit upset, the mayor. Quite a bit upset. You know—(*Hand on his heart.*)—never so good. Gets those palpitations. And now all these crowds out at the grotto. Disorder, you know. Gives the city a bad name. You understand.

ABBE. Yes,—I understand,—perfectly.

JACOMET. Fine, fine. I'm glad you're here, Abbe. Sit down, little girl.

(BERNADETTE *perches stiffly on the edge of the chair and* JACOMET *takes out a notebook and pencil.*)

Now, what is your name, please?

BERNADETTE. Bernadette.

JACOMET. Bernadette what?

BERNADETTE. (*Looks at the* ABBE *and then back to* JACOMET.) But you know it is Soubirous.

JACOMET. (*Smiles.*) That's right. It's just a matter of record. We get everything in writing just as the witness tells it.

BERNADETTE. What witness?

JACOMET. (*To the* ABBE.) Cute kid, isn't she? Likes to tease. (*To* BERNADETTE) How old are you, little lady?

BERNADETTE. Fourteen. Going on fifteen.

JACOMET. Oh, come now! You're not more than twelve.

ABBE. (*Curtly.*) She is in her fifteenth year. She's small for her age, the smallest in the catechism class.

JACOMET. (*Not interested.*) You don't say. And now what was it you saw at the grotto of Massabielle? A woman?

BERNADETTE. A girl, Monsieur, a young girl in a white dress with a blue sash.

JACOMET. Did you ever see her before you saw her up there among the rocks?

BERNADETTE. No, Monsieur.

JACOMET. Then she's not from Lourdes?

BERNADETTE. No, Monsieur.

JACOMET. Where, then?

BERNADETTE. I don't know.

JACOMET. Didn't you ask her?

BERNADETTE. No.

JACOMET. Why not?

BERNADETTE. Because I think I already know.

JACOMET. Ah, now we are getting somewhere. Where do you think she is from?

BERNADETTE. (*Looks directly at him for a moment, but then addresses her words to the* ABBE.) I think she is from Heaven.

JACOMET. Oh ho! And how does Mademoiselle Soubirous know who comes from Heaven? Have you been there? (*He winks at* ABBE, *who gives disapproving look;* JACOMET *is embarrassed and clears his throat.*)

BERNADETTE. No, Monsieur. But the lady is so beautiful that whenever I see her, I think at once: This is how they must look in Heaven! She is too lovely to belong to the earth.

JACOMET. (*Smiling broadly.*) We have some mighty good-looking ladies right here in Lourdes, plenty of competition for your beautiful lady, don't you think so?

BERNADETTE. Oh, Monsieur! It is like an insult to compare her with them.

JACOMET. So? Well, what's the name of this beauty with the blue sash?

BERNADETTE. (*Slowly.*) I don't know.

ABBE. (*Leans forward.*) Do you *want* to know?

BERNADETTE. Yes, oh, yes, I do! I ask her every time she comes to tell me her name.

ABBE. And she never does?

JACOMET. Maybe she can't talk, eh?

BERNADETTE. Monsieur, she speaks Patois as well as you do! Like she was born here! She tells me many things.

JACOMET. But not her name?

BERNADETTE. No.

JACOMET. Why not?

BERNADETTE. I don't know. But—(*Looks at the* ABBE) I think she likes me to ask her. I think maybe she will tell me some day.

ABBE. Why?

BERNADETTE. Because when I ask her, she looks at me like this (*Jumps up and folds her hands.*), like she was just going to tell me. But then she only smiles instead.

JACOMET. What does she tell you?

BERNADETTE. (*Sits down again slowly.*) Mostly secrets, Monsieur.

ABBE. Indeed! (*To* JACOMET.) Here is as fine a little monster of pride as a curé could hope to find. Can't even read her French catechism but she knows secrets too deep for me. (*His face works, and his voice is brittle and strangely toneless.*)

BERNADETTE. No, Your Reverence. They are not too deep—it is only that—they are only for me. (*Rises and looks slowly over at the* ABBE.) But one secret I can tell, Your Reverence. (*Bows her head.*) The beautiful lady said that she would not promise to make me happy in this world, but only in the next. (*Looks up timidly.*) The other secrets, I cannot tell. (*Looks at* JACOMET.) Not for any price.

JACOMET. (*Narrows his eyes.*) Sounds like a plot. Now let me tell you something, girl. If all this crazy business *were* just for you, I'd be a happy policeman with nothing to worry about but thieves and cutthroats, people I can deal with. But this affair is for all Lourdes. And it's creeping all over France. Didn't the mayor find an article in a Paris paper about the tomfoolery in Lourdes! Aren't we being made fools of! Now you tell me the truth! (*Slams his notebook shut.*) Who is paying you to tell all these lies?

BERNADETTE. Paying me? I don't understand you, Monsieur.

JACOMET. Yes, you do! (*Waves the notebook at her.*) I have it all here, black on white—You say you can't tell the secrets the lady tells you except for a certain sum of money. You said you could tell them for a price.

BERNADETTE. (*Rises and steps back, as though struck, her hand across her mouth.*) Monsieur! I never did!

JACOMET. It's here, I tell you. (*Stands up and slams the notebook on the table.*) And either you tell me who is behind all this, or I'll throw you into jail.

ABBE. (*Rises.*) Wait a minute now, Jacomet.

(*Enter* TOINETTE, *flinging the door wide.*)

JACOMET. I mean it! Bernadette is going to tell the truth or I am going to throw her into jail.

TOINETTE. (*Running to* BERNADETTE.) I'll go with her! You'll have to throw me in, too. And Mama. And Papa.

BERNADETTE. (*Smiling through her silent tears.*) We *are* in jail, Monsieur. The cachot is the only home we have.

JACOMET. (*Embarrassed. Gathers up his notebook.*) Well, you think over what I said, girl. The mayor wants this business settled once and for all, and I have to follow orders. Now, I forbid you to go back to the grotto any more. Understand?

BERNADETTE. I understand you, Monsieur.

JACOMET. You won't go back?

BERNADETTE. Yes, Monsieur, I will go. I must go. The lady told me to come back.

ABBE. Why don't you submit to authority, child? (*Softened voice.*)

BERNADETTE. I do, Your Reverence. It is the lady I must obey. (*Her eyes begin to shine, and she moves slowly downstage, Center and Left, all during*) She is greater than anyone here. She is a queen, I think. Everything obeys her. When she stands on the rocks, they turn to gold. And when she speaks, the air accompanies her like music.

(BERNADETTE *is downstage now, oblivious of all. The* ABBE *moves downstage and stares at* BERNADETTE.)

She is so beautiful, it breaks my heart with joy to see her. And I would die to see her even once more. (*Looks off into space.*) Dear Lady, I would gladly die to see your face for only a minute more.

JACOMET. (JACOMET's *face works with emotion and then blazes into anger again. To far Left.*) Who taught you that speech?

BERNADETTE. (*Turning back, she becomes suddenly aware of those around again.*) What do you mean, Monsieur?

(ABBE *drifts to Down Center.*)

JACOMET. I mean that you are a clever little actress, but you don't fool me. This is all a pack of lies.

TOINETTE. (*Crosses Left and plants herself directly in front of* JACOMET, *arms akimbo.*) I wish I weren't too old to spit!

JACOMET. (*Startled.*) Eh?

TOINETTE. When I was little, I used to spit at people I didn't like. (*Sadly.*) But I am too big now.

ABBE. (*Smiles despite himself.*) Hush, Toinette. Remember who this gentleman is.

TOINETTE. Your Reverence, every time I say anything, someone says: Hush up, Toinette! Why is that?

JACOMET. I'm going. But you watch out, girl, or you are going to be in more trouble than you bargained for. There is plenty behind all this. What is it you're after? There's something you want very much, isn't that right?

BERNADETTE. (*Her sad little smile.*) Yes, Monsieur.

JACOMET. I knew it! What is it?

BERNADETTE. To make my First Communion.

ABBE. (*Starts and then leans forward.*) Suppose I promise you that I will let you make your First Communion if you admit you have lied about the Lady? Suppose I tell you that I will help you myself and take all the responsibility for your training, if you confess this is all make-believe? What would you say to that?

BERNADETTE. I would say: No, Your Reverence.

ABBE. (*Straightens up again, steel in his voice.*) Then you certainly do not really want to make your First Communion.

BERNADETTE. I do! (*The tears come again.*) But I cannot tell a lie. I cannot offend our Lord, not even to receive Him in my heart.

(RAP *at the door;* TOINETTE *looks at the* ABBE *and then goes to the door and admits* JEANNE.)

JEANNE. (*Wide-eyed.*) Oh! Is something going on?

ABBE. No, nothing is going on. What do *you* want?

JEANNE. (*Offended.*) I just wanted to tell Bernadette that her mother is crying, Your Reverence, and all upset. And we feel very bad because Bernadette won't obey and makes her mother sick.

BERNADETTE. (*Quickly.*) I will go to my mother. I will make her understand. (*Quick curtsey to the* ABBE.) Excuse me, Your Reverence. (*Her voice catches on a sob.*) Toinette, you stay with his reverence. (*She rushes out the door.*)

JEANNE. Well, did you ever see such rudeness! No manners at all!

TOINETTE. You shut up, Jeanne Abadie, or I'll pinch you black and blue.

ABBE. Hush, child!

TOINETTE. You see, Your Reverence! Everybody says it to me!

JEANNE. What a house! No wonder Bernadette is off balance in her head.

TOINETTE. (*Glares at* JEANNE *and then runs over to the* ABBE *and snatches his hand.*) Your Reverence, please put him out (*Points at* JACOMET.) and give Jeanne a penance because she thinks she's smart, and I'll get Mama and Bernadette and then we will all say the rosary together like we used to do every evening before life got so mixed-up. (*Kneels down swiftly and kisses the* ABBE's *hand and then runs out the door, calling.*) Bernadette! Bernadette! Wait for me!

JACOMET. What a miniature shrew that one is!

JEANNE. What is a shrew?

ABBE. A shrew is a sharp-tongued woman. (*Looks levelly at* JEANNE.) The kind of woman no one likes.

(JEANNE *flushes and looks away.*)

JACOMET. I'll leave you to your instructions, Abbe. I have to report to the mayor. I'll tell him I gave Bernadette a good scare so she won't dare show up at the grotto again. The lady can talk to the birds. (*Coarse laugh.*) Good-day, Abbe,—young lady. (*Exits.*)

JEANNE. Does he really think Bernadette won't go back to the grotto, Your Reverence?

ABBE. Evidently.

JEANNE. Well, I bet she will. And I know something—my mother said they expect ten thousand people to be at the grotto tomorrow. Just to think! Are *you* going, Your Reverence?

ABBE. (*Indignantly.*) Since when do young ladies question their abbe about his plans?

JEANNE. (*Quick curtsey.*) Beg your pardon. (*Not ruffled.*) You know what *I* think, Your Reverence? I think Bernadette made it all up because she is so vain.

ABBE. So? And how do you know she is vain?

JEANNE. Why,—uh,—well, I *know* it, Your Reverence. She just *is*. She doesn't mean any harm. She's real kind. But she likes a lot of attention, so she made up this story. I know it.

ABBE. Do you want me to tell you how you know it?

JEANNE. Please, Your Reverence? Pardon?

ABBE. You know what is in your *own* heart.

JEANNE. Pardon?

ABBE. Yes, pardon. Beg pardon of God that you plant your own vanity in the innocent heart of Bernadette.

JEANNE. (*Head high.*) I don't understand you, Your Reverence.

ABBE. I think you do. You project your own vanity into her so that you can despise it. (*Turns away and speaks very slowly.*) Just as a proud man, yes, a proud priest might project his own pride into her so that he could abominate it without pain to himself.

LOUIS. (*Excited* RAPPING, *and* LOUIS *enters before anyone can answer the knock. He carries a large sign; comes Center, above table. Not realizing who is present.*) Look! I've got it! Had it painted by an old friend of mine. (*He holds up the sign so that the audience can see it:* HEAR BERNADETTE TELL ABOUT HER VISIONS, 10 A.M. and 4 P.M. DAILY. TAKE HOME A PICTURE OF BERNADETTE, BEARING HER TENDER KISS. *He stops short, lowers the sign and comes below table as he makes out the form of the* ABBE.)

ABBE. (*Eyes blazing.*) What do you think you are doing, man?

LOUIS. (*Wavers and then decides to brazen it out.*) I'm going to use my God-given opportunities. Isn't that what you preach to us? If God hasn't time to take care of my family, I'll just provide for them myself. It's my idea. (*Holds up the sign again.*) I'm going to cash in on it. I'm going to put this sign up, Abbe, and things are going to be quite a bit brighter for me and for the Soubirous, too, when the coins start ringing down. (*Looks about him.*) I'm going to put it up right now.

ABBE. You are going to do nothing of the kind.

LOUIS. (*Furious.*) Who is going to stop me?

(JEANNE *shrinks back in fright and begins to cry as the* ABBE *steps up to* LOUIS.)

ABBE. A proud man is going to stop you. Or, at least a man who has seen a brave and humble child. (*He takes the sign from* LOUIS' *hands and breaks it in two over his knee.*)

CURTAIN

ACT THREE

SCENE I

SCENE. *The Grotto of Massabielle, some days later.* JACOMET *stands at the Left of the stage, arms folded meaningfully over his bayonet.* LOUIS *is beside him. There is a distant murmuring of many voices, like an immense crowd approaching.*

LOUIS. She'll be here, you can bet your life on it.

JACOMET. Let her come, then. I was wrong to try to keep her away. Let the people see for themselves that she's just an empty-headed little fool.

(*The sound of* VOICES *grows steadily louder to give the impression of the crowd advancing.*)

(*Moving and looking off, Right.*) Good God! Look at them coming! Like a million black beetles.

LOUIS. (*Towards* JACOMET, *bitterly.*) Don't tell a near-blind man to look at them.

JACOMET. (*Towards* LOUIS.) Well, listen, man!

(*The* VOICES *grow louder.*)

(*Back to Right.*) Lord, there must be thousands of them. I'm glad I've got gendarmes posted all around the grotto. There might be trouble.

LOUIS. For the gendarmes, maybe.

JACOMET. Don't be so sure. She can't go on like this, deluding the people with words. They will want to see something for themselves. And Heaven help Bernadette if that crowd ever turns on her.

(BERNADETTE *appears Right, walking between her parents. She advances steadily, and* JEANNE *and* TOINETTE *then appear, Right.*)

BERNADETTE. (*To Center, turning back.*) No, stay there, please. Do not come closer.

(JEANNE *and* TOINETTE *halt Right Center and* JEANNE *waves back, as though transmitting this message to the crowd just behind her, only a few of whom need appear on the stage.*)

JACOMET. (*Barring* BERNADETTE'S *path, Down Stage of her.*) Where do you think you are going?

BERNADETTE. (*Staring straight ahead Down Left.*) Just right here, Monsieur, where the lady told me to come. Please step aside. You are in the way.

JACOMET. (*Raises his bayonet.*) Stand back!

(LOUISE *screams and* FRANCOIS *puts an arm around her.*)

LOUISE. Don't hurt her!

FRANCOIS. (*Leaves* LOUISE *and goes to put his arm on* BERNADETTE'S *shoulder.*) What are you doing, Monsieur?

JACOMET. My duty.

JEANNE. (*Crosses Right, shouting to the crowd Offstage.*) He won't let her pass!

(*Great* ROAR *from the crowd.*)

LOUIS. You had better take care, man! That mob could tear you limb from limb.

JACOMET. (*Lowers bayonet and speaks in a surly tone*.) All right, my little actress. What's next on the program?

BERNADETTE. (*Smiling at him.*) Thank you, Monsieur. I will ask the Lady to bless you.

(JACOMET *blushes and falls back a few steps.* BERNADETTE *comes to the extreme Left, holding her arms out in back of her to indicate that her parents and the children should stay back.*)

JEANNE. (*Shouting Offstage.*) He let her by.

(*Great* ROAR *of acclaim from the crowd;* BERNADETTE *kneels and takes out beads.*)

She's kneeling down. Taking out her beads.

(*Crowd* NOISE *up and down at each of these.*)

LOUISE. (*Left Center, nervously.*) Francois, we should have forced her to stay home.

FRANCOIS. (*New dignity.*) She said she had to come. We belong here with her.

LOUISE. But there are gendarmes all around. Maybe they will kill her. Oh, Francois, our first baby! Our little girl! Why did all this have to happen to us? (*Begins to cry.*)

FRANCOIS. I don't know. I've never bothered much about why things happen the way they do. What's the use? You can't change them. But nobody's going to kill Bernadette. At least, not without killing me first.

LOUISE. (*Crosses Up Left of* BERNADETTE *and then back Center; distracted.*) Francois! (*Pulls at his sleeve.*) Look at her!

(BERNADETTE *has been passing the beads of her rosary through her fingers, oblivious of all the* OTHERS. *Now her face begins to glow with a celestial light and an unearthly smile makes her ethereally lovely.*)

TOINETTE. (*Down Right Center.*) Oh, Jeanne! Look at her! Isn't she beautiful?

JEANNE. (*To* TOINETTE, *hands against her cheeks in wonderment.*) Yes. Ye-es, Toinette! (*Takes* TOINETTE's *hand.*) I think I made a mistake. (*Pause, and the tears start to course down her cheeks as she watches* BERNADETTE.) Toinette, I wish I were like Bernadette. I wish I weren't so mean.

TOINETTE. (*Philosophically.*) Well, go ahead and be good then. (*Squeezes* JEANNE's *hand in both of hers.*) Jeanne, she must be looking at the lady. And talking to her! See, her lips are moving!

JEANNE. (*Crosses Up Right, to the crowd Offstage, in a new, awed voice.*) The Lady is here!

(*The confused murmuring dies to complete silence.* FRANCOIS *pulls off his cap and* LOUISE *blesses herself.*)

LOUIS. What is happening?

JACOMET. (*Strangled voice.*) I—I don't know.

LOUIS. Why is everything so quiet?

JACOMET. (*Drops his bayonet on the ground, startling everyone except* BERNADETTE *who remains transfixed and smiling.*) God in Heaven!

LOUIS. (*Grabbing at his arm.*) What is it, man?

JACOMET. (*Down a few steps.*) I am a fool. Oh, God, I am a sinner, a sinner and a fool.

Louis. Are you going mad, Jacomet?

Jacomet. No, I am going sane.

Louis. (*Frightened voice.*) You,—mean,—you mean, you see something? You—you—see—the Lady?

Jacomet. No, I do not see the Lady. (*Voice breaks.*)

Louis. (*Relieved.*) Well, what's the matter, then? What do you see?

Jacomet. (*Voice full of tears.*) I see the face of Bernadette. (*Falls to his knees, continuing to look at her.*)

Jeanne. (*Importantly.*) Kneel down, Toinette! Just look at Monsieur Jacomet, would you!

Toinette. (*Kneels.*) No, but look at Bernadette! Oh, Jeanne! Jeanne! (*Pulls the older girl down beside her.*) She is too beautiful to live! It hurts me to look at her. (*Toinette rises and runs to Louise and Francois Up Left of them.*) Mama, is Bernadette going to die? She looks like a little bird when it spreads its wings to fly!

Louise. (*Falls to her knees.*) Oh, dear God, dear Lord in Heaven, don't take my child!

Toinette. (*Poised in indecision for a moment, she then runs impulsively forward and throws her arms around Bernadette, kissing her on both cheeks. Bernadette remains unmoving, looking up. Toinette steps back and looks at her and then runs back to her parents and buries her face in Francois' shabby blouse.*) Papa, she is dead!

Francois. No, no, she's moving. Look at her, Louise! Toinette! Look!

Bernadette. (*Bernadette slowly rises, looking off in the direction of the grotto, as though receiving orders. She walks uncertainly downstage and then looks back toward the grotto, appearing surprised.*) Oh? That way? (*Points backstage. She nods her head obediently and goes toward the back, looks at the ground, hesitates, and looks inquiringly off toward the grotto. After a few moments, she nods her head.*) All right. Yes, my Lady. (*She kneels, her back to the audience, and begins energetically scraping the earth with her hands.*)

Louise. What is she doing, clawing at the earth like that?

Francois. Maybe she lost something.

Louise. (*Louder, frightened.*) Francois, something is wrong! Look at her!

(*Bernadette bends down almost to the ground, smearing the mud over her face and scooping some into her mouth. She pulls at a few blades of grass, looks at them dubiously for a moment, and then puts them into her mouth.*)

Francois. My Lord, she must be going mad! (*Steps forward.*) Bernadette! Put down that grass! Take that grass out of your mouth!

Toinette. (*Starts to cry afresh.*) I'm afraid!

Jacomet. (*Rises unsteadily from his knees, his face working and his fists clenched.*) What are you doing, girl?

(*Bernadette rises and comes back to her former kneeling position, turning her muddied face toward the audience. She is not aware of those around.*)

JEANNE. (*Comes to Center, the crowd closing in behind her, murmuring.*) Look at you, Bernadette Soubirous! Aren't you ashamed? Acting like a dunce!

JACOMET. (*Hoarsely.*) Mad! She's mad! (*He reaches down for his bayonet and advances toward the* SOUBIROUS *and* JEANNE.) Step back, all of you! We have an insane girl here!

LOUISE. No! I don't believe it!

FRANCOIS. Our child can't be mad!

TOINETTE. She's just muddy, Monsieur!

JACOMET. (*Shouting now.*) Stand back, I say! Bernadette nearly fooled me, too. I admit it. She almost roped me in. But she's mad, do you hear? Do you see?

JEANNE. (*Hand on her cheek.*) Crazy! (*Up Right and off to crowd.*) Bernadette is crazy!

(*The* CROWD *takes up the word, and it grows and grows in volume to a steady chant.*)

VOICES. $\left\{\begin{array}{l}\text{Mad!}\\\text{Crazy!}\end{array}\right.$

(LOUIS *gradually moves Down Left closer to Left of* BERNADETTE. *He has not been able to make out her movements and he cannot see the mud on her face. He looks with squinting eyes from the crowd to* BERNADETTE.)

JACOMET. (*Left, crosses Center.*) Go home, all of you. Clear out of here. (*Flourishes his bayonet.*) I'll get this mad girl safely put away where she belongs.

LOUISE. Francois, stop him!

FRANCOIS. (*Weakly.*) I don't know what to do. What shall I do? (*Looks around blankly.*)

TOINETTE. (TOINETTE *looks from one parent to the other and then very suddenly, giving the impression of an irresistible impulse, runs straight to* LOUIS, *pulling vigorously at his arm.*) Louis, save her! She prays the rosary for you every single day.

(LOUIS *looks down at the child dazedly.*)

(*Shakes his arm violently.*) Louis! Louis! She says you are a good man. (*Ingenuously.*) Nobody ever liked you but Bernadette.

JACOMET. (*Turning back.*) Get away, little girl, I'm taking care of this.

LOUIS. (*Shakes off* TOINETTE'S *hand and digs his two fists into his dimming eyes.*) Wait a minute, Jacomet.

JACOMET. Get out of the way, Louis. I'm handling this.

LOUIS. (*Lowers his arms and stands up very straight.*) No, you're not!

JACOMET. (*Sneering.*) No? Who's going to stop me?

LOUIS. I am! I am, by God.

JACOMET. You don't believe in God. Why are you getting so excited about Him all of a sudden? (*Short laugh.*) Come on, let's get going.

(BERNADETTE *slowly stirs, opens her eyes wide and stares around at the* OTHERS.)

(*Rough hand on her shoulder.*) Come along with me, girl!

LOUIS. (*Voice of thunder.*) Let her alone!

(*He steps forward so imposingly that* JACOMET *involuntarily falls back.* LOUISE *stops crying, and* FRANCOIS *steps forward a little.*)

JEANNE. What's the matter with him?

JACOMET. (*Gentler voice.*) I don't want to hurt you, Louis.

LOUIS. You'll have to kill me before you touch Bernadette.

(*Complete silence falls, and all the* OTHERS *stand motionless.* BERNADETTE *looks up at* LOUIS *calmly and expectantly.*)

(LOUIS *looks toward the* OTHERS, *and then in the direction of the grotto—a great anguished cry breaks from his heart; Down a step and then towards Down Left.*) Oh, God, if You exist, give me back my faith in You! Mother of God, if you are here, give me peace. Mother of God, let me see!

(*Another great sob breaks from him, and* BERNADETTE *reaches out shyly and touches his hand.*)

CURTAIN

ACT THREE

SCENE II

SCENE. *The same, some days later.* JACOMET *is holding his bayonet menacingly against a crowd pushing against ropes strung halfway across the stage.* LOUIS *is in the foreground, with* LOUISE *and* FRANCOIS *close behind him.*

JACOMET. Stand back! Stand back, I say.

(*He raises the bayonet threateningly, and the crowd falls back a little, muttering.*) We're going to have order, do you hear me? (*To* LOUIS.) Why don't you stay away from here? They troop out here to gape at you as though you were a marvel of creation. If you'd stay home, maybe they would, too. (*Shakes the bayonet at* LOUIS, *and angry murmurs break out from the crowd.*)

CROWD. { Let him alone!
{ Be careful, Jacomet! — He belongs to our Lady!

LOUIS. (*Turns Right, raises his arm, and the crowd falls almost silent; turns back.*) You ask me to do the impossible, my friend.

JACOMET. (*Exhausted.*) I ask only that you stay away from here. Is that impossible?

LOUIS. Yes.

JACOMET. I'd like to know why.

LOUIS. Look, my friend, I came here a bitter, low-minded man. I couldn't see three steps in front of me. I had venom in my heart, and a vacuum where other men have souls.

JACOMET. So what?

LOUIS. So, a little girl prayed for me here. And she drained all the venom out of my heart. She gave my soul back to me. And her Lady gave me my eyes back again. Then you ask me to stay away from the place where I found my eyes and my soul!

JACOMET. (*Sneering.*) Bravo! Bravo! Sounds like the actress herself.

(*Muttering from the crowd.*)

CROWD. { She's no actress!
She's a saint.
Our Lady will strike you down!

LOUIS. These people want to drink from the miraculous stream, Jacomet. What's wrong with that?

JACOMET. And then we'll have another whole crop of miracles by noon! Mass hypnotism, that's what it is!

LOUIS. Do you hypnotize a blind man into seeing?

JACOMET. You never were blind. You could see some. (*Back a step and gestures toward Up Left.*) That water has curative chemicals in it, that's all. You kept on massaging your eyes with it,—and there you are! Therapy. Just physical therapy. And everybody's gone crazy just because you can see a little better.

VOICE FROM THE CROWD. You're the crazy one!

FRANCOIS. Where did the stream come from, tell me that?

CROWD. { That's right!
There was never a second stream here before.
Bernadette gave us the miraculous stream!

JACOMET. (*Brandishes the bayonet at* FRANCOIS, *and* LOUISE *screams.*) I won't have another word out of you, loafer! Tramp! Good-for-nothing!

LOUISE. (*Pulling at* FRANCOIS' *arm.*) Let's go home. Let's get out of here.

LOUIS. Don't be afraid, Louise. Nothing will happen to us.

LOUISE. (*Crying now.*) There is nothing left to happen to us, except to be killed. (*Pulls at* FRANCOIS' *arm again.*) Come on. Please, please come on.

JACOMET. (*Top of his voice.*) Clear out! I'm telling you for the last time. I've got orders from the mayor. Clear out, before I throw the whole lot of you into jail!

LOUIS. (*Raises his arm again, and the muttering of the crowd subsides.*) All right, Jacomet. We'll clear out. (*Turns back to those behind him.*) Come on, my friends, do as the law here says. Our Lady won't be stopped by a bayonet and a few ropes!

(LOUIS *begins to push those nearest him with both arms and they gradually drift Offstage, muttering low threats, and frequently turning back to raise fists at* JACOMET.)

(*To* JACOMET.) We will go, because we agree to go, not because we are forced. And we will come back.

JACOMET. (*Finally only* JACOMET *remains. He puts down the bayonet and takes out his handkerchief to wipe the sweat from his face.*) Damned fools. It's enough to turn your stomach. And to think she actually took *me* in for a while! Sickly brat! I'll never live it down! Me, Jacomet, chief of police,—and almost fooled by a whining girl! (*Begins moving Right, and goes through ropes.*) I'm the lucky one. I'm the man to see the truth. (*Straightens up.*) So what if I did make a mistake once? Only a big man can admit his mistakes. That's Jacomet! A big man. A man that's willing to say he acted like a jackass for a few minutes. But not a born jackass like the rest of them around here! (*Short laugh.*) I think I'll go home. They're all gone now. (*Slight lift of his shoulders.*) This place gives me the jim-jams. Maybe that Soubirous brat is a witch for all we know. (*Crosses Left under rope; shake of his head.*) I just don't like the air here. I'll wade the stream and go home. (*Exits Left.*)

(BERNADETTE, TOINETTE *and* JEANNE *appear at the Right after a few moments, looking around cautiously.*)

JEANNE. (*To Center.*) He's gone! (*She slips under the ropes.*)

TOINETTE. (*Pulling* BERNADETTE'S *arm.*) Come on, Bernadette! Nobody's around. Hear the stream gurgling, Jeanne?

(*The* TWO SISTERS *follow, through the ropes.*)

JEANNE. Uh-huh.

(BERNADETTE *starts to drift Down Left.*)

TOINETTE. Let's get a drink from it. It isn't muddy at all now. (*Points Offstage, Left.*) See! (*Turns back proudly.*) I guess they're all sorry now they said Bernadette was crazy when she scooped up that mud! Look at the water gushing out!

JEANNE. (*Importantly.*) Louis said it's giving ten thousand gallons a day now. And from just that little hole Bernadette scratched in the ground!

(*Crosses Down Center and peers at* BERNADETTE *who is looking Offstage, Left, oblivious of the other two.*)

Do you see something, Bernadette? (*Excitedly.*) Do you see the Lady?

BERNADETTE. (*Turns back with a wistful smile.*) No, Jeanne. I don't see her.

JEANNE. What were you looking at?

BERNADETTE. Memories.

TOINETTE. (*Crosses Down to Left of* BERNADETTE.) Maybe she'll come back again.

BERNADETTE. (*Very slowly.*) No, she will never come back to me.

JEANNE. How do you know?

BERNADETTE. I just know it,—in here. (*Hand over her heart.*)

JEANNE. (*Good-natured laugh.*) That's where you always know things! But won't you really ever see the Lady again at all?

BERNADETTE. Not until Heaven.

TOINETTE. (*Worriedly.*) You think I'll get there all right?

BERNADETTE. (*Gives her a big hug.*) I do! Oh, yes, I do, Toinette!

JEANNE. (*Embarrassed humility.*) And I, Bernadette? Will Our Lady want me near her?

BERNADETTE. (*A tiny pause and then she kisses* JEANNE *very lightly on the cheek.*) She has always wanted you near her, Jeanne. Didn't you bring me here to gather sticks, that first day? It was all your idea to come here. It's really all your doing.

JEANNE. (*Very pleased, but embarrassed, too.*) Oh, go on!

BERNADETTE. We'll have to be together, Jeanne, in case Our Lady needs some sticks for a fire! Haven't we the best eyes in Lourdes to find sticks!

(*All three laugh.*)

TOINETTE. I'll bet Our Lady will want Louis very, very close to her. And he'll be able to *see* her, too!

JEANNE. (*Her ordinary superior tone.*) Everybody can see in Heaven, silly.

TOINETTE. (*Ruffled.*) Yes, but he's getting started on earth, isn't he? I like him much better since he can see.

JEANNE. But he's so quiet. He doesn't even like it when everybody asks him questions. Wouldn't you think he'd be all excited like everybody else is? Goodness, it's a *miracle* for him to see again!

BERNADETTE. But *we* don't get excited about miracles, Jeanne.

JEANNE. Huh! *I* would if a miracle happened to me! (*Crosses Up Left.*) If I washed in the stream and got my eyesight back, I'd jump and shout and—well, I don't know what all I'd do.

BERNADETTE. (*Smiling, fanning, look Up Left and then Down Right.*) But you *do* wash in the stream, Jeanne.

JEANNE. (*One step towards* BERNADETTE.) Yes, sure I do. All the people do now, when that old Jacomet doesn't shoo them away.

BERNADETTE. (*Crosses Up Left to* JEANNE.) And you can see, can't you?

JEANNE. Of course, I can. What's the matter with you?

BERNADETTE. Well, that is a miracle. It's a miracle that we can see and hear and walk and talk. Only we never pay much attention to it.

TOINETTE. I never thought of that.

BERNADETTE. (*Leading* JEANNE *toward Down Center, warming to her subject.*) And we can love people. We can love Our Lady and Our Lord. That's a big miracle, the biggest there is. But it doesn't make anybody want to shout. It makes me almost want to cry. (*She looks away Down Left, seeming to forget the* OTHERS, *and drifts Down Left, speaking in a tone of wonder.*) What have we done that Our Lord should let us love Him? That He should *want* us to love Him and His Mother?

(JEANNE *and* TOINETTE *look vaguely at each other.*)

TOINETTE. (*Matter-of-factly.*) I don't know. But I do love Him, yes, I do! (*She begins a little skipping step crossing one foot in front of the other, and chanting in a high sing-song.*) Yes, I do, yes, I do! Lord, I love You, love You, love You!

(BERNADETTE *laughs and then begins to cough.*)

JEANNE. That's irreverent.

TOINETTE. No, it isn't. That's the way I pray. (*Stop and laughs.*) Come on! Let's climb up the rocks to the rosebush before we go home. I want a little branch for Mama. It will make her smile. She cries too much. Come on! (*Taking* OTHERS *by hands and tugging.*)

BERNADETTE. I don't know. I can't get my breath very well. You go. I'll wait for you. I like to listen to the stream sing.

JEANNE. All right. Come on, Toinette. I'll race you!

(*They run off Left.* BERNADETTE *sits down on the little stump and spreads her skirt out carefully.*)

BERNADETTE. (*Smiles.*) It makes music all day long for you, my Lady! (*She cocks her ear and begins to move her right hand back and forth as though directing the music of the water. She begins to sing softly in the Lourdes melody.*)

Ave, Ave, Ave, Maria! Ave, Ave, Ave, Maria!

(*Enter* ABBE *and* LOUIS, *Right,* ABBE *Down Stage as* BERNADETTE *repeats her song.* LOUIS *is carrying a squarish box very carefully.*)

ABBE. Very pretty!

BERNADETTE. (*Jumps up, startled; smiles and curtsies.*) Excuse me. I did not see Your Reverence. (*Another quick little curtsey.*) Louis! Good afternoon! I'm waiting for Toinette and Jeanne. They went to get a branch of the rosebush.

(LOUIS *and* ABBE *toward* BERNADETTE.)

LOUIS. Jacomet must have thought the place was safe without him and his bayonet. I see he's gone. (*Slowly looks around like a man inspecting a new house.*) And I see the rosebush. I see the buds. I see the little green leaves. And I see the thorns.

ABBE. You are fortunate if you can see the thorns. Too many people see only the roses and then curse God for surprising them with the thorns.

BERNADETTE. (*Shyly, to* LOUIS.) We did not know you were coming. I'll go after them and ask Toinette to get another branch for you. And for Your Reverence. (*Her little curtsey.*)

(*The two men look after her as she exits Left, and* LOUIS *hands his box to the* ABBE, *takes off his cap and turns it nervously in his hands.*)

LOUIS. I need another miracle, Abbe.

ABBE. We all need them by the dozens.

LOUIS. I was satisfied with myself when I was blind. (*Kicks a pebble from his path.*) Sure, I was bitter. Hadn't God given me a raw deal? I thought I'd go Him one better. Nothing was too low for me. (*Clenches his fists, squeezing the cap into a ball.*) Not even cashing in on a saint. Remember that sign I wanted to put up?

ABBE. Forget it, man. It's all behind you.

LOUIS. (*Slowly.*) Yes. (*Jerks back to the* ABBE.) Everyone wants to see me now. I'm the prize exhibit. The blind man who can see again. Not that I blame them. But I'll tell you this, Abbe.

It's a terrible thing to be cured. (*Voice rises.*) It's a terrible thing to have the self-pity and bitterness stripped off you. (*Turns toward the grotto.*) I have to look at myself now. And God in Heaven, what a sight it is!

ABBE. (*Gently.*) You're a very fortunate man, Louis.

LOUIS. I know it. Yes, I know it. I can see. I believe. But—

ABBE. That's not what I mean. You are fortunate to have learned what few men do.

LOUIS. What's that?

ABBE. That every miracle is a kind of crucifixion.

LOUIS. (*Staring.*) How could *you* know that?

ABBE. (*Smiles.*) A real miracle means that measures and compromises can no longer exist. A miracle is the most terrible of God's demands. (*Turns Down Right away a little and speaks very slowly.*) Not everyone is able to survive being loved by God.

LOUIS. (*Taking step Down Right.*) How do you know that?

ABBE. (*Ghost of a smile.*) Not all miracles are worked on the eyes, my friend. Some take place in the heart of a proud man.

(*Enter* BERNADETTE, *Left, carrying one branch. She gives it to the* ABBE. *She stays Left of rope;* ABBE *crosses Up Center to her.*)

I thought Louis was to get one.

BERNADETTE. (*Her shy smile.*) Toinette wants him to come and climb. She says he ought to use up the seeing he's been saving.

LOUIS. (*Smiles, too.*) And she's right. As right as a theologian. How about it, Abbe?

(*He slips through the ropes, laughing, and goes out, Left. The* ABBE *slips through after him.* BERNADETTE *starts to cough, and the* ABBE *motions her to sit down on the stump. She gracefully demurs, offering it to him with the graciousness of a hostess and seats herself on the ground.*)

ABBE. Well, what is going to happen now, Bernadette? (*Sets the box carefully in front of him.*)

BERNADETTE. I don't know, Your Reverence.

ABBE. (*Studying her face.*) Your parents could be rich now, do you realize that? Everybody wants to bring you gifts.

BERNADETTE. My parents don't want gifts, Your Reverence. Neither do I.

ABBE. Isn't that ungrateful?

BERNADETTE. No, Your Reverence. Why should people bring me presents because I saw Our Lady? I'm no different than I ever was. I'm nobody of any importance, only Bernadette Soubirous who has a bad chest and a worse head. (*She laughs very softly.*)

ABBE. But don't you want life to be easier for your parents?

BERNADETTE. (*A moment's pause, and then she looks directly up at him.*) No, I don't think so, Your Reverence. Our Lady did not promise to make me happy in this world. I think she meant it for all the Soubirous. We are not intended to be great or important. We are just meant to show that nothing matters very much in this life because Heaven is coming afterwards.

ABBE. How do you know that, child?

BERNADETTE. (*Smiles.*) I know it,—in here. (*The familiar gesture over her heart.*)

ABBE. But have you no plans for the future? (*Rests his hands on the box.*)

BERNADETTE. No, Your Reverence.

ABBE. You can't go on like this forever, having people gape at you and question you. Surely you don't like it?

BERNADETTE. (*Looks down.*) No, I hate it. I dread each rap at the door.

ABBE. Wouldn't you like to go away?

BERNADETTE. (*Looks up again and smiles.*) No, Your Reverence.

ABBE. But you just said you hated all the crowds and the questions.

BERNADETTE. Yes. But you told us in Lent we should learn how to mortify ourselves,—learn how to die. There are many ways to die. This is my way.

ABBE. (*Visibly moved.*) And that is all the future you see for yourself, Bernadette? Just to stay in Lourdes and let people pick the skin off your soul?

BERNADETTE. It is all I am good for. (*Her sweet, quick smile.*) Maybe when they pick enough skin off me, the catechism answers will get through my head and I will be able to make my First Communion. (*Serious again.*) After I make my First Communion, I will be able to suffer more. I will be strong then.

ABBE. Are you afraid of me, Bernadette?

BERNADETTE. No, Your Reverence,—not any more.

ABBE. (*Hiding his smile.*) Indeed? You have changed, then?

BERNADETTE. No, Your Reverence, I don't think I have changed. But you have.

ABBE. (*Laughs outright, and then quickly sobers.*) You are right enough. I have changed. Thank God for that. But if you're not afraid of me, how is it you don't ask me to let you make your First Communion as you did before?

BERNADETTE. (*Clasps her hands together and looks up at him.*) I used to ask when I was afraid of you. But now I do not ask because I love Your Reverence, and I know you will do what is best for me without any asking.

ABBE. (*The* ABBE's *eyes film with tears and he stands up abruptly to hide his emotion, taking up the box as he rises.*) So? So, that is how you scheme, is it?

BERNADETTE. (*Gets to her knees and smiles up at him*) There *is* something I want to ask Your Reverence, though.

ABBE. (*Sets the box on the ground.*) Which is—?

BERNADETTE. (*Very serious now.*) It is the name Our Lady told me. The name I told Your Reverence. You know it.

ABBE. (*Looks down at her fixedly.*) Yes, I know it. I know the name she told you. "I am—(*his voice breaks just a little.*)—the Immaculate Conception."

BERNADETTE. Yes, Your Reverence. Those were her very words. But—(*She frowns a little.*)

ABBE. But what?

BERNADETTE. Your Reverence,—what does it mean?

ABBE. (*Her simplicity throws him off his poise for a moment and he struggles to get hold of himself, leaning down to flick some imaginary dust off the box.*) You don't know what it means that Our Lady called herself the Immaculate Conception?

BERNADETTE. Not very well. I only know it is something that belongs to being God's mother.

ABBE. (*His hand on her shoulder.*) Yes, it belongs to God's mother. For her, it means beauty and blessedness. For Bernadette, it means your martyrdom.

BERNADETTE. What do you mean, Your Reverence?

ABBE. I mean that you have seen what is spotless. Life will be spotted and lonely for you now until you die.

BERNADETTE. (*Very simply, as she lowers her gaze.*) Thank you. I thought it meant something like that.

> (*Enter Up Left* LOUIS *crosses Down Center;* JEANNE, *who stays Up Left, and* TOINETTE, *who crosses Up Center to Right of* LOUIS, *waving small branches of the rosebush.* BERNADETTE *rises.*)

LOUIS. What a pair of sober faces for Our Lady to see!

TOINETTE. Are you sick, Bernadette?

BERNADETTE. (*Laughs.*) No, Toinette. Why?

ABBE. She means you must be sick of talking to such an ancient person as Abbe Peyramale.

TOINETTE. (*Wide-eyed.*) My goodness! Don't tell Mama that, Your Reverence! She'll box my ears. I think maybe I won't talk at all any more.

JEANNE. I'll bet you two beans and a button you will never stop talking until you die.

JACOMET. (*Enter* JACOMET, *Left, purple with anger, and coming Down Left.*) Maybe some people are going to die sooner than they think if the law isn't kept here.

> (TOINETTE *and* JEANNE *shrink back against* LOUIS, *as the* ABBE *steps forward.*)

ABBE. Are you out to frighten children today, my friend?

JACOMET. (*Shouting.*) I'm out to keep order! Nobody is to come past those ropes, you hear! (*Little milder voice.*) And that means the clergy, too, Abbe. Now this is my last warning. Get back there!

> (*Enter* LOUISE *and* FRANCOIS, *Right, as* JACOMET *brandishes his bayonet.* LOUISE *screams.*)

LOUISE. Don't you kill her!

> (*She runs up to the rope and* BERNADETTE *quickly wriggles through and throws her arms around her mother.*)

BERNADETTE. He won't, Mama! See, I'm all right.

LOUISE. (*Shaking her off, in her stress of emotion.*) Why did you come back here today? I've been frantic, looking for you.

FRANCOIS. (*Coming several steps behind.*) I told you she'd be here, Louise. No need to get all upset. I like it out here myself. Smells nice. Good air.

JACOMET. (*Groans.*) Listen, go home, will you?

LOUIS. (*Laughs and steps Down.*) No! We *all* like it here, Jacomet.

JACOMET. (*His rage fully enkindled again at this, rushes Center;* ALL *fall back except* LOUIS.) You fools! Why don't you stop acting like jackasses! (*Up to* LOUIS *and to his Right.*) I've got a good notion to punch your jaw loose.

ABBE. (*The* ABBE *steps forward, picking up the box and holding it before him.*) You touch him and I'll let you have this,—right through your heart!

JACOMET. (*Blinking.*) What's in there?

ABBE. Enough to shut your mouth forever. (JACOMET *falls back a little.*) Now, you listen to me, Jacomet. You're just like the rest of us. You take all the dark, crawling things in your own miserable little soul and try to fasten them on the soul of Bernadette.

JACOMET. (*Stepping forward and trying to get the upper hand again.*) Who do you think you're talking to, Abbe?—somebody in the catechism class?

ABBE. No,—to Jacomet, who never really learned the answers.

JACOMET. (*Doubles his fist.*) Watch yourself, Abbe!

(BERNADETTE *slips through the rope again and looks fixedly at the* ABBE, *and then crosses Up Left to* JEANNE.)

ABBE. (*Lifts up his box.*) You better watch out for yourself. Do you want me to drive this through your miserable heart?

JACOMET. (*Drops back again, and* FRANCOIS *also slips through the rope as* LOUISE *stops crying in her interest over the scene.*) What's wrong with you, Abbe?

ABBE. There's not so much wrong with me now as there used to be. There wouldn't be so much wrong with *you* if you would stop being such a snivelling coward.

JACOMET. (*Doubles his fist again.*) Who's a coward?

ABBE. (*Stepping up to him.*) You are!

JACOMET. (*Shouting.*) There's not a man alive I'm afraid to face!

ABBE. You're a liar. You're frightened to death of one man. And you bully everybody else just because you are so afraid of that one man.

JACOMET. You're crazy! Name him!

ABBE. (*Measured tones.*) Monsieur Jacomet, chief of the police of Lourdes.

(JACOMET'S *body droops as though he had been struck a heavy blow, and he drops back a step, lowering his fist. The* ABBE *continues in a milder tone:*)

You came face to face with yourself here one day when you watched Bernadette talking with the Mother of God. It broke you in two. And who is a man until he *has* been broken into pieces? But you couldn't stand it, Jacomet. You used a child with mud on her face to patch up your own bravado again. *You're* the jackass, Jacomet! That's why you keep on shouting that everyone else is.

LOUIS. (*Quietly.*) I know what you mean. I claimed Bernadette was out for money because *I* was. I thought she must be shallow, because my own soul didn't run an inch deep.

JEANNE. (*Steps back and catches* BERNADETTE'S *hand.*) I said she was vain because *I* am.

ABBE. (*Very slowly.*) And I called her proud because I am proud,—may God help me.

TOINETTE. (*Skips forward.*) You mean that every time Monsieur Jacomet calls Bernadette a jackass, he really means that he is one?

LOUISE. (*Coming Down Center on Right of rope; force of habit.*) Hush up, Toinette. (*Pulls her back,* TOINETTE *still on Left of rope.*)

FRANCOIS. I guess everything is all right. I knew everything would turn out all right. (*Slips back behind the ropes and puts an arm around* LOUISE, *on her Right.*)

JACOMET. (*Looks around dazedly and speaks weakly, going Up Left to where* FRANCOIS *had been.*) Clear out of here, will you? Let me alone.

ABBE. (*Backing Up Left.*) Not before I stab you straight through the heart! (*Holds up the box and takes off the lid.*)

(LOUISE *shrinks back against* FRANCOIS.)

FRANCOIS. Wait a minute now, Abbe! You're all excited.

LOUIS. (*Crosses Down Right, a hand on* FRANCOIS' *arm.*) Let him alone.

ABBE. (*Very deliberately sets down the lid of the box.*) Every blackhearted sinner in Lourdes has been accusing Bernadette of his *own* sins. Everyone has been blaming her for coveting the things he wants himself,—money, praise, fame. But there is only one thing she has wanted. And she's going to have it, do you hear me, Jacomet? Stand back, man! I'm going to put a knife right through your heart!

(*He reaches into the box as* JACOMET *stares at him. All the* OTHERS *except* LOUIS *and* BERNADETTE *fall back in fright.* ABBE *waves* BERNADETTE *forward; she crosses Down Center. He slowly sets the box on the ground and draws out a long white veil with wax orange blossoms. He pulls a drab little shawl off* BERNADETTE'S *hair and places the veil on her head.*)

She is going to have the only thing she wants in life. She is going to make her First Communion, Jacomet. Louis sold his lambs to buy her dress and veil.

BERNADETTE. (BERNADETTE *stands at Center, looking like a very small bride, the tears streaming down her face. She turns to* LOUIS.) Oh, Monsieur! (*She clasps her hands very tightly over her heart as though it pained her.*)

LOUISE. (*Forgetting all her worries.*) Oh, my pretty! My little girl!

ABBE. (*Takes a sheer white dress and long cape out of the box and crosses Center, hands them to* LOUISE.) Here, take these home and see if they fit her.

LOUISE. (*Holds them up and presses the lovely stuff against her cheek as her own tears begin to flow.*) It's the Mother of God has done all this!

FRANCOIS. Didn't I tell you everything would turn out all right? There's never any use getting excited about things. Come on now, Louise, come on, Bernadette! Toinette! (*Starts marshalling them importantly before him.*) Jeanne! Get along now! Come with us, Louis?

Louis. (*Shyly.*) No, I guess I'll go along home. You better come with me, Francois. They have women's business to do.

(JEANNE *and* TOINETTE *begin fingering the dress, and* LOUISE *slaps* TOINETTE *smartly on the fingers.*)

Louise. Don't you touch it! (*Gestures right.*) March! Home with you! Bernadette, you thank the Abbe and Louis properly and then come along.

(*Exeunt* LOUISE, TOINETTE, JEANNE, *Right. The women have forgotten all about* JACOMET *who is staring at* BERNADETTE *in the streaming white veil. The* ABBE *watches him a moment and then backing Left motions* FRANCOIS *and* LOUIS *to go. Exeunt* LOUIS, FRANCOIS, *right.*)

Abbe. Well, man?

Jacomet. (*Turns away at last.*) Let me alone. For the love of God, go away and let me alone.

Abbe. (*Crosses Up Left, strangely tender voice.*) All right, my friend. (*Grips* JACOMET'S *shoulder and then walks off, Left.*)

(JACOMET *stumbles over to the stump and sinks down on it, dropping his bayonet on the ground.* BERNADETTE *follows him, a strange little figure in the billowing veil with her rough skirt and heavy sabots.* JACOMET *stares at her again and then abruptly covers his face with his hands and begins to sob.*)

Bernadette. (*Timidly places her small hands over his large ones.*) It's all right, Monsieur. I have to cry hard sometimes, too. Nobody else will know. And I don't matter. I am nobody important. (*She picks up his bayonet, crosses Down Center and looks at it wonderingly, as all* LIGHTS *fade to out except a pencil of light on the bayonet pointed towards her heart.*)

SLOW CURTAIN

The End

Smallest of All
Property List

ACT ONE

SCENE I

Stage Props:

Two tables

Three chairs

Two stools

Washtub, bucket, stove

Hand Props:

Dishes

Pots, pans, etc.

Table cloth

Two cloths for drying dishes

Wooden mixing bowl and wooden spoon

Large crucifix (for wall above fireplace)

Four pairs of large rosaries

Pipe (for FRANCOIS)

Matches (strike anywhere kind)

Cane (for LOUIS)

Breviary (for ABBE)

SCENE II

Two stumps

Three bundles of sticks

ACT TWO

Stage Props:

Same as ACT ONE, SCENE I

Hand Props:

Sign (for LOUIS)

ACT THREE

SCENE I

Stage Props:

Same as ACT ONE, SCENE II

Hand Props:

Mud and grass (for BERNADETTE) (Chocolate cake-mix and shredded cocoanut dyed with vegetable green solve this.)

Bayonet (for JACOMET)

SCENE II

Stage Props:

Same as previous scene, with mud and grass removed and rope barrier added. This barrier can be done quite simply by suspending rope between three rough wooden tripods, from Up Center to Down Right

Hand Props:

One long thin box with First Communion dress and veil.

Four long stemmed yellow roses.

ELECTRICAL PLOT

The only special lighting needed is for the apparitions in ACT ONE, SCENE II and ACT THREE, SCENE I. To give the impression of BERNADETTE's being in a state of ecstasy when the BLESSED VIRGIN appears and speaks to her, the girl should be bathed in a soft golden light, streaming from the left and above stage level.

Smallest of All
Scene Design
Act One, Scene I ~ Act Two

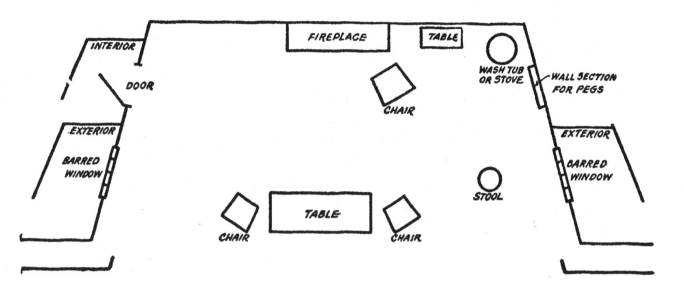

Smallest of All
Scene Design
Act One, Scene II ~ Act Three

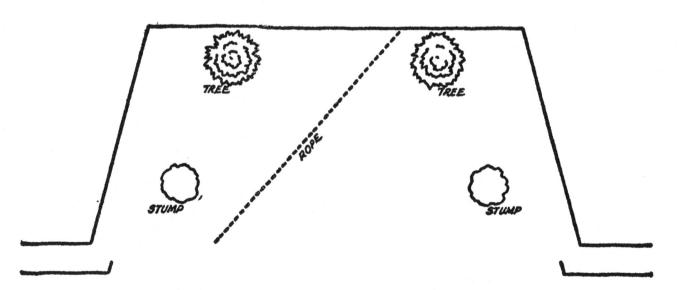

The action of the play takes place in Lourdes, a small town in the foothills of the Pyrenees, near the southern border of France, during February, 1858.

ACT ONE

SCENE ONE: "Le Cachot," the abandoned jail of Lourdes, which serves the Soubirous family for home, February 11, 1858.

SCENE TWO: The far end of a field adjoining the Grotto of Massabielle, alongside the River Gave, the same day.

ACT TWO

"Le Cachot," ten days later.

ACT THREE

SCENE ONE: The Grotto of Massabielle, some days later.

SCENE TWO: The same, some days later.

Candle in Umbria

The Story of Saint Clare of Assisi

© 2000 The Community of Poor Clares of New Mexico, Inc.

Imprimatur: Edwin V. Byrne, D.D.
             Archbishop of Sante Fe

In the Year of Saint Clare's Jubilee, February 26, 1953

Cast of Characters
In Order of Appearance

ORTOLANA . . . . wife of the Count Favarone Offreduccio,
mother of Saint Clare

PENANDA . . . .

AGNES . . . . } sisters of Saint Clare

BEATRICE . . . .

CLARE

THE LADY POVERTY . . . . mystic bride of Saint Francis and Saint Clare

PACIFICA GUELFUCCIO . . . . sister of Bona Guelfuccio, cousin of Saint Clare

BROTHER GILES . . . . one of the first friars of Saint Francis

FRANCIS BERNARDONE

BROTHER SYLVESTER . . . .

BROTHER RUFINO . . . .

BROTHER FILIPPO . . . . } among the first friars of Saint Francis

BROTHER BERNARD QUINTAVALLE . .

BROTHER PETER CATANII . . . .

SISTER ILLUMINATA . . . . one of the first Poor Clare Nuns

SISTER AMATA . . . . Clare Nun, cousin of Saint Clare

SISTER FRANCESCA . . . . one of the first Poor Clare Nuns

SISTER BALVINA . . . . Poor Clare Nun, cousin of Saint Clare

SISTER FILIPPA . . . . one of the first Poor Clare Nuns

TWO SARACENS

BROTHER LEO . . . .

BROTHER JUNIPER . . . . } among the first friars of Saint Francis

BROTHER ANGELO . . . .

THE CHORUS OF VIRGINS

THE BLESSED VIRGIN MARY, MOTHER OF GOD

THE MODERN-DRESS CHORUS

Story of the Play

Clare Offreduccio was born in Assisi, Italy, in 1194. Wealthy, of noble blood, and extraordinarily beautiful and gifted, she turned her back on the world when she was eighteen years old, to become the first spiritual daughter of Saint Francis and the Foundress of his Second Order, the Poor Clare Nuns. The purest mirror of the ideals of Saint Francis, Saint Clare remains through the centuries a candle to light the world on the dark path to eternity.

Candle in Umbria

ACT ONE – PROLOGUE

SCENE. *The stage is dimly lit. A woman enters from the Left, walks restlessly to the Right, and retraces her steps to center stage. She is carrying a piece of embroidery which she takes into both hands and half-folds against her breast.*

ORTOLANA. I wonder, would Favarone laugh or frown,
      If I should say what mysteries
      Hang like cherry blossoms in my heart?
      Each morning teases all my careful plans
      For polishing of silver and ordering of meats
      And making lace. I do not understand
      Myself why I am so entrapped by song
      And feel the whole world's music locked in me,
      Yet cannot quite—no, cannot set it free!

(She laughs ruefully, and clasps the work more tightly to her.)

      Child beneath my heart, what will you be,
      I wonder, that my life seems all unmade
      Because yours is in making! Everything
      Is always on the very verge of joy
      To me these days, and yet, and yet . . .   *(her face grows grave)*
      Fingers of shadow filigree the sun;
      And in the very center of my songs
      Lies a hard core, as though the mirth in me
      Had a demand to make upon my soul.

(She walks to back center where a crucifix is hanging, and drops to her knees.)

      My Lord, sweet Christ, I do not understand
      The mystery of mingled mirth and tears
      That sets my whole soul quivering, and robs
      My days of ordinary blunt designs.
      What manner of child is this astir in me,
      Whose flesh and bone are mine, though yet unseen,
      But kindles song at once and fear in me?

THE VOICE. Ortolana, O fear not!
     This child shall be
     A LIGHT
     Illuminating all the world.

(Full Orchestration)

CURTAIN

ACT ONE

SCENE I

SCENE. *The family home, January, 1212. Three young girls are gathered around a small organ.* CLARE, *about 18, plays; while* AGNES, *about 14; and* BEATRICE, *about 12, sing with her.* PENANDA, *about 19, is working at a piece of lace. There is a pause after the song, broken by* PENANDA.

PENANDA. Clare, I think your hands that play
And lips that sing are all we own of you
These days. Your eyes are far away as skies!

BEATRICE. I heard our father say, Clare is in love!—

AGNES. And will not tell his name!

PENANDA.   It seems you two
Are wise indeed for tender little plants!

CLARE. (*smiles*)
I like that word, Penanda, "little plants!"
It were the total height of my ambition
To bloom a little in some secret garden
And give God fragrance for my life's short hour.

(*She pauses and looks away.*)

But little plants need tending. Who would care
To prune and water such a plant as I?

PENANDA. (*laughing*)
Clare, you talk in mysteries these days.
I think, indeed, my sister *is* in love!
Chattering on of plants and clinging flowers
To ease the burden of the heart's bright weight.
(*wisely*) I knew it, too, before my wedding day.

BEATRICE. Two years ago! —and hear our sister say it
Quite as though she counted four score years!

CLARE. Laugh away, my darlings, but I vow
To you, the secret reaches of my soul
Go further than the love of any man.

BEATRICE. (*drops down on her heels at* CLARE'S *knee*)
I know! You mean to be a nun! I think
It fine to sit upon a throne, and sing
Out of a great red book, and have a staff,
And make the others bow and kiss my ring!

(*They all laugh.*)

(*insistently*) I saw the nuns at San Paolo, and
I think it fine to be an abbess. I
Should have the longest mantle of them all

And wear a jewelled cross upon my breast!
        Clare, will you be a lovely nun like that?

CLARE. (*embraces her, laughing*)
        My darling, I should languish on a throne
        And use my staff for walking-stick to go
        Glad miles across the meadows in the spring
        When the wind trifles with my hair, and thyme
        Assaults my heart like vandals! Surely I
        Should quite belie the graces of the throne!

        (*rises and sobers*)

        My dreams find readier pivot than your own.
        How shall I tell you how I love the shades
        Of morning, when the fields are half-awake
        And God's breath is the scent upon the day!
        When every blossom does Him homage, I
        Reach an ambition wilder than their own:
        To bloom a while, then die upon His Heart,
        Giving Him back the perfume He has poured
        Down all my veins and flooded in my heart.

(*Enter* ORTOLANA, *Left.*)

ORTOLANA. What judges' faces my four girls display!
        Tell me, what war is being lost or won?
        Or, has the world brought all its troubles here,
        That my four flowers turn such solemn petals?

        (*They laugh and go to her*)

BEATRICE. (*delightedly*)
        Mother you talk of flowers,
        Just like Clare!

PENANDA. But not with such a tone of mystery!
        Clare's head is full of mystic horticulture.

(*They laugh again, but* ORTOLANA *looks sharply at* CLARE *who turns slightly away.*)

ORTOLANA. Penanda, go make sure the fire is roaring
        High enough to suit your father's mind.
        He and your lord will be here in an hour.

BEATRICE. Is the cake ready, Mother, and the wine?

(ORTOLANA *smiles at her. Exit* PENANDA, *Right.* ORTOLANA *sits down, and the three girls gather around her.*)

ORTOLANA. Really, my dears, our city is astir
        As if its whole bloodstream were set to boiling.

AGNES. I know!—you mean that Francis Bernardone!

ORTOLANA. Yes, Francis Bernardone. Those who threw
    Stones yesterday, are still enough today;
    For Bernard Quintavalle has gone mad
    As ever Francis was! I saw them pass
    Along the road today. Though it was cold,
    Their feet were bare; and both of them were singing
    As though the taste of God's own joy were burning
    The hearts out of their breasts.

CLARE.   I heard them, too,
    And thought of Paradise when it was morning,
    Earlier than sin, and all things sang
    Like all the bells of innocence together.

AGNES. Mother, if Francis has gone mad, I think it
    Must be very lovely to be mad!
    After the Mass on Sunday, when I saw him
    Laughing in the sunlight, do you know,
    It seemed he was the partner of its shining!
    How can I tell you what passed in my heart,
    Seeing him in his ragged tunic, laughing
    As though he had inherited the stars!

CLARE. He was a gay enough captain of the revels
    Once in the city, yet none ever saw
    Francis so gay as now. Mother, how can it
    Be such joy in poverty is mad?
    I heard him speak like thunder in the crowded
    Square, and yet as gently as the rain
    On a spring evening.

(*Enter* PENANDA, *Right. She sits at the edge of the group.*)

                His habit was dishevelled
    And gathered with a rope around his waist;
    His feet were bare and travel-stained . . . but, somehow,
    The beauty of an angel would seem less
    Than was the look of Francis Bernardone,
    His face turned upward to the curving skies.
    Never, as I shall live, shall I forget
    The mystery of joy that would transfigure
    His thin brown face into a blaze of gladness
    Each time he spoke the holy Name of Jesus.

(*All turn toward* PENANDA *as she begins to speak.*)

PENANDA. Our cousin Martin told me just this morning
    The tide of thought has sharply turned toward Francis
    Now; and those who only lately mocked him,
    Crowd into San Giorgio's to hear him

Discourse of God and this strange, novel highway
He walks to Heaven, poor as any beggar
That haunts Assisi's streets, but strangely claiming
His poverty as royalty instead.

(BEATRICE *rises and tilts up on tiptoes, stretching her arms out lazily.*)

BEATRICE. Has Francis never any cake or wine
Or any fire upon the hearth at evening?
Is poverty to have no shoes or stockings,
Mother?—and what is beautiful about it?
Can't we love God with shoes on? I should rather
Keep my white kid boots and have my cake,
Than be a beggar!—But, Oh! I do love it
When Francis sings so gaily in the square!

(*They all laugh.*)

ORTOLANA. My darling, you most certainly can prosper
In holiness, and keep your white kid boots!
I do not know myself why Francis rotates
His love of God around this poverty;
But this I know, he has a little prayer
For ending every discourse; and it troubles
My heart and moves my spirit so,
That I recall it through each day like music.

PENANDA. What is it, Mother? Tell us what he prays!

ORTOLANA. He lifts his eyes so that one feels his spirit
Has slipped the bonds where ours are languishing,
And says: "Now I beseech Thee, my Lord Jesus,
Lap up my soul from all things under Heaven
With the fierce-hot honey of Thy love,
So that for love of Thy love, I may die,
With joy, since Thou hast died for love of me."

(*There is a long pause; then* ORTOLANA *rises.*)

But there's enough grave talk for one short evening!
Clare, now—some music! I like my girls to sing
Together as the twilight closes on us,
And peace comes down like starlight on our home.

(CLARE *begins to play: "Salve Regina" and they all sing, gathering around the organ again.*)

Now gather up your work. But you, Penanda,
Go fetch the wine.   (*turns to* BEATRICE)
                    And you, my darling, run
And be the very first to greet your father.
A kiss for him!—and two, if he is tired!

(BEATRICE *laughs and runs ahead. Exit, Right.* ORTOLANA *and* PENANDA *follow.* CLARE *and* AGNES *begin to gather up their embroidery.*)

AGNES. Clare, when we talked together now of Francis
        You spoke as one who knows some secret thing
        And cherishes the thought! We had no secret
        Ever before, alone. Why does that glimmer
        Of secret gladness light your eyes whenever
        The others talk of Francis and poverty?

(*There is a little silence, and then* CLARE *takes* AGNES' *hands in her own, and looks at her a long time.*)

CLARE. My sister, truly your soul knows the rhythm
        That swings my own! I did not speak to you
        Of Messer Francis, less to guard a secret,
        Than that my words have all been drowned in joy.
        Agnes, I've gone to him! Madonna Bona
        And I have sought him out a dozen times.
        His love of God has burned all hesitation
        Like dry leaves from my heart, till now I know,
        Obscurely, that my destiny is simple
        Beyond all dreaming, simple as his own.

AGNES. (*wide-eyed*)
        Clare, you surely cannot dream of walking
        Assisi's streets like Francis and his friars!—
        Singing and laughing and ragged as a gypsy!
        What will our mother say?—And, oh! our father!

        (CLARE'S *face clouds for a moment.*)

        My dearest, dearest, know I, too, have guessed
        Some hint of Francis' meaning in his talk
        Of poverty and utter, utter giving.
        I held my tongue before the others, lest
        They think me much too strangely wise; but I
        Can see no place for women in his plan
        To give God back a joyous world again.

CLARE. (*smiles*)
        Nor I! But this I know: if he would have me
        For his small plant, I'd bloom beneath his tending
        As I can never bloom in other gardens.
        Agnes, for this pray God: that Messer Francis
        Find me a little plot in God's broad acres
        And plant me there where God alone shall see
        My face. And God alone shall be the meaning
        Of all my hours. (*pauses*) Agnes, Francis calls
        His poverty, a Lady and a Queen!

He means to give her all, and he has told me
How his bare feet and threadbare habit are
The merest symbols of the secret wedding
Of his whole heart to Lady Poverty!

AGNES. But, Clare, what of the dozen suitors pressing
Our father for your hand? Can you not love
A husband, and this poverty besides?

CLARE. How shall I tell you, Agnes?—how the length
Of love within my heart is great enough
To circle all the world, yet that world cannot
Hedge my own love again! Oh, understand,
God owns me wholly, for His love has bid
A higher price for me than any man's!

ORTOLANA. (*voice Offstage*): Agnes!

(AGNES *gazes at* CLARE *a moment, then turns to leave Right.* CLARE *turns to the crucifix on the left wall and stands in silence for some moments.*)

CLARE. My Lord, give me one glimpse of Messer Francis'
Sweet Lady Poverty, that I may be
As wholly hers as ever, ever he is! (*drops to her knees*)
Give me to see the face of Poverty!

(*Lights dim. Enter the* LADY POVERTY, *Left. She wears a loose white robe with a silver cord around her waist; her feet are bare, her beautiful long hair hangs loosely down her back, and there is a golden crown on her head. She advances toward* CLARE, *repeating her name and stretching out her bare arms to her.*)

THE LADY. Clare! Clare! Clare!

CLARE. Godspeed you, Lady! You call me by name,
Although a stranger to me. Still, my heart
Seems now to know you. Tell me, please, your name?

THE LADY. (*Gathering in the full-arm gesture, she half folds her hands, the fingertips touching very lightly, and her head slightly tilted.*)
I am a royal Princess long in exile.
I am a Queen whose throne has been usurped
By arch-pretenders. Avarice and caution
Have driven me from out my splendid palace.
And now I dance my exile in the aisles
Of crowded earth, and few have eyes for me;
But once a man does look down the pure cloisters
Of my eyes, he is never earth's again.
I am the bride of Francis Bernardone.
And I have come for you, my lovely Clare,
To dance you to the highest and the merest
And whitest Heaven of the Love of God!

(She stands erect, and flings both arms upward so that the elbows are on a level with her shoulders, and the forearms half-bent outward. In a ringing voice of proclamation:)

You shall shed earthly cares like useless garments!
You shall fling all earth's desires away
Like ribbons down the Breath of the Holy Spirit;
You shall own neither thing nor wish nor will!
You shall be free, as God is free in His Heaven,
Free as the poor in spirit whose legacy
Is the wide Kingdom of Heaven, the House of God.

(The Ballet:* Wedding of Clare with Poverty. During the ballet, Clare casts down her jewels, one by one. The ballet ends in the embrace of Clare and the Lady Poverty.)

Curtain

End of Act I

Act Two

Scene I

Scene. *The lower floor of the home, March 18, 1212. Clare and her cousin, Pacifica Guelfuccio, are holding a low-voiced conversation. The house is wrapped in the darkness of night, and the lanterns in the girls' hands cast wavering light about them.*

Pacifica. Clare, the thunder of my heart will wake them!
Here, feel it crash against my ribs like stone!

(reaches for Clare's hand)

Clare. Not so, Pacifica!—but nuptial music
For me! Oh, firm and glorious and great!

Pacifica. I tell you, Clare, my bones are all dissolving!
My throat's a desert place of sun and sand.
What if we rouse the servants? What if Beatrice
Goes searching for you in the night as often
She does when nightmares frighten her, and find
Your room abandoned and her sister gone!
Fancy the wail that child will raise! Imagine
The court of outraged love we two shall face!

Clare. *(laughing)*
Pacifica, if I *were* frightened, truly
My cousin's fear would tease me back to smiles!

---

* *The Ballet may be improvised or omitted.*

What a dear trembling reed my heart has chosen
To lean upon this night. Come, darling,
Gather your forces. Man this sinking ship!
Take courage! You're here to be my sturdy staff;
But I begin to think, instead of leaning
Upon it, I had better take the staff
And carry it upon a satin cushion,
For fear it go to splinters on our way!

(*embraces* PACIFICA)

PACIFICA. (*ruefully*)
  It's true enough, I am a woeful coward.
  Forgive me, Clare. You know that I have faith
  In you beyond all measure, but the substance
  Of me is simply not the stuff of Clare.

CLARE. Oh, no! that is not so! How long our two hearts
  Have burned with a single, yearning flame!
  One is the substance, one the dream—you know it.
  Tonight small cautions plague you; that is all.
  Think of it, sweet, we go to meet the Bridegroom.
  Shall we dishonor Him with least distrust?
  We need not know His future plans. Sufficient
  To know He calls and waits and will do all
  Things sweetly. Oh, Pacifica, my own heart
  Is singing like a river under stars!

(*She steps back and holds the lantern away from her in her right hand, holding her skirt out slightly with her left.*)

Tell me, Pacifica, is there any other
Final touch to make me beautiful
Tonight as I can ever be? I want Christ
To cull his little flower when its head
Is most, most brightly-petalled and its leaf
Is veined with golden threads of utter giving.

(*She turns slowly about.*)

It is my best gown, and the jewels mother
Has treasured for my wedding, little dreaming
The King of kings had claimed me! Afterward,
You must return them to her, darling, saying
They are her pledge I go a brighter way
Than any road her love could pave for me.
These new gold sandals shall be yours, my cousin,
After my Bridegroom spurns them from my feet.
But now I must be lovely for a Lover
More beautiful than all the sons of man!

PACIFICA. (*her eyes fill with tears, and she speaks very simply*)
Yes, you are beautiful, Clare, like a shining light.
I have no other word to say tonight.
But this I know: strange courage has come flooding
Into my quaking soul! My fear is pilfered
Out of my heart, but I adore the Thief!

CLARE. Come, then, we go—No, wait! where is my palm branch?
I want to bear it with more devout Hosanna
To my lover than He's heard before!

(*She takes up the palm branch from a heavy buffet at the right. They pass through the door on the Left, out into the night.*)

PACIFICA. How they have talked for hours of the Bishop
Leaving the rail to place it in your hand
This morning! None of the elders can remember
That ever Bishop paid such due as that
To a mere girl!

CLARE.   Oh, not to me, sweet cousin,
But to Christ Who claims my hand! His Lordship
The Bishop Guido knows tonight's elopement
Ends for me in poverty where Francis
Waits with his friars. He has said his blessing
Would meet me at Saint Mary of the Angels.

PACIFICA. Saint Mary of the Angels!—what a contrast
Tonight will mark with this bright morning's splendors
In the cathedral! Who on earth save Francis
Would think that little ruin of a chapel
Worth the rebuilding! Yet it seems already
To catch the coruscations of his heart,
For when we two have knelt there, something
Of Heaven's brilliance seemed to light the place.

CLARE. I know it well! It seems the full white circle
Of love keeps tracing pure circumference
From Tabernacle there to heart of Francis
And from Sir Francis back to Christ again.
It is the perfect place for Christ to claim me;
For I, quite like Saint Mary of the Angels,
Require Sir Francis to rebuild and raise me
To a new life. Come, darling, let us go!

(*exit, Left.*)

CURTAIN

ACT TWO
SCENE II

SCENE. *Outside the chapel of Saint Mary of the Angels. Six friars, including* RUFINO, *the cousin of* CLARE, *are gathered around* FRANCIS. *All carry lighted torches, save* FRANCIS *who has a large crucifix in his two hands.*

GILES. They should be coming soon, good Father. Listen
    How the small noises of night grow quiet,
    Waiting the footsteps of the Lady Clare!

FRANCIS. (*smiles*)
    I mark it, Brother; and I see our Sister—
    The moon has burnished up her lamp exceeding
    Bright to light a pathway for the bride
    We give to Christ our Lord this secret evening.

SYLVESTER. My Father, what if some ill-chance has thwarted
    Young Clare's design? What if the household waken
    And bar her path? Or what if stern Monaldo . . .

RUFINO. (*breaks in laughing*)
    What if!—Suppose!—And it might be! Sylvester,
    It's plain enough you do not know my cousin!
    Clare Offreduccio may look fragile as a flower,
    But she has strength of will to fit ten men
    With courage for a dozen wars! I tell you,
    Clare will be here. No one will stay *her*, nay!

FRANCIS. Rufino speaks in truth, for I have tested
    Her spirit if it be of God or mere
    Whim of a woman. She has stood refining
    And come out what I thought her—purest gold.
    This is a Christian woman. Mark it, brothers,
    Tonight's a night my friars will remember
    And cherish when the hurricanes shall beat
    Against our brotherhood and bruise and smash it.

FILIPPO. Tell me, who threatens our fraternity!
    And I shall teach him better things, my Father!
    Give leave—I'll tame this Brother Hurricane!

FRANCIS. (*smiles*)
    I pardon your belligerence, good Brother,
    Because you only walk the ways of peace yet
    As a weak-limbed child. The day will break when
    Filippo adds, "The Gentle" to his name.

BERNARD. But, what is your meaning, Father? I discover
         Fingers of mystery haunting all your words
         Tonight. You speak so plainly to us always:
         And yet you seem, this night, a prophet born!
         We only just begin the life of penance
         And peace; how do you talk of storms?

FRANCIS. Now press me not, good Bernard. I speak simply
         Enough of what Christ whispered down my soul's
         Glad avenues that morning when I beckoned
         The people to come help me carry stones
         To old San Damiano; and I told them,
         In words surprising me as much as them,
         How one day God's ladies from that ancient pile
         Would waft new perfumes of their own pure lives.
         I spoke that pulsing morning, not with Francis
         Bernardone's tongue; no wit of mine
         Inspired those words. I only knew their thunder,
         Not mine, would roll until the end of time.
         Neither tonight can I translate to common
         Parlance what I no less know is true
         As sunlight is, and strong as Brother Fire!

(He looks off into the distance, and holds the crucifix suddenly aloft in his right hand.)

         My brothers, hear and remember what I tell you
         This night, though do not press me for a gloss
         Upon it! There will come a day when only
         One woman's loyalty will buoy me up
         In a great raging sea of desolation
         And bring our brotherhood, through storm, to port.
         Let not your eyes rest ever on a woman's
         Face, nor dwell upon a woman's name,
         Save only hers whose name is light and splendor.
         Only the face of Clare may claim your gaze.

(There is a silence, and all gaze at him intently.)

PETER CATANII. Father, behold, she comes! I see the two small
         Lanterns laughing down the aisles of trees!

(The friars hold up their torches, and form in two uneven lines on either side of FRANCIS. *Enter* CLARE *and* PACIFICA *Right. Both make deep court bows first to* FRANCIS, *then to the friars on left and right.)*

FRANCIS. Christian woman, what do you seek of us?

*(*CLARE *drops to her knees, before him. She is carrying the palm.)*

CLARE. Sir Francis, for the love of Christ my Lover,
         I beg you, give me leave to call you: Father,
         And join your tryst with Lady Poverty.

FRANCIS. Will you, then, trade these jewels and these garments
    For robe as rough as ours, and walk to meet
    My Lady Poverty with unshod feet?

CLARE. (*very simply*)
    I wore my best apparel that my Lover
    Christ might see my only thought of it
    Is but to spurn it for His royal Name.

(FRANCIS *motions to* SYLVESTER *to open the double doors of the chapel, and turns to* PETER CATANII.)

FRANCIS. Because this Christian woman has no other
    Desire on earth save that she be allowed
    To walk our way of peace and penance, summon
    Upon her, Brother, the Spirit of Light and Love.

(PETER CATANII *intones the* VENI, CREATOR SPIRITUS, *which all the friars take up. At the fourth stanza,* FRANCIS *motions them to enter the chapel; and they enter in procession, ranging themselves in two lines on either side of the altar.* CLARE *and* PACIFICA *follow, stepping aside before the altar to bow to* FRANCIS *who enters last. He ascends the second altar step, lays the crucifix on the altar, and turns to face* CLARE *who kneels on the first altar step before him.*)

1. Veni, Creator Spiritus,
    Mentes tuorum visita
    Imple superna gratia
    Quae tu creasti pectora.

2. Qui diceris Paraclitus
    Altissimi donum Dei,
    Fons vivus, ignis, caritas
    Et spiritalis unctio.

3. Tu septiformis munere,
    Digitus Paternae dexterae,
    Tu rite promissum Patris,
    Sermone ditans guttura.

4. Accende lumen sensibus,
    Infunde amorem cordibus
    Infirma nostri corporis,
    Virtute firmans perpeti.

5. Hostem repellas longius
    Pacemque dones protinus:
    Ductore sic te praevio,
    Vitemus omne noxium.

6. Per te sciamus da Patrem,
    Noscamus, atque Filium;
    Teque utriusque Spiritum,
    Credamus omni tempore.

7. Deo Patri sit gloria,
    Et Filio, qui a mortuis
    Surrexit, ac Paraclito,
    In saeculorum saecula. Amen.

FRANCIS. (*looks to Heaven*)
    Behold, good Lord! see how this virgin wishes
    To put aside the ornament of woman
    And doff her crown of hair to wear instead
    A veil for sign her heart is Thine alone!

(FRANCIS *cuts* CLARE'S *long hair, leaving the beautiful golden locks about the floor. The friars lean forward, watching every movement.*)

FRANCIS. Hear now, our sister, how the Royal Master
    Gives you a pledge your lifetime to remember:
    "The Lord Himself is my bright legacy's portion.

CLARE. (*repeats after him*)
     "The Lord Himself is my bright legacy's portion

FRANCIS. And He Himself the filling of my cup.

CLARE. And He Himself the filling of my cup.

FRANCIS. The Lord, my faithful Lover, surely one day

CLARE. The Lord, my faithful Lover, surely one day

FRANCIS. Will my inheritance restore to me."

CLARE. Will my inheritance restore to me."

(GILES *takes the shears from* FRANCIS, *and the friars begin to sing.*)

THE FRIARS. Come, now, * spouse of Christ, receive
     That bright crown He has woven
     Out of His infinite love for thee to wear
     Unto everlasting glory!

(PACIFICA *unclasps* CLARE's *mantle and takes it from her, holding it over her own arm.* PETER CATANII *extinguishes his torch, and turns to a table at the extreme Right where a habit has been placed. He hands it to* FRANCIS *who throws it over* CLARE's *shoulders; she rises, and its folds fall to the ground.* FRANCIS *girds her with a rough cord, and she kneels again.*)

FRANCIS. Preserve this robe of Poverty, our sister,
     For pledge of your betrothal to a Prince
     Richer than any lord of earth. Be faithful
     Never to plight a troth with earth again.

     (*pause*)

     This is a holy place!—cast down the sandals
     From off your feet, and the more swiftly run
     Down the sweet tanglewood of penance into
     The everlasting arms of Christ our Lord.

(CLARE *stands, and stoops down to remove her gold sandals which she hands to* PACIFICA *with a smile.*)

THE FRIARS. (*sing the antiphon again,* PETER *intoning:*)
     Come, now, * spouse of Christ, receive
     That bright crown He has woven
     Out of His infinite love for thee to wear
     Unto everlasting glory!

(PETER CATANII *hands* FRANCIS *a black veil, taking it from the same table which held the habit.* FRANCIS *drapes it over* CLARE's *head; she then crosses her arms on her breast and bows her head.*)

CLARE. Christ has set a seal upon my forehead
     That I admit no lover but Himself.
     My Lord has robed my soul with cloth of gold
     And covered me with jewels of His love.

THE FRIARS. (*bravissimo voce!—this time,* FRANCIS *intones:*)
>Come, now, * spouse of Christ, receive
>That bright crown He has woven
>Out of His infinite love for thee to wear
>Unto everlasting glory!

CURTAIN

ACT THREE

SCENE. *A morning in 1240, at San Damiano.* SISTER CLARE *sits in an invalid's chair on the balcony, at the back, toward the door of the house. Two nuns stand on either side of her, and three are sitting on their heels at her feet. All sewing on linens, even* SISTER CLARE.

CLARE. (*to* SISTER ILLUMINATA, *seated at her feet*)
>Child, I see too many grooves of worry
>Etched in your cheeks.

(*She tilts up* ILLUMINATA'S *chin.*)

>   Have faith. Did I not tell you,
>The Lord, our Spouse, will never let His own
>Perish? If He has counted every hair
>On all our heads, do you suppose He's wanting
>In knowledge of the threat those Saracens
>Lay to our dear Assisi? We shall wound Him
>Deep in His loving heart, if we display
>A trace of worry for ourselves, when truly
>We are the little sheltered plants of God.

(*She lays her hand on* ILLUMINATA'S *cheek for a moment, then looks around at the others.*)

ILLUMINATA. Mother, I've made a thousand acts of worship
>Toward God's great providence. Forgive me that
>My heart is stubborn in its fear. Oh, Mother,
>I've heard their arrows are as long as swords!

CLARE. However long they be, Illuminata,
>God's love is longer; and we dwell with Him.

AMATA. What shall we do if ever, oh! if ever
>They ride on us! Dear Mother, will they kill
>Us all together, do you think, or might they
>Bear us away?

FRANCESCA. (*breaks in*)
>If we could die together
>Here, with our Mother, I should be content.
>But not alone!

CLARE. (*places her hand lightly over* FRANCESCA'S *mouth*)
Francesca, never, never
Let that false word, "alone," deceive your heart!
How can we be alone, whose Lord and Lover
Is with us always?

BALVINA.   Mother, do you never
Feel the hard drag of fear upon your heart?

CLARE. (*smiles*)
Never, my daughter! Since the day our Father
Francis signed my soul for Christ, my life
Has been quite lost in God; and in *Him*, never
Flutters a breath of fear! All suffering
Is scented like a flower, once we place it
Upon that heart of His that bled for us.

FILIPPA. Mother, you have a way of sweetly calming
The panic in my breast. Indeed we are
Safe in God's garden, and He surely somehow
Will save us from these Saracens.

(*She drops down to her knees and kisses* CLARE'S *left hand, while* CLARE *lays her right hand on* FILIPPA'S *head in blessing.*)

AMATA. Is not the heat too much for you now, Mother?
Permit us to return you to your cell.

(CLARE *smiles, and the nuns begin to move about to help her rise.*)

CLARE. If it will please you, daughters, let us go.

(ILLUMINATA *walks over to the balcony railing to pick up her work basket, gazes in horror out into the distance, and then gives a shriek.*)

ILLUMINATA. Mother, the Saracens!
(*the others rush to the railing.*)

BALVINA.   O God, defend us!
We perish! See the foaming horses speed
Against us!

(CLARE *struggles to her feet, and* FRANCESCA *and* AMATA *rush to her side, supporting her. The sisters begin to weep and gather around* CLARE, *some falling on their knees and holding on to her hands.*)

FILIPPA. We are doomed! Oh, we are doomed!

CLARE. (*sternly*) Silence, my daughters! Such a women's clamor
Ill suits the spouses of the most High King.

(*They quiet down, some still weeping softly. The sound of hoofbeats and shouting can be heard very faintly in the distance, gradually growing more distinct.*)

CLARE. (*raising her eyes to Heaven, begins to pray very calmly*)
Sweet Christ, defend your handmaids, or we perish.
Deliver not to beasts the souls of them

Who trust in You! We have no strength to parry
A single blow, nor shield to turn aside
One arrow of the Saracens, yet gladly
We cast our quivering lives upon Your power
And lean our women's trembling on Your arm.

(*There is a silence, and all the nuns look expectantly at their Mother, while the sound of hoofbeats and shouting grows louder.*)

CLARE. (*turns to* FRANCESCA, *placing her hand on* FRANCESCA'S *shoulder.*)
Go you into the chapel. Kiss the floor
Before the Tabernacle Box; then take it
Into your arms, and bear it here to me.

FILIPPA. (*wide-eyed and trembling*)
Mother!—and dare I touch the Tabernacle!

CLARE. Question me not, my daughter. What I say
Is a command my own soul has been given.

(*The stamping and shouting increases.*)

Bear the Lord Jesus here to me; I cannot
Walk to Him, but He will come to me. (*exit* FRANCESCA, *Right*)

(*to* BALVINA *and* AMATA)
Go after her, and take you two blessed candles
To worship Christ our Lord upon the way.

(*They run after* FRANCESCA. *The noises grow louder still, and the sisters are rigid with anticipation. There is a silence.*)

CLARE. Illuminata, start that little song our Father
Francis loved so well—the "Jesu, tibi!"

ILLUMINATA. (*trembling*)
Mother, I vow to you, my heart is willing
To do your wish, but my poor throat is pasted
Shut beyond all singing, and my tongue
Is stricken like a boulder in my mouth!

CLARE. (*Looking out into the distance, she herself begins to sing in a clear, sweet, steady voice.*)
Jesu, tibi vivo! Jesu, tibi morior!

(FILIPPA *joins her, in a shaky voice.*)

CLARE AND FILIPPA. Jesu, sive vivo, sive morior, Tuus sum!

CLARE. (*smiles*)
My daughters, well you know, if our Father
Were here with us, he'd surely bid us sing!
If Sister Death is stirring in the sunlight,
Our Father Francis would not fail to greet her
With courtesy of song and smiling mien.

(*She again begins:*)
Jesu, tibi vivo!
(*and this time, the other two join her with steady voices*)

ALL THREE. Jesu, tibi morior!
Jesu, sive vivo, sive morior, Tuus sum!

(*There is the sound of a small bell tinkling, and* BALVINA *and* AMATA *emerge from the door, carrying candles.* BALVINA *rings the tiny bell she carries in her left hand.* CLARE *motions them to either side of her, and* FRANCESCA *appears in the doorway bearing a silver Box encased in ivory. She carries it in both arms, against her breast, as a woman would carry a child. There is a moment of electric silence, and then all save* FRANCESCA *fall to their knees,* ILLUMINATA *assisting* CLARE, *and kiss the ground. Kneeling with bowed heads, they join in* CLARE'S *spontaneous song.*)

CLARE. Jesu dilectissime,

ALL. Miserere nobis!

(*The shouting and clamor grow earsplitting, but the nuns' clear voices pierce through the din.*)

CLARE. Jesu suavissime,

ALL. Miserere nobis!

CLARE. Jesu potentissime

ALL. Miserere nobis!

(CLARE *rises, supported by two sisters.*)

CLARE. Deliver not, my Lord, the souls of Your handmaids
Trusting Your love, into the hands of these men!

(*She drops to her knees and draws a small key from her bosom. Inserting it in the lock of the silver Box, she reaches inside to take out the lantern-like Pyx containing the Sacred Host, while the sisters prostrate to the ground, the two candle-bearers kneeling with bowed heads.* CLARE *holds the Pyx in both hands, and walks to the edge of the balcony just as two scarlet-turbaned heads appear over the railing, amid unspeakable din, pawing of horses, and shouting of rough men. As the first* SARACEN *leaps over the railing,* CLARE *lifts the Pyx high, and repeats in a loud, proclamatory as well as supplicating voice.*)

CLARE. Deliver not, sweet Lord, Your poor, weak handmaids,
Trusting Your love, into the hands of these men!

(*The first* SARACEN *stands transfixed, the second remains with both hands on the railing of the balcony, his eyes bulging . . . There is a long moment of pregnant silence, and then a* VOICE *unutterably sweet and calm and light as a caress.*)

THE VOICE. I will always take care of you, till the end of time!

(*The Pyx is bathed in light—spotlight it, triple; the first* SARACEN *falls back, stricken, against the low railing, clutching at his breast with his left hand, and his right hand against his forehead. He falls to the ground. The second plunges over backward from the railing. The sisters kneel up with arms stretched out full-length toward the Sacred Host. The two with candles hold the candles out toward the Pyx in both hands, while* CLARE *gazes directly into the Face of the Sacred Host, and her face lights with an unspeakably beautiful smile. The lights go down, leaving only the spotlight focussed on the Pyx.*)

THE VOICE. I will always take care of you, till the end of time!

(Full chorus Offstage, while the nuns hold the tableau.)

Chorus Offstage. Christus vincit! Christus regnat! Christus imperat!
Christus vincit! Christus regnat! Christus imperat!
Christus vincit! Christus regnat! Christus imperat!

CURTAIN

ACT FOUR

Scene. *The cell of* Saint Clare *at San Damiano. It is August of the year 1253, and "Sister Death" is hovering close by.* Clare *lies on a low couch, supported by pillows, clothed in her habit, and her veil thrown loosely about her head. Six nuns crowd around the bed,* Agnes *kneeling by her pillow and a few weeping softly with their hands covering their faces. Three of the friars are also present, and* Brother Leo *is reading the Passion from a large Bible open before him on a crude lectern.* Brother Angelo *tries unsuccessfully to hide his tears from the sisters.* Juniper *stands at the foot of the couch, gazing fixedly at* Clare, *his hands clasped against his mouth and his head slightly tilted.)*

Leo. And when Jesus had tasted the vinegar, He said:
It is finished. And bowing His Head, He yielded up His Spirit.

(All go down on both knees. Rising, Leo *closes the book and looks at* Clare.*)*

Clare. *(looking at* Leo*)*
Now if it please you, Brother, bless me once
Again before you go. Then I am warmed
With every consolation, seeing I
Have heard the tale of how our most sweet Lord
Suffered and died for love of me, and now
Permits that I should suffer and die for Him.

Angelo. Remember, Sister, that your pains are mere
Prelude to bliss. Take comfort in the thought!

Clare. Sir Angelo, I vow to you that never since
Our Father Francis led me toward the way
Of Christ's dear love, have I once let a pain
Or sorrow go uncherished in His Name.

Juniper. Lady, commend us to our Father when
You join him. Tell him Juniper now waits
With some impatience, to be summoned home!

Clare. *(smiles at him)*
Nay, rather, bid me tell Saint Francis that
God's jester keeps our days still merry with
His lilting joy, and weary earth requires
For some space yet good Juniper's bright song!

AGNES. (*kneeling on left side of the couch*)
  Mother, before our Brothers leave you, beg
  Them once again to sing our Father's song
  Of Brother Sun and Sister Death, and cheer us
  With one last pledge of unity and love.

CLARE. Oh, yes! for Christ's dear sake grant we may hear
  Our Father's Canticle once more, since it was here
  He sang it first; and we have loved it well.

(*The friars look toward* ANGELO *who steps forward and raising both arms slightly outward with hands shoulder-high, begins to sing. All join in, after the first line.*)

SAINT FRANCIS' CANTICLE OF THE SUN

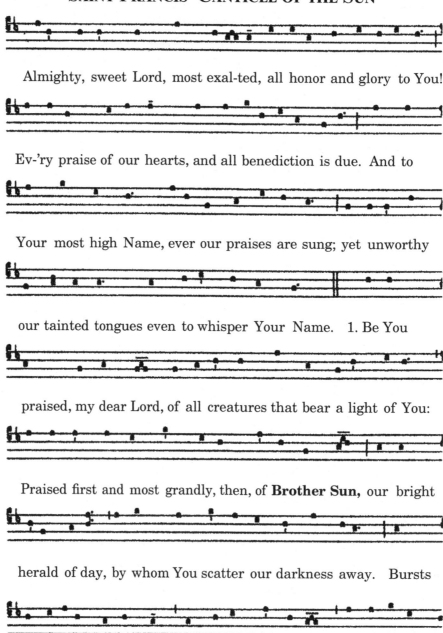

Almighty, sweet Lord, most exal-ted, all honor and glory to You!

Ev-'ry praise of our hearts, and all benediction is due. And to

Your most high Name, ever our praises are sung; yet unworthy

our tainted tongues even to whisper Your Name. 1. Be You

praised, my dear Lord, of all creatures that bear a light of You:

Praised first and most grandly, then, of **Brother Sun,** our bright

herald of day, by whom You scatter our darkness away. Bursts

his radiance on our sight with a splendor of light: for his shining is

bright with a rumor, my God, of You! 2. Be You praised, my dear

Lord, through our **Sister** the **Moon** and the Stars that stud the

night; in the heavens You set them for our light, gracious, gleaming

in beauty bright! 3. And be praised, my sweet Lord, through little

Brother the **Wind**. And through days that are clouded or days

most serene, be You praised! And through varying weathers,

wherein our goods we find. 4. Be You praised again, Lord, through

our **Sister Water**, so great is she and yet remains so humble,

shining in her crystal chastity! 5. Still be praised, my great Lord,

through our most ardent **Brother** the **Fire**. With his flames, You

dispel all our night! He is joyous and strong: to him, power

belongs! 6. Ever praised be my Lord, through the **Earth,** our

mother and our sister: as a loving mother, she sustains us with all

her sundry fruits, while she delights our hearts with riotous

blossoms! 7. Then be You praised, my Lord, through **hearts** that

love as You have loved with sweet compassion, and through

Cross-laden hearts bearing pain that never knows surcease!- thrice

happy hearts, dwelling in Your peace, for by You, most high

God, these shall be   crowned! 8. Lastly, praised be my Lord

through our sweet and most beloved **Sister Death**! No man lives

but shall feel one day the kiss of her breath! Woe and woe again

to them who greet her with a soul in sin: yet how blessed those

who do Your Will, ever holiest Will; for death that never ends,

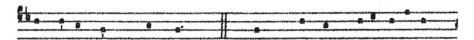

no power wields o'er them! Praise and bless eternally my

Lord; ever thank Him, ever serve Him with a most humble heart.

(ANGELO *lowers his arms after the first line, and sings like the other friars, hands in sleeves, but with up-raised eyes and very joyful faces. At the beginning of the lines to Sister Death,* CLARE *reaches out her hands to clasp those of* AGNES *on the left and* BEATRICE *on the right.*)

CLARE. (*loosens her clasp on the sisters' hands and folds her hands together*)
My Lord, most gracious, how I thank You
For creating me with infinite courtesy!

(LEO *steps close to the couch and raising his hands, blesses her, tracing the Sign of the Cross over her.*)

LEO. May God Almighty, Father, Son and Spirit,
(*he extends his hands out over her*)
Bless you and keep you, Sister Clare, forever.

(*As the friars leave, Left,* AGNES *buries her head in* CLARE'S *pillow and begins to weep.*)

AGNES. (*raising her head*)
Oh, leave me not alone! I beg you, Mother,
As once you drew me from our father's house
To serve the most high King, now draw me
After you to Heaven, else this little plant
Shall droop and die, untended, on the earth.

CLARE. (*placing her hand on* AGNES' *head*)
Weep not! Know that our Bridegroom summons
You shortly, little sister, after me!
You shall see marvels yet, beyond all telling
Before you die.

(*There is a slight pause, and* CLARE *turns her head toward the Right, as though someone had called her. Her face lights with a wonderful smile.*)

Oh, Sisters, do you see
The King's bright court, as my eyes now behold it!

(FLOOD THE STAGE WITH LIGHT. *Enter a* CHORUS OF VIRGINS *in soft white garments, each wearing a crown. They are all smiling, and begin to sing joyously together.*)

THE CHORUS. Come, now, spouse of Christ, receive
            That bright crown He has woven
            Out of His infinite love for thee to wear
            Unto everlasting glory!

(*The nuns draw back, hands slightly up-raised in delighted wonder, taking their places behind* CLARE'S *couch, as the virgins form in broken lines on either side of* CLARE. *But the* VIRGIN *who entered in their midst, wearing a blue mantle over her white garments and a crown far more glorious than the others, stands directly over* CLARE *who gazes up entranced into the beautiful face of the* MOTHER OF GOD.)

THE BLESSED VIRGIN MARY. Put away now the penance and the sorrow
            And claim the crown of those who love my Son
            Past measure. Leave at last the secret cloister
            And walk the shining acres of His love.
            Now, for the rough robe, take the robe of glory.

(*The* BVM *begins to spread over the bed a very thin, exquisitely beautiful veil, gradually covering* CLARE, *as she continues to speak.*)

THE BLESSED VIRGIN MARY. Now, for the weary vigils, claim the feast!
            Now, for the naked faith, the splendid vision!
            Now, for the silence, everlasting song!

(*Just before covering the face of* CLARE *with the veil, the* BVM *stands holding the veil in her hands and looks up to Heaven.*)

THE BLESSED VIRGIN MARY. Let earth behold its judgment turned against it!
            The thoughts of God are not the thoughts of men.

            (*She covers* CLARE'S *face with the veil.*)

            Hear how my Son proclaims the dream of Francis
            And Clare shall light the earth till time is done!

            (OUR LADY *sings with the* CHORUS OF VIRGINS.)

THE CHORUS. Come, now, spouse of Christ, receive
            That bright crown He has woven
            Out of His infinite love for thee to wear
            Unto everlasting glory!

CURTAIN

EPILOGUE

SCENE. *Only the outmost curtain is opened, for a flashback to the prologue.* ORTOLANA *kneels, exactly as before, before the crucifix.*

ORTOLANA. My Lord, sweet Christ, I do not understand
            The mystery of mingled mirth and tears

That sets my whole soul quivering, and robs
My days of ordinary blunt designs.
What manner of child is this astir in me,
Whose flesh and bone are mine, though yet unseen,
But kindles song at once and fear in me?

THE VOICE. Ortolana, O fear not!
This child shall be
A LIGHT, illuminating all the world!

(Full Orchestration)

(Open inner curtain, to reveal SAINT CLARE *in glory. She stands on a high pedestal, wearing her habit and mantle. One bare foot is slightly extended. Her hands are clasped on her breast, and she is smiling slightly. There is a great halo of light about her head, and lilies are banked on either side of her. A single tall candle burns at her feet.*

GIRLS *in modern dress, each different, enter singly from opposite sides of the stage. Each carries an unlighted candle which she takes to light from the candle burning before the saint. Each new entrant takes her place in the two lines forming obliquely at either side of the saint; and as each one takes her place with her lighted candle, she speaks, in such a way that while the first girl is speaking, the second girl is coming onstage to light her candle, etc.)*

FIRST GIRL. This light burned only, sent no fissured atom
Shivering down some miles of naked space.
This light just flickered, faithful, till the final
Sputter of yearning burst her drift of flesh.

SECOND GIRL. She was a small light burning. All the arc lamps
Of noise are shattered, all the spotlights gone
Away to weep in their unhappy ruins,
But the Clare-candle whispers on and on.

THIRD GIRL. Where was the famous dictum, where the flashing
Deed, the policy taken, history turned?
Who would remember Clare wrapped in her silence,
Once the bare feet were cold, the eyelids closed?

FOURTH GIRL. Fool of a woman! Laying down her shining
Hair for a wisp of dream in a madman's heart!
Who will remember Clare, after the gentle
Hands are still, the kept heart only stone?

FIFTH GIRL. Ah, but the weary, weary, generations
Each after each has flung its noise away,
Broken its own too terrible searching arc lights,
While the Clare-candle flickers on and on.

SIXTH GIRL. This light just burned, too small for any notice.
This light just let its pale, pure beam seem lost
In all the rocket flashes of a brilliant
And dreamless world as practical as Hell.

SEVENTH GIRL. And who shall witness bear the very tender
 Paradox, the irony of God—
 That the small light has filled the earth and heavens
 Past flame and torch and glare and beam, if not
 The thousands strong who say no word, and lightly
 Spurn the strange earth with their unslippered feet.

EIGHTH GIRL. Who fling their gleaming hair away like laughter
 And turn their faces toward a nameless spring.

NINTH GIRL. (*She kneels directly in front of* SAINT CLARE, *her back to the audience*)
 And sing! because one small light flickered, faithful,
 And the Clare-candle lights the weary world!

(*The* SAINT *lifts the two front ends of her mantle, so that as she speaks, she stretches her mantle out over the chorus.*)

SAINT CLARE. May Almighty God bless you,
 May He look upon you with the eyes of His mercy
 And give you His peace.
 On earth may He pour forth His graces on you abundantly.
 And in Heaven, may He place you among His saints!

FINAL CURTAIN

The End

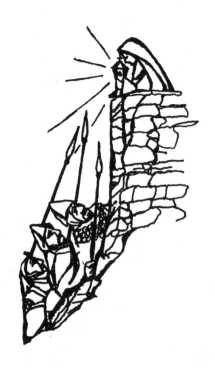

Musical Settings for lines that are indicated to be sung:

On pages 158, 159, and 168:

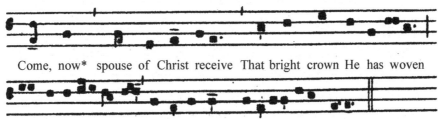

Come, now* spouse of Christ receive That bright crown He has woven

Out of His infinite love for thee to wear Unto everlasting glory!

On page 162:

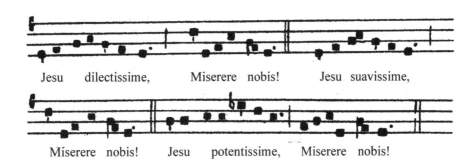

Jesu dilectissime,   Miserere nobis!   Jesu suavissime,

Miserere nobis!   Jesu potentissime,   Miserere nobis!

On page 170:

The Blessing of Saint Clare

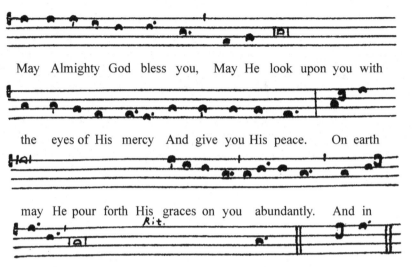

May Almighty God bless you, May He look upon you with

the eyes of His mercy And give you His peace. On earth

may He pour forth His graces on you abundantly. And in

Heaven, may He place you among His saints! All: A -men.